FROM MUSHROOMS TO THE MESSIAH

*One Man's Journey up a Mountain
Called "Commitment"*

MATTHEW JONES

WESTBOW
PRESS®
A DIVISION OF THOMAS NELSON
& ZONDERVAN

WestBow Press books may be ordered through booksellers or by contacting:

WestBow Press
A Division of Thomas Nelson & Zondervan
1663 Liberty Drive
Bloomington, IN 47403
www.westbowpress.com
1 (866) 928-1240

ISBN: 978-1-5127-2038-9 (sc)
ISBN: 978-1-5127-2039-6 (hc)
ISBN: 978-1-5127-2040-2 (e)

Library of Congress Control Number: 2015918992

Print information available on the last page.

WestBow Press rev. date: 12/7/2015

To my faithful God, loving parents, patient mentor, and amazing wife. Thank you for supporting, encouraging, and praying for me through this journey. I am forever grateful.

CONTENTS

This book is based on a true life experience.

MY MOUNT EVEREST

Imagine opening the newspaper to browse the classified ads. As you sift through the countless sea of singles, free stuff, casual encounters, employment postings, and other services, you stumble across the following ad:

WANTED

Provider of the following: all-inclusive vacations, first-class world travel and accommodations, personal chef, chauffer, graduate school tutoring, counseling, paid mentorship, food stipend, health club membership, debt consolidation, nutritional supplements, tax advising, resume builder, poker, snowboard, tattoo sponsor, and other duties as assigned.

Now, if you were to see such an ad, what would you think of its author?

Some words that come to mind are delusional, narcissistic, detached from reality, deranged, or even mentally ill. I would personally think that the author created the ad while snorting fairy dust with Peter Pan and "thinking happy thoughts." In other words, this person was in desperate need of an unemployment application and a reality check.

Although posting something so preposterous may seem far-fetched and futile, that was exactly what I received from my ad on a well-known dating website. My personal ad may not have resembled the one above, but I did manage to walk away with all the perks listed and more!

Before we begin, please let me clarify that this is not a story about dating websites, hiking, or a snow-covered mountain in Nepal. This is my personal encounter with the miraculous and transformational power of God—scripted long before I was born, which was created for consumption by atheists, believers, skeptics, and seekers. These experiences are a gift from God so that people can comprehend the very real presence and power of Jesus Christ today.

This is also a story about overcoming the fear of commitment. Let's be honest—each of us has fear in life. These fears, no matter how big or small, prevent us from actualizing our potential.

My greatest fear was commitment. For me, making and keeping commitments was like climbing Mount Everest: nearly impossible. Each opportunity to make a commitment sounded really good at the time, but as I started to experience any form of resistance, I quickly gave up.

The problem with this particular fear is that commitments are required to complete anything of significance in life. Every good marriage, business idea, academic endeavor, fitness plan, or personal goal begins with a commitment.

For me, to fear commitment was to stifle any potential success in my life. I would be forced to settle for less than God's best because I was unwilling to face the obstacles standing in my way. Unfortunately, my fear was mountainous. My inability to commit left me with a trail of broken relationships, unfulfilled goals, and empty dreams. I found myself skating through a life of mediocrity, making minimal effort, taking minimal risks, and therefore experiencing only minimal satisfaction and success. Ultimately, my failure to keep commitments left me feeling insignificant, unaccomplished, and ashamed as a result.

For me to overcome this fear of commitment, I would have to embark on the greatest adventure of my life, my Mount Everest …

SPECIAL THANKS TO ...

My God, who saved me, loves me unconditionally, and
gave me his best when I deserved his worst.
My wife and best friend, for her mountain-moving faith,
sacrificial service, patience, and passionate love.
My mom, for her unceasing prayers, unwavering
spirit, and unconditional love.
My dad, for never giving up on me, even when this road
was dark and directionless and didn't make sense.
My mentor, who obeyed God and endured the pain and
suffering of our commitment journey together.
All my friends and family who lovingly supported me
through listening, prayer, and encouragement.
Stephanie Leisenring, for her editorial expertise
and faithful friendship to my wife.

ATTENDING MY OWN FUNERAL

Despite my growing up in the church, attending Bible studies, getting baptized, and volunteering annually in children's summer camps, I decided in high school that the Christian life was not for me, at least not yet.

I remember telling my Christian friends and pastor when I first started to break away from the church, that I would follow God again when I was done having fun. Before committing my life fully to Christ I wanted to experience a spring break in Cancun, join a fraternity, have a one-night stand, smoke pot, and do all the things of which college was made and the Bible forbade.

I knew about God, Jesus, and the Bible, but his "plan for my life" would have never aired on MTV, so it was time for us to part ways.

Like for many American teenagers, my path of rebellion progressed from house parties in high school to full-blown ragers and keggers in college.

MTV would have been proud; I was an athlete on the lacrosse team, shredded like Jersey Shore, and the "fratiest" of frat boys. I had different girls in my bed, drinks and drugs in my hand, money in my pocket, and not a care in the world.

During the summer before my senior year in college, I started working as a bartender at a resort on the Russian River. On a good day at the resort, I was making upwards of five hundred dollars cash in tips. This money went straight to my vacations in Las Vegas, tab at the bar, and recreational drug use.

That summer, my weekend drinking binges and occasional marijuana use turned into weekly lines of cocaine, tabs of ecstasy, and caps of magic mushrooms. Not only that, but my partying was no longer confined to the weekend. I now found myself using narcotics on Tuesday nights just because they were available.

I realized things were starting to get out of hand when I accompanied a close friend to purchase a large amount of ecstasy to distribute around campus. Just one pill was enough for a felony charge and jail time, and we had enough to lock us away for life.

Also, although in the prime of my partying career, I realized that my drug use was taking a severe toll on my body. I started becoming depressed from the lack of serotonin in my brain. There were even the occasional thoughts of suicide as my highs were decreasing in height and my lows increasing in depth. I hated the feeling of sobriety, but I also hated knowing that I could experience such pleasure and happiness only while I was high. I justified the resulting depression as a "necessary evil" and continued bingeing on special occasions. I remember one night in particular like it was yesterday ...

CHAPTER 1

"GATEWAY" DRUGS

December 19, 2008, was the last night in college before Christmas vacation. Most of my friends were preparing for the long winter break, but I was preparing a party. This particular party had been in the planning process for weeks because our celebratory intentions would require much preparation. My friend Kory and I had been discussing our party options for some time and decided that taking psilocybin "magic" mushrooms would be a great way to end the fall semester.

I wanted to experience our tasty treats on the beach or at the national redwood forest, but Kory, being a first-timer, wanted to be in the safety of his own home. This actually worked out for us, because on that Friday, it began to rain heavily.

Kory purchased a large bag of mushrooms from his sister's friend for this special occasion. Since we had a surplus of mushrooms, we invited our friends Brandon and Jason to join the adventure. Word got out that we were planning on shrooming, so others naturally became curious and eager to participate. Unfortunately, there were not enough mushrooms for the other five guests, so they decided to purchase a large amount of marijuana instead.

The plan for our mushroom trip included music, movies, food, and fun. Kory created a special mushroom music mix to get us in a magical mood. He also had the movie *Step Brothers* and the documentary *Planet Earth* prepared for our viewing pleasure. We had wisely prepared a variety of munchies and drinks, creating a self-sustaining environment for our trip. It was important for us to make sure we had everything we needed so that we wouldn't have to leave the house or worry about anything for the next six to eight hours.

To begin our adventure, Kory made BBQ bacon cheeseburgers to mask the taste of the mushrooms. We washed our burgers down with orange juice because some believe the vitamin C increases the intensity of a mushroom high. As we sat on the couch waiting for the hallucinogens to kick in, Kory turned on *Step Brothers*.

The first stage of any mushroom high is uncontrollable, gut-busting laughter. Watching *Step Brothers* made it difficult to discern when I was actually feeling the effects of the drug or responding to the hilarity of Will Ferrell's unabashed antics.

After nearly thirty minutes, I finally realized that the shrooms had begun to take their effect, because John C. Reilly's face began to melt on the screen. It was now officially safe to say that I was "tripping balls," or was just really, really, really high—whichever you prefer.

> The snozzberries taste like snozzberries.
> —*Super Troopers*

While I was high in Kory's apartment, each room had a different feel and offered a unique experience. Simply turning my head to access a different perspective opened new windows of opportunity for my magical journey. It was as if each new glance contained its own dimensions of a world completely independent from the one before.

Once I realized that my mushroom high was in full effect, I walked over to the bathroom to see what adventures awaited me there. I remember locking the bathroom door and looking into the mirror. The whitewashed walls behind me began morphing into different dreamlike shapes and figures. Like a kaleidoscope, the pictures projected upon the walls were constantly changing with the hallucinations in my mind. My dreams seemed to be materializing into reality through these bathroom hallucinations.

Although having the time of my life, I remember an intense paranoia developing while I was in the bathroom. I began to stress that my friends were worrying about me taking too long. My worst fear was that they would call the police or an ambulance while thinking that I was hurting myself or in danger while I was locked away in the bathroom. I could have spent my entire trip in there if I hadn't been so worried about the other people in the apartment. In no way am I an advocate for illegal drugs, but magic mushrooms are most definitely best experienced in solitude.

Paranoia is a common side effect associated with psychedelic drugs. It often corrupts the psychedelic experience with thoughts that others are watching you judgmentally and critically. These thoughts can quickly turn a great trip into a frightening one. When one is under the influence of psychedelic mushrooms, everything hinges upon perception—but then again, life is all about perception. What you value and believe changes how you perceive the world to be.

Once I left the bathroom, I stumbled into the family room to discover that three new people had joined our party. I remember repeatedly yelling, "You guys wish you were on my level! Get on my level!" I tend to feel like Superman—invincible and ultra-arrogant—when I'm loaded, so these statements were deemed normal for me. They laughed condescendingly, knowing how messed up I was, but they urged me to sit down on the couch.

I began to feel an uncontrollable silliness that could be contained only while I was sitting upside down on the couch with my back flat on the floor. Yes, as strange as it sounds, I felt normal only by lying on the ground with my feet in the air, being supported by the legs of the couch. To intensify the peculiarity, in an effort to remain "grounded" while my mind wandered the apartment, I clamped my jaws to the underside of a coffee table. What a sight that must have been for the sober people in the room. I was eating wooden furniture while lying upside down on the couch. Magic mushrooms are one heck of a drug.

Being high on magic mushrooms is an introspective experience that makes you think, meditate, and dissect the complex issues of life and the happenings all around you. Although I was upside down with my feet in the air, my eyes were open and my mind was still stimulated, which are all that seem to matter when you're hallucinating. After a while, my biting the coffee table made me realize how insanely high I was and that I needed to sober up before I lost my mind or teeth completely.

Now, the last thing you want to do while hallucinating on magic mushrooms is to harbor any negative thoughts. Feelings of overdose or thoughts of a good trip going bad are enough to enable temporary psychosis. I unfortunately had lost control and was on the verge of a psychological meltdown. I knew that I needed to sober up and fast, but I was only two hours into my high.

Shrooms are much like a roller coaster. Once you are on, there is no way to get off until the ride is over. The ride of a mushroom high lasts anywhere from six to eight hours, depending on potency and amount of caps consumed. Being an extremist, I consumed the highest dose humanly possible without the risk of going insane. After forty-five minutes, I was having the most intense visual hallucinations I had ever experienced while on mushrooms. I decided the trip was too intense and that it needed to stop immediately. The problem I was having with this impossible strategy was that it was … well, impossible. I was already on the roller coaster; my only option was to ride this out and hope to walk away with my sanity. Although I could not stop the hallucinations, I figured if I was to lie down on the couch, I could sleep through the remainder of my high. So I unclenched my teeth from the coffee table, got up from the floor, and lay down on the couch. I then closed my eyes and began to talk myself to sleep.

Am I Dreaming?

I don't know exactly how long I slept, but as I regained consciousness, I realized that something was different. It was dark outside, and I was sober. How long had I been asleep? I felt fully rested, which meant I had probably slept for a solid four to five hours, but to my surprise, the clock on the wall read 5:00 p.m. That meant I had been asleep for only an hour. How could I possibly be sober?

I stood up to survey the once brightly lit room, which was now illuminated only by multicolored Christmas lights. Kory had draped these lights across the ceiling, giving the room an eerie glow.

Where had everyone gone? I suddenly realized that not only was I sober, but I was also very much alone. I could faintly hear the sound of Kory, Brandon, and Jason in the back bedroom, but everyone else had left. As I walked around the apartment, I felt weightless, as if I were floating. I felt no discomfort, no anxiety—not much of anything. An overwhelming sense of peace swept over my body as I attempted to comprehend what was happening around me. Do not ask me why, but the only thought in my mind was that I had overdosed and died.

I started to think about life after death. What would it be like?

If I had died, why was I still in Kory's apartment?

Thoughts of heaven, hell, purgatory, and other afterlife options flooded my mind. I didn't experience any bright light and my life did not flash before my eyes, but I could not help but think that I was dead. Before I woke up, all I could think about was not ending up in the hospital, but I guess that would have been a better option than death.

How does one accept one's own death? And if I did die, where was heaven or hell? I was still in Rohnert Park. Some may consider that hell, but it was not what I was expecting.

I began to think about my family and what they would think about their "golden child" overdosing on hallucinogenic drugs. Wow. What a disappointment I would be. Approaching my final semester of college and dying of a drug overdose … Way to go, kid!

How had I gotten here? Not in this physical place but in this situation?

Looking back, I remembered my DARE class from elementary school. They made the kids who were experimenting with drugs look so lost and evil. We all swore and even signed a pledge to never be those kids, yet here I was.

How had I slipped so far?

It had started off with alcohol in high school, and then a little pot; then came the ecstasy, cocaine, and now mushrooms. Talk about a slippery slope. I think the craziest part about the descent was how I convinced myself that drugs weren't as bad as I had once thought and that others were ignorant for judging otherwise. The sin I was currently involved in was truly blinding. If you had told me even a year before that I would overdose on narcotics, I would tell you to fly a kite. No way was that happening to me; I was invincible. Yet this was my reality.

I continued thinking about my parents. My dad, a police officer … he was supposed to arrest people like me. What would he think? And my mom—my poor mom! I could just picture her crying, tears turning into anger. "Why, Matt, why? Was it worth it? Putting us through this torture … was it worth it?"

No, it wasn't worth it. I remember thinking to myself, *If I wake up from this dream, I will never do drugs again. I don't want anyone to go through such pain on my account.*

As I pulled away from these thoughts, I floated to the back of Kory's apartment and knocked on his door. "Hey, guys, what are you doing in there?" Kory opened the door, and he looked at me with soft, compassionate eyes as if he felt bad for me. I was confused, as I had never received such a look from any of my friends before. I then asked him, "Hey, man, what's going on here? I feel nothing. I'm not high anymore. I feel completely sober, and I am honestly a little confused." He looked at me as if I had lost my mind. Saying nothing, he led me and the other two guys into the living room.

As I followed them, I noticed that something was different about my friends. I felt as if they had some kind of authority over me or something. I could not understand what it was about their affect or posturing that gave them this authoritarian appearance, but I felt as if they were supposed to guide me somewhere or teach me something. I asked Kory, "Honestly, man, I don't understand what is going on. Help me out here."

He gave me a look of perplexity. "Matt, I don't know what you're talking about."

Not getting anywhere with my interrogations, I plainly came out with what was on my mind. "Are you guys, like, supposed to be … my guardian angels? I honestly feel as if I have died and you guys are supposed to lead me somewhere or tell me what to do from here."

Brandon laughed and made a gesture with his arms as if he were outlining imaginary wings around his back. "Do I look like an angel to you, Matt? If I'm an angel, where are my wings?"

Frustration and discouragement began to seep in as I begged them to explain why I felt the way I did and what was happening to me.

They then began to mess with me and said, "You're right, Matt. We are your guardian angels, and we are supposed to lead you somewhere … so let's go!"

Although I was slightly relieved to hear them finally admit to my suspicions, I became highly anxious. Was I going to have a *Christmas Carol* experience and see my life played out before my eyes? Would I have to see the hurt and pain that I had caused to my family and the type of person I would become if I continued on my current life path?

Where were they going to take me? Was I currently sitting in a waiting room? Having been raised in the church, I began to recall what the Bible says happens to people when they die: all people must go before the judgment seat of God, where they are either ushered into heaven or are condemned to hell based on their faith in the life, death, and resurrection of Jesus Christ. I could not help but think that Kory's apartment was the waiting room before the judgment seat. My anxiety and imagination spiked as my mind wandered through all the possibilities of what heaven would be like. As Kory opened the door to walk outside, I noticed that there was nothing different about his apartment complex.

Why should anything be different? you may be asking.

I was expecting him to open the front door and see a blinding light that would lead us to heaven, but only darkness poured in.

As we walked down the steps toward the parking lot, I grew more and more afraid of the possibilities that awaited me. I suddenly lost strength in my legs and reached out for Jason and Kory to keep from falling. When we reached Kory's carport, I saw a bright light in the distance and thought that I should investigate. In my mind I thought that these three guys were leading me on some interpersonal journey that would result in a greater understanding of myself or teach me some great life lesson.

I approached the light only to find a couple of college kids drinking beers on their balcony. As I looked around perplexed, I could hear my friends laughing in the background. I asked them where I should go, and they told me to follow them back to the apartment. They led me back to the house laughing hysterically because I thought they were supposed to take me on a journey. I was the butt of their stupid joke, and they were really enjoying my fragile, vulnerable state. As we climbed the stairs back into Kory's apartment, I felt overwhelming peace cover my body once more. It was as if something were telling me that everything would be all right, that I was safe inside Kory's apartment.

Once inside the apartment, Kory, Brandon, and Jason stood in a circle talking amongst themselves. As I stood on the outside looking in, I asked once more, "Guys, seriously, what is going on here?" I thought they were conspiring against me or something.

Finally, after what felt like hours of my begging for an explanation, Kory said, "Matt, why don't you just sit on the couch and enjoy yourself."

Enjoy myself? How was I supposed to "enjoy myself" when I felt like death was staring me in the face?

Still confused, I followed Kory's directions and sat on the couch. As I sat there, I felt a sense of submission as if I were a mere child taking orders from his father.

Still unclear of what I was waiting for, I sat expectantly while Kory turned on the television. He put *Planet Earth* into his DVD player, the movie we had all agreed to watch before beginning our adventure. To intensify the experience, Kory muted the television and plugged his iPod into the surround sound speakers. Becoming increasingly impatient, I asked once again, "Guys, what do you want me to do?" They calmly encouraged me to remain seated and enjoy the experience.

I kept trying to figure out why they kept using the word *experience*. Were they talking about my mushroom trip experience, thinking that I was still hallucinating, or the "experience" that I was waiting to have with them while watching this movie? Still confused and slightly frustrated, I stared at the television waiting for the show to start.

As *Planet Earth* began to play, the heavenly sound of flutes came pouring through the speakers. It was as if an angelic choir was orchestrating a concert in Kory's living room. *What are we listening to?* I asked myself. There was no way that Kory had acoustic flutes on his mushroom music mix, and seeing the "mute" icon in the corner of the television, I knew this wasn't part of the movie either. In my mind, I was convinced that I had officially died. In the book of Revelation, the apostle John describes the end of the world commencing with a loud trumpet blast and the King of Kings, aka Jesus Christ, coming from the heavens on clouds of fire. Although there were no clouds of fire or visions of Jesus, I was convinced that this sound was a representation of my death. The flutes continued, but now the song "Heartless" from Kanye West began to play.

This was the first time I'd heard this song, and I became fixated on the lyrics: "In the night I hear them talk, the coldest story ever told, somewhere far along the road, he lost his soul, to a woman so heartless.

How could you be so heartless?" The lyrics seemed to be speaking directly to me as I started to ask myself the question, *How could you be so heartless?* I felt strangely connected to the lyrics; they were a seemingly perfect depiction of how I had left my faith in God to pursue the world, "a woman so heartless," and lost my soul in the process.

As I sat there with flutes blaring, the opening scenes of *Planet Earth* began to stream across the television. Beautiful oceanic landscapes appeared while a voice, independent from the actual narration of *Planet Earth*, began to speak. As I watched the cinematography, the voice, booming with authority, began speaking to me.

Now, I know what you psychologists and skeptics must be thinking: *This kid is having "ideas of reference." Nothing was talking to him; he must still be high.*

That's fine. Keep reading ...

As the movie continued to play, the voice explained that he had created all of the beautiful scenery before my eyes. He said that he had intended for me to enjoy these things in fellowship with him but that I traded his truth for a lie. Instead of enjoying a loving relationship with him, I chose to live my life selfishly, indulging in the lusts of the flesh and pleasures of the world.

The narrator's words sounded relatively biblical; was this some kind of "divine intervention"?

Looking back on my time at church, I remembered feeling like an outcast among my peers. They would often say super-spiritual stuff like, "God totally spoke to me today" or "I could feel God's spirit moving inside of me." Truth be told, in my twenty-one years of church attendance, I had never felt God, heard his voice, or "experienced his presence" like my peers had so often claimed. Yet, here I was, in Rohnert Park, watching *Planet Earth* with my buddies, who were high on magic mushrooms, and I was hearing a voice talking as if he were God. Still not completely convinced, I continued to watch.

The scenes from *Planet Earth* changed from pictures of oceans, mountains, deserts, and forests to a dark, damp cave.

As the camera examined the cave, bats were shown hanging from the ceiling while the floor of the cave appeared to be moving. When the camera zoomed in for a closer look, I could see that the cave floor was covered with thousands upon thousands of cockroaches.

The voice began to speak again as he described his intended purpose for my life. He explained that instead of enjoying the beauty that he had created, I had decided to indulge in "bat dung."

As the voice spoke the words *bat dung*, the television displayed bat guano dripping from the ceiling of the cave and into the mouths of the cockroaches. As I sat there, my jaw dropped in disbelief. How could a voice, independent of the *Planet Earth* narrative, have been synced so perfectly with the movie?

I realized that outside our relationship with God, we are all cockroaches who are eating the "bat dung" of this dark world. The guano represented sin, I was the cockroach indulging in the sin, and the darkness represented separation from God.

If this depiction wasn't enough to convict me of my sin, what was happening in the apartment would do the job just fine.

When the bat scene had ended, the television faded out as if there were an intermission in the DVD sequence. While the movie was at a standstill, my friends began acting out what felt like a choreographed skit in the living room. Kory, Jason, and Brandon were all laughing and joking with one another while passing around a big glass bong. When Jason received the bong, he inhaled deeply and blew the smoke into the room. He then looked at me with glassy eyes and a childish grin and said, "You wanna hit this?"

Now, this may not seem strange to you, but he asked me in a sarcastic tone as if he was taunting or tempting me with the weed. I had just received a message about how I defiantly chose my selfish party lifestyle over the one God had intended for me, and here was Jason, asking me to smoke pot with him. It felt like a test; amazingly, I had no interest in the marijuana.

I was now sitting on the couch staring at my "friends" passing around drugs and alcohol and laughing at me as if to say, "This is what you would rather do than have a relationship with the Creator of the world?" I felt embarrassed and a little angry with them, as they were once again making fun of me.

"Come on, Matt. Take a hit! You don't wanna smoke, huh? Still enjoying your trip? You want to take some shots?" Jason asked.

Listening to these words made me cringe and hate the sin in which I was so deeply submerged. As I watched my friends acting out this party scene, I felt dissociated, as though I were watching from behind my eyes like a turtle watching from inside his shell. The television then lit up once more, and *Planet Earth* continued to play.

A black stallion was then shown galloping through an open field of wildflowers and tall grass. As this beautiful black creature galloped freely through the pasture, the voice began to speak. The mustang was described as being wild and free, without a care in the world and no thought about anyone else but itself. The voice seemed to be comparing me to this horse while stating that it was nearly impossible to contain such a prideful creature.

I felt a deep sense of conviction while hearing the voice's description of the horse. Reflecting upon the words of the narrator, I realized that this comparison was spot-on. I had no concern for anyone but myself and treated others as social stepping-stones.

Hearing these words and applying them to my own life made me sick. How could I be so "heartless"? The lyrics of that song began to resonate with me once more. I came to understand how wretched a man I truly was. How could I live so selfishly, and why would God want to love someone as prideful and arrogant as me?

Catching Crabs

The sequence following the horse in the pasture was extremely strange. As the mustang galloped into the sunset, the scene suddenly changed to an underwater view of the ocean floor. After examining the sandy depths, the camera focused on two crabs in the midst of a mating ritual. As the crabs conducted their business, provocative reggae rhythms provided by Damian Marley emanated from the surrounding speakers. I had never heard this song before, but the seductive sounds and lyrics seemed to play along perfectly with the sexual performance of these kinky crustaceans. It was almost comical how calculated this sequence seemed to be.

11

While we were watching the mating ritual, one particular part of Marley's lyrics captivated my mind: "Junior, you're a genius; you think with your mind and not your penis." Although this line was only sung twice in the actual song, the words *think with your mind and not your penis* spun around and around like a broken record in my brain. I couldn't help but think of my sexual sin.

God's voice was loud and clear. He wanted me to stop allowing my untamed sexual appetite to drive my reasoning. I could also sense him saying that there were severe consequences for sexual immorality. The king crabs seemed to represent a sexually transmitted disease that might come as a consequence of my actions. I was terrified.

As if this wasn't enough, the television unexpectedly changed to a picture of the Comcast On Demand menu. The TV show that appeared in the preview section was an episode of *South Park* titled, "Eek a Penis." These phallic references continued to confirm that God was trying to speak to me about my impure sexual lifestyle. The message was crystal, but God wasn't done.

Adding insult to injury, my "friends" began acting out another scene of my life in the living room. Jason and Brandon were sharing a dialogue that I had previously had with a recent girlfriend. Neither of these guys was aware that I even knew the girl they were imitating, yet they reenacted our conversation perfectly. Brandon played the part of my ex-girlfriend, and Jason played the part of yours truly. They were replaying a memory that I wished would go away, as it wasn't one of my proudest moments, when I told this girl a lie so she would fall for me. The dialogue was a perfect replication of what had actually occurred.

How could they have known?

I continued to watch in embarrassment. It was at this point that I was convinced I was no longer in the presence of my friends, but angels using their bodies to communicate God's conviction.

It's true what is written in the Bible—all of our actions here on earth are viewed by the heavenly host of witnesses. I couldn't help but laugh at myself for how ridiculous I appeared in the reenactment. My lines sounded as if they came straight from a *Tool Academy* textbook.

Brandon and Jason continued acting out this scene from my life, but the conversation suddenly shifted. The dialogue pertaining to my ex-girlfriend had ended, but their conversation continued on. Jason seemed to be bragging to us about all the drugs he had tried and the experiences he had had while partying. The topic of conversation fit with the theme of the evening, but what struck me was his choice of words.

Jason began boasting about his experiences while on ecstasy, something that I enjoyed bragging about also, since it happened to be my drug of choice. When Brandon asked him what the high felt like, Jason explained that while peeing, it felt as if he were having an intense orgasm. I had had that exact conversation only weeks prior. How did these guys know all of this about me? I was positive that neither of these guys was present when I had explained my experience on ecstasy before, yet he had my description memorized word for word.

Realizing that my sin was out in the open and feeling the intense presence of God, I turned to Brandon, who was currently sitting next to me and said, "Man, I'm such an 'f'-up."

Brandon then responded by saying, "Come on, Matt, you don't need to talk to me like that. We're on a different level."

The image of Brandon's face when he uttered these words has been branded in my mind ever since. His face appeared angelic, as if made of porcelain. Brandon was now also wearing glasses, which made him look more intelligent and innocent than ever before. His words burned in my mind as I realized the weight of his statement. I was no longer talking to Brandon. I still cannot confirm if it was Jesus or an angel from heaven, but it definitely wasn't Brandon. This man swore like a sailor and would never have paused at my profanity, but tonight was different.

The way Brandon spoke melted my heart and once again made me feel like a little boy being scolded by his father. *Scolded* may be the wrong choice of words, but each syllable seemed to cut deep into my soul. His words, although cutting, were offered with sincere love. I could feel his heart breaking as he heard me swear, which was so uncharacteristic of Brandon. The pain in his eyes made me hate what I had become. How could such a small statement make such a large impact? I felt ashamed of my choice of words and offered a sincere apology. Brandon responded with a gentle, sincere smile and continued to direct my attention to the television. I believe the next DVD sequence truly brought me to a place of repentance.

As Brandon turned his head toward the television, I followed his lead. I felt comforted knowing that these angelic forms had my best interests at heart. Although still confused as to what was truly happening, I could feel the conviction of the Holy Spirit as I sat and watched the events before my eyes.

The next scene depicted a pack of wild dogs roaming a desertlike plain. God's voice spoke once more. As I listened to his words, I could only think of him as a lion. In the Bible, Jesus is called the Lion of Judah, which was fitting for how his words roared out of the speakers with great authority. As I watched the television and listened to him speak, I imagined the powerful embodiment of God's voice. His words sounded condemning, but I knew they were coming from a place of love. He said, "Matt, I love you. I have a brilliant and wonderful plan for your life, but you have to leave your old sinful ways behind and follow me. You cannot procrastinate any longer. This is your last chance; if you do not turn from your sin now, you never will. Choosing to deny me and to continue in this life of sin will bring you to the place of weeping and gnashing of teeth."

I was outright terrified by these words, but what frightened me even more was the imagery on the television. As he said, "the place of weeping and gnashing of teeth," the camera zoomed in on two wild dogs attacking one another. Their teeth gnashed against each other while the sounds of dog whimpering and crying could be heard from the speakers. As I watched this sequence in horror, my mind rushed to a verse in the Bible that described hell as the place of "weeping and gnashing of teeth." The last place anyone wants to go is hell, yet that was exactly where God would send me if I didn't turn away from my sin and follow him. Only God can strike this type of fear in the heart of a man.

I had grown up believing in hell, but the thought of my going there never crossed my mind. Unfortunately for me, this place was becoming a vivid reality, and I knew that I needed to give my life to the Lord. I just didn't know how.

Shell-shocked and broken, I sat in front of the television on the verge of tears.

The next scene was of a large group of penguins huddled together on a freezing Antarctic night. A dark storm was raging as violent winds attacked the rookery of emperor penguins. These flightless birds would be without sunlight for the following four months. Their only job was to protect their eggs in the midst of the harsh winter. To survive, the penguins huddled together tightly to warm each other with their body heat. Each member served as a protective shield to its neighbor from the deadly cold winds and Antarctic temperatures.

While watching these creatures fight to stay alive, I heard God's voice speak to me again. He said, "If you want to live for me, you must surround yourself with other believers in the faith. In order to survive the storms of life, you need to find Christian community. Temptation, trials, and tribulation will inevitably come, but if you are surrounded by your brothers and sisters in Christ, you will persevere."

After the penguin scene ended, the DVD sequence started over from the beginning.

I knew what I needed to do.

As I sat on the couch, I closed my eyes and began to pray. I remember telling God, "I know what you are asking of me; I just do not understand how to do it. Help me. I want to give up my old life of sin and live for you, but I need your help. I cannot do this on my own. Please forgive me of my sins; I do not want to live that way anymore."

I took a pause from praying because I felt like nothing was happening. Was I praying wrong? How was I to do this? I thought I should be feeling something, but I felt nothing.

When I opened my eyes, I could see my three friends staring at me. What were they looking at? I felt awkward, so I closed my eyes to avoid making eye contact and continued to pray. Suddenly, my mouth became painfully dry. It felt like I had eaten a handful of sand.

In waking up from my mushroom coma, thirst was the first physical feeling I had. I longed for water, and I was painfully parched. I could not pray any longer; I needed water now. When I opened my eyes again, before me was a bright green Nalgene container on the table. This bottle of water seemed to be glowing as if to say, "Drink me. I'm here for you."

Where had this bottle come from? When I had closed my eyes to pray, there was nothing but a glass bong, lighter, and a few empty beer bottles on the table, but this glowing green bottle of water had suddenly appeared. Neither Brandon, Jason, nor Kory had moved since I had been on that couch. I looked at my three friends to see if any of them knew what had happened, and they all stared compassionately at me and then back at the bottle. Their eyes were seemingly telling me, "Drink the water. We know you are thirsty—take it!"

I couldn't do it.

I sat there in protest looking at that bottle of water as if it were placed there to poison me.

Why was I so afraid?

I so badly wanted the water, but something was holding me back. Maybe I wasn't truly ready to let go of my old ways. Maybe God knew my heart and saw that I wasn't ready to dive into this new life that he was graciously offering. I sat there hesitantly and closed my eyes to pray again, but I felt as if my prayers were coming back empty.

While sitting there, I could hear my friends talking to each other. "Maybe he's not getting this; he must still be high. You still enjoying your trip? Come on, you know what you need to do!" I thought they meant repent of my sins, but their eyes remained fixated on the bottle of water in front of me. Prayer did not seem to be working, so I opened my eyes once more and seriously considered drinking the water. My mouth was so dry, I couldn't take it any longer.

As I reached for the bottle, the voice said, "Drink of me and you will never thirst again." I knew those words! Those were the words of Jesus! "Whoever drinks the water I give him will never thirst. Indeed, the water I give him will become in him a spring of water welling up to eternal life" (John 4:14).

I was done hesitating; it was time to dive in. I grabbed the bottle of water and spun off the cap with great excitement. The moment that water hit my lips, I felt an indescribable sense of peace flood over my body … not just peace, but electricity. I sensed a surge of new life flowing through my veins. It was as if I could feel the blood of Christ washing over me, covering my body completely and cleansing me of all sin.

As I finished the bottle, my thirst was completely satisfied and I felt refreshed … not just physically, but spiritually. For the first time ever I felt the love and grace of God's forgiveness removing the heaviness of my sin, leaving me weightless and free. I knew at that moment that I would never be the same again; after what I had just experienced, how could I stay the same?

The Bible says that when people receive Jesus Christ as Lord and Savior, they become dead to sin and alive in Christ. The once dead sinner is then resurrected to new life as a new creation in Christ. I felt new. I felt alive. I felt forgiven. God had reached down into the darkness of my sin and pulled me into his glorious light. I had been forgiven, redeemed, rescued, renewed, refreshed, and restored. I was born again!

Not a minute after my spiritual rebirth there was a knock at the door. Seconds later the apartment door flung open. There in the doorway stood our friend Dustin. With two six-packs in hand and a devilish grin on his face he said, "It's time to get wasted! Who's with me?"

No one responded.

Dustin could sense the serious tone of the room and asked, "Whoa, what is going on in here? Come on, it's Friday night. Let's go to the bar." Then Dustin looked me right in the eyes and said, "Come on, Matt, you know you wanna get faded tonight. Besides, there are plenty of babes at the bar waiting for you. You know you wanna get some tonight!"

I was speechless and overwhelmed by the darkness of Dustin's presence. Thankfully, Kory spoke up and said that we were all staying in tonight and that we had had a long day. Dustin then turned again to me and tempted me with the promises of girls and good times, but I found the courage in my heart to say no.

Brandon looked at me with endearing eyes and said, "You do get it." I knew what he meant, and I felt a sense of accomplishment having turned down this temptation. Dustin realized that we weren't going to party with him, so he left.

I then turned to Kory and asked if I could crash on his couch. He said, "Good call, Matt. I'll make you a bed." I thanked Kory and went to sleep.

Hello, Hangover

When I awoke the next morning, I gathered my stuff and snuck out the front door making sure not to wake Brandon, who was asleep on an adjacent couch.

On the drive home I felt great. My conscience was clear, and my heart was at peace. I waited until eleven o'clock before contacting Kory. When I got him on the phone, I invited him to Sonoma Bagel for breakfast. I was excited to see him even though we had just spent the entire day together. I was curious to hear his recollection of the evening's events. As we sat down, I asked him how he was feeling, and he told me that he felt terrible. Apparently Kory had awakened with a horrible hangover, which I found peculiar. I asked Kory if he had gone out to the bars after I had gone to sleep, but he denied doing so. This was strange to me because I had never had a hangover after taking mushrooms. I figured he had had a few drinks after I went to sleep, but this wasn't the case. With this mystery in mind, I continued with my questioning and asked what he remembered from the evening. Most of what he said was subjective to his personal mushroom experience, so I cut to the chase. "Kory, do you remember anything strange happening last night? I mean something truly out of the ordinary?"

Kory just laughed and said, "Matt, a ton of strange things happened last night; we were all on magic mushrooms!"

This was not the answer I was looking for, so I prodded further. "No, I mean, do you remember anything about watching *Planet Earth*?" He responded with a vague account of the movie we had watched and explained that nothing particular had stood out to him. I explained the evening from my perspective, and he looked at me as if I had lost my mind.

"Well, we were on shrooms last night. Our experiences are completely our own, but no, to answer your question, I do not recall playing your 'guardian angel' last night."

I let the conversation go, as I could tell that my account was worrying him.

After breakfast I decided that I had better check in with Brandon and Jason. Maybe they would remember something that Kory had forgotten. I called Brandon asking how he was doing, and he responded, "I don't know about you, but I woke up this morning feeling like I had been hit by a semi truck!"

"A semi truck?" I asked. "You have a hangover or what?"

"Yeah, man. I feel terrible!"

Curious as to where these hangovers were coming from, I asked Brandon if he remembered anything peculiar from the night before. He remembered taking the shrooms, but he couldn't seem to recollect any further details.

This was odd.

I had had the most significant experience of my life, and none of my friends could corroborate my story.

I still had one shot, so I asked about Jason. "Brandon, have you heard from Jason at all this morning?"

"Yeah, man. Apparently he's feeling pretty bad this morning too."

All three of my friends had ended up with hangovers, while my head was perfectly clear and I could recall every detail of the *Planet Earth* incident as if I had caught it on camera!

CHAPTER 2

WALKING THE FENCE

After having experienced something so powerful, I was left in a strange transitory phase. I now knew without a doubt that God was real and that I could no longer live the way I had grown accustomed to living in college. With newfound conviction in my heart and my "God experience" fresh on my mind, I was contemplating what to do next.

I decided to call my mom since she was the only solid Christian I had any contact with. My mom had been praying for me to know God since I was a child, and she had always made an effort to encourage the growth of my faith. Apparently God was teaching my mom a painful lesson in patience, because it took twenty-two years for her to receive an answer to her prayers.

My mom sounded really confused on the phone as I told her about my encounter. It wasn't so much that she didn't believe me, but she sounded very apprehensive and maybe a bit skeptical about what she was hearing. Nonetheless, she was excited that I now desired to change my life and follow Jesus.

During Christmas vacation I began reading a book titled *Every Man's Battle* by Steven Arterburn. This book helped me confront many ugly truths about my sexually immoral lifestyle and provided helpful strategies to overcome my sinful desires.

I personally thought that I was a sex addict, since I had been struggling with pornography and sexual immorality since high school. The truth was that I simply had no boundaries in my relational life and used sex as a way to feel a sense of worth. I idolized women and worshipped sex. These two vices had placed me in bondage and slavery to my sexual appetite. If I was going to follow Jesus, I would have to get this under control.

An Unexpected Rescue Mission

I discovered something after my initial encounter with God; Jesus wasn't lying when he said, "The thief comes only to steal and kill and destroy; I have come that they may have life, and have it to the full" (John 10:10). I quickly found that anytime I desired to do something good for God, my enemy was right there trying his best to thwart my plans.

Before leaving Sonoma for winter vacation, I made a promise to one of my fraternity brothers that I would take him to the bars for his twenty-first birthday. Ricky lived in Livermore, which was a mere ten-minute drive from my parents' place in Pleasanton. None of Ricky's hometown friends were twenty-one yet, so I was his only hope for a night out on his birthday. This promise was of course made before I had decided to follow Jesus.

The day of Ricky's twenty-first birthday presented my first real battle with temptation. I spent the entire day anxiously awaiting Ricky's text in hopes that he would forget about my promise. I was praying about bailing on Ricky all day and finally felt peace about my decision: "When Ricky calls, I'm going to apologize to him for not being able to go out and courageously explain why. He's a good friend; he'll understand."

Almost instantaneously, Ricky's name flashed on my caller ID. In a panic I forwarded his call to voice mail. After a few minutes of freaking out, Ricky called again. This time I picked up the phone and nervously began to explain why I couldn't go to the bars with him. Ricky then proceeded to make me feel like a terrible friend for ditching him on this monumental occasion. I couldn't take the guilt trip and decided to go along for the ride. I compromised with Ricky and told him that I would be his chauffeur, but that partying was out of the question.

My mom overheard this conversation and asked what I was thinking, going to the bars after my experience with God. I explained to my mom that I intended to fulfill my promise to Ricky by providing him with a sober ride and that I wouldn't be drinking or doing anything crazy. It's true what they say, "The road to hell is paved with good intentions."

Ricky drove to my parents' place in Pleasanton and jumped into my car. Although my plan was to remain sober, or at most have a beer and still drive Ricky as promised, Ricky needed to stop for alcohol.

We then headed to a small liquor store down the street. I should have stayed in the car, but I wanted a pack of gum. While in the store I began to peruse the frosty beverage aisle. I intended to avoid alcohol and instead grabbed my favorite energy drink. At the counter, Ricky once again gave me a hard time about not drinking on his birthday. He also wanted to buy a certain bottle of vodka but didn't have enough cash. Ricky then asked if I was willing to split the bottle with him as a birthday present, and I agreed. With me still intending not to drink, we left the store brown bag in hand.

In the car Ricky continued with his barrage of belittling remarks and temptations. "Come on, Matt. It's my birthday! You promised to take me out, and you're not gonna party with me? How lame! Can't you just have a little? You don't have to get drunk; just take a couple shots with me. Where's the harm in that? Can't you stop partying tomorrow?"

I was frustrated with this conversation and with myself because I could sense that my boundaries were breaking down. All day I had planned to bail on Ricky and not respond to his calls, but I folded under pressure and compromised.

How did I go from canceling on this evening to compromising my convictions after the personal experience I had had with God? It was as if I had an angel and a demon duking it out on my shoulders. Each one was fighting for my soul as I weighed the decision in front of me.

A wise man once told me that there will always be two wolves fighting over my soul. That wise person then asked me which wolf would win, and then he explained, "The wolf that you feed."

As we sat in the parking lot of the nightclub, a group of girls pulled up next to us. I knew right then that my convictions weren't strong enough to withstand the temptations in my mind.

I found myself justifying the idea of drinking by telling myself that I needed the alcohol to socialize and enjoy this evening. I told myself that it wasn't fair to Ricky if I was a "wet blanket" or a "negative Nancy" on his twenty-first birthday. Besides, I had made a promise, and I wouldn't completely fulfill my promise unless I partook in the evening's events.

I was feeding the wrong wolf.

All of this conversation took place in my head while I was sitting in the car. It probably lasted forty seconds, but it felt like an eternity. After Ricky turned up the music in my car, I grabbed the bottle from his hand, pounded half of it, and chased the nasty-tasting vodka with my energy drink. And just like that my convictions were out the window.

Welcome to the Jungle

The club was like a high school reunion. Had I not recently consumed a large amount of liquid confidence, this would have been a painfully uncomfortable situation. As we entered the club, I saw a sea of familiar faces. I beelined toward the bartender and ordered beers for myself and Ricky. I couldn't walk around the club empty-handed, right?

Almost immediately she caught my eye. Seemingly out of place among my high school friends and others in my peer group was a "wild cougar." No, they did not allow killer cats into the club. On the contrary, this was the type of cougar that only hunted younger men. These women are usually in their midthirties to early forties, often divorced and looking for a man to make them feel young again.

I approached her on the dance floor and initiated some friendly conversation. The cougar explained that she was with a group of friends but had incidentally separated from the pack. I offered to buy her a drink, which she gratefully accepted. We then began dancing together and eventually started making out in the middle of the dance floor. We ended up dancing and kissing all night without much attention paid to Ricky. At the end of the night the cougar invited me home to her house in Tracy. I accepted her invitation, and we headed out the door. At this point I was intoxicated, consumed with lust, and couldn't care less about the God encounter I'd had. There was only one thing on my mind, and it was not how Ricky planned on getting home.

When we finally located her friends, I was introduced to the man who was planning to be our driver. He looked intoxicated, which made me have second thoughts about accompanying this woman home. As our driver started the engine and backed out of the parking space, my suspicions were confirmed; the guy was wasted.

Before I was able to have a full-blown anxiety attack, the girls realized that they were still missing one of their friends. Our driver immediately stopped the car in front of the club. This sudden interruption gave me an opportunity to get some fresh air to collect my thoughts.

The moment I stepped out of the car, I heard the authoritative voice of my sister yell, "Matt! What are you doing? Get in my car right now; we're going home!"

Where my sister came from, I have no idea, but the timing was miraculous, so I didn't ask questions. Without hesitation I ditched my date and jumped into my sister's car. Ricky had apparently called my sister for a ride, which turned out to save me from a potentially dangerous drive home and a sexual encounter that I would most definitely have regretted.

I woke up the next morning with a throbbing hangover and an unnerving sense of condemnation. What had I done last night? God had just pulled me out of this pit; why would I voluntarily walk back in? I guess Solomon was right—"Like a dog returns to its vomit, so a fool returns to his folly" (Proverbs 26:11).

Compromise was killing me.

Looking back on the night, I could see the cancerous consequences of compromise, but in the moment, I had been blinded by the temporary pleasure. I needed a better strategy. Overcoming sexual sin would require much more than self-control; I would need to stop placing myself in tempting situations. Although I couldn't become a monk and completely hide myself from all women, I could certainly stop getting drunk around them.

Still not taking complete responsibility for my actions, I was now blaming my drunkenness for my sexual sin. I hoped this new discovery would help me avoid further slipups during the winter vacation.

Red Coats Reunion

A few nights later I received a phone call from a fraternity brother who also lived near my parents' place. Nate's call came in around nine o'clock;

he asked if I wanted to join him at the Redjacket bar in downtown Pleasanton. I respectfully declined his offer, explaining that I was trying to leave the party scene and felt that meeting at a bar would only tempt me to compromise.

Nate explained that he wasn't trying to get drunk and that his mother was at the bar with him. "Matt, come have one beer with me and my mom. What's the big deal? We haven't hung out in days, and my mom would also love to see you."

I had developed a close relationship with Nate and his mom throughout college and justified my outing by telling myself that I wasn't an alcoholic and that one beer wouldn't kill me. With compromise already kicking in before even leaving the house, I was setting myself up to fail.

As I walked up to the Redjacket, I could see a long line of people waiting to get into the packed bar. I took my place at the back of the line and called Nate. His mother immediately came outside and whispered something into the bouncer's ear. I was then escorted to the front of the line past the now impatient hopefuls still waiting to enter.

Once we were inside the bar, Nate's mom told me that her tab was open and that my drinks were on her tonight. I thanked her for the kind offer but declined to take a drink.

So far, so good.

Then I heard Nate's loud, drunken voice yelling my name from across the room. He approached me staggering with a tall glass of Jack and Coke in hand. "Come get a drink with me!" he said, slurring.

I followed Nate to the bar, where he ordered me a Jack and Coke. After a few sips, I lost all conviction. One drink turned into ten, and I once again found myself trashed at a bar.

Why did this keep happening?

How could I have this little conviction and self-control?

Thankfully, I was able to avoid the ladies at the bar that night and took a cab home with Nate instead.

The next day I woke up with another headache and decided that I had a real problem. I had no self-control, boundaries, or lasting conviction. Women weren't the problem; drinking wasn't the problem. I was the problem. I couldn't continue to blame others for my actions. If I wanted to follow Jesus, I would have to completely surrender.

The Party to End All Parties

My final test came on New Year's Eve. For the holiday I decided to visit my best friends from high school, Andrew and Chris, who both lived in Sacramento. The three of us traditionally spent the New Year's holiday together, and this year would be no exception. I arrived in the early afternoon to help the guys prepare for their "ugly sweater" themed party. After all the preparations were in place, the guys started drinking as we usually would. They asked if I wanted a beer, and I explained what had happened to me a few weeks prior when I met Jesus. They were surprised to hear my story but still encouraged me to have a beer.

The conversation was all too familiar. "Come on, Matt. It's New Year's; can't you have a couple beers with us tonight? You don't have to get drunk—just have a couple."

The temptations seemed like a combination between the first two tests, and I once again buckled under the pressure of my friends. I promised myself that I would have no more than three beers over the progression of the night, and to my surprise I actually followed through.

Andrew threw an awesome party, we all had a great time, and I was able to stick to my convictions. However, at some point during the night I called a girlfriend from Sonoma State to join our party, and she did. When the night ended, we all crashed at Andrew's place, and I slept on the couch with my date. Thankfully, nothing happened between us, and I was able to fall asleep without feeling any condemnation.

I woke up the next morning to what seemed like a scene from *The Hangover*. There were cups, bottles, and cans strewn about the house, strangers on the couches and floor, dogs and cats licking up puddles of liquor, Guitar Hero playing on the TV in the background, and the musty smell of hard alcohol and beer hanging in the air.

As I examined the remnants of the evening's shenanigans, I felt the strangest sense of freedom. Today was a new day, the beginning of a new year. I was free to choose a life of wholehearted devotion to Jesus. I didn't need to hold on to the past any longer. I had no more excuses and no reasons to keep me chained to my sinful lifestyle any longer.

The feeling was exhilarating.

I had been a slave to my sin, but on this first day of January 2009, I could throw my chains to the ground, walk away, and never look back. I was free to live for Jesus!

As I drove home from Sacramento, I prayed and repented of my sins once again and dedicated my life to following Christ. I vowed to give up the things that enslaved me so that I could walk in freedom with my Savior.

Shortly after returning home I broke up with my girlfriend and informed my friends that I wanted to give up drinking and drugs. No one understood my decision and many tried to dissuade me, but my convictions were strong and there was no going back.

From that moment on I withdrew from friends who would not support my decision to stop partying and began to focus my time and attention on Jesus. I began to watch online sermons from Pastor Craig Groeschel and spent my free time reading the Bible.

This may sound strange, but after New Year's Day, God placed a desire in my heart for his word. I honestly thirsted to know him more, an experience that was previously foreign to me. I then joined a Bible study with some friends from college who eventually brought me to their church, Calvary Chapel Petaluma. This was the first time in church when I felt free to worship God without judgment.

I remembered attending a high school youth group feeling restricted from worship. I vividly remember a sermon that called Christians "walking billboards for Jesus." I was terrified about the accountability associated with claiming to follow Christ. I still had sin in my life that I was unwilling to give up, and I thought that if I worshipped God that I would be considered a hypocrite. The fear of hypocrisy and not wanting to make Jesus look bad kept me from worshipping him in high school, but not today, not anymore. The moment I walked into this church, I knew that I was home. I knew that I was free to worship. I was hungry for worship, thirsty for God's word, and I craved the sermons that were preached in that place. There was a freedom that I had never experienced before, and my eyes were finally open to God. He was real, he was in that place, and he was changing my heart.

The spring semester of my senior year was an exciting time of spiritual growth for me. I was cultivating a relationship with my Creator and felt an inexpressible joy in my heart as I grew closer to him. I tried to explain this feeling to my roommates, but they didn't understand. Although my roommates had known my frat boy antics and witnessed the transformation of my life, they still refused to embrace the fact that Jesus was changing me—I wasn't changing myself.

I really don't understand how they could attribute these changes to anything other than the power of God. I had everything a college kid could want; what could possibly explain an overnight transformation such as the one I had experienced?

Honestly, I had enjoyed my sinful lifestyle before I began following Jesus. It's like my pastor Craig says, "Anyone who thinks that sin isn't fun, clearly isn't doing it right!" It was fun to live life without accountability or commitment and to pursue selfish gain and pleasure without boundaries. It's not like I woke up one morning and decided that I was bored of sex, partying, and irresponsibility.

God definitely intervened at a really inconvenient time in my social career. Everything I had dreamed of becoming in terms of social status during high school was currently my reality. I had friends in every sorority, fraternity, sports team, and unaffiliated group of students at Sonoma State University. I could attend parties any night of the week with the group of friends of my choice. I was living the college dream. It wasn't as if an unplanned pregnancy or death in the family had awakened the responsible adult in me. No, something miraculous had happened, something so significant that I was willing to forsake everything I had been enjoying— the parties, girls, drinking, drugs. All of it went out the window overnight, and all for a relationship with Jesus Christ.

As I look back, I believe my roommates must have thought that I was crazy. Instead of going out drinking, I would be the designated driver. Instead of spending hours playing Call of Duty, I was reading the Old Testament. If I went to a party, I would play beer pong with soda, and for the first time in my life I didn't care what others thought about me. I knew that following Jesus was unpopular, but I was realizing that his promises were so much more appealing than any party or sinful pleasure.

CHAPTER 3

MIRACLE ON TWO WHEELS

The Bible says that God will consume the wealth of the wicked like a moth (Psalm 39:11). Although I was now following Jesus, I soon discovered that I was not excluded from experiencing the consequences of my sinful lifestyle. The guy who once had piles of cash from bartending was now jobless and broke. With only a semester before graduation, I needed some income.

I applied everywhere in my college town, but to no avail. I couldn't even get a job at In 'n' Out Burger. That was a discouraging day. The rejections continued, and my confidence dwindled just as fast as my bank account.

With no money or job prospects, I began losing hope. Sitting in the parking lot of a Taco Bell, I did the only thing that I believed would work. I prayed, telling God that I was discouraged and at the end of my rope, that I desperately needed his help and didn't want to accept any more handouts from my mom. In that prayer, I promised that if God would provide a job for me that I would be generous to the poor and would tithe my income to his church.

After that conversation I had a little more hope, but the reality of being completely broke eventually had me back in a depressing place.

When I got home, I turned to the one activity that usually lifted my mood. Last summer while I was bartending, one of my major purchases was a really nice mountain bike. I finally had the money to buy the bike of my dreams, so I purchased one with full suspension, disk brakes, and all the other bells and whistles that make an expensive mountain bike so attractive.

Exercise almost always made me forget about my troubles, at least until the adrenaline wore off, so I decided to take my bike for a spin. The bike was lying in my garage without the front wheel attached from the time when I last transported the bike in the trunk of my car. It took me almost an hour to get the wheel back on. When it was finally in place, I realized that part of the tire locking mechanism had broken off during my last ride. Without this crucial piece, I wouldn't be able to ride my bike. I couldn't believe it. Why was this happening? I had no job and no money, and I couldn't even ride my bike to help deal with my frustrations about the whole situation.

Thankfully, I remembered that I had a warranty on the bike. I immediately called the sporting equipment store to report my broken bike. As if my day couldn't get any worse, the store informed me that the warranty company had gone out of business and that they could not replace my bike.

Are you kidding me?

The associate placed me on hold to talk to her manager.

Boiling in anger and slipping into further depression, I sat on the other end of the phone waiting for more bad news.

The associate picked up the phone and apologetically thanked me for my patience and understanding.

If she only knew.

"You have two options, Mr. Jones. We can either give you store credit to buy a new bike, or we can refund you the total amount of your purchase." And just like that, my prayer was answered. I wanted a new bike, but God wanted to give me something greater. He was meeting my real need instead of my superficial desire. God knew that I needed gas and food much more than a new bike, and he provided accordingly.

That day I learned that God, as my Heavenly Father, is a faithful provider.

An Arresting Development

Jesus was a realist. He did not sugarcoat anything. Instead, he told his followers exactly what to expect. Jesus also offered the assurance of his promises, backing them up with miracle after miracle.

Jesus promised to provide abundant life for those willing to follow him, but he also promised hardship, persecution, and trouble. Jesus never promised smooth seas, but he did promise to sail with us through our storms.

My first major storm came on February 26th, 2009. I was on my way to a Bible study at school when I received the following text message from my dad: "Son, I want you to hear this from me before you turn on the TV, read the newspaper, or hear any rumors about what's going on. I was arrested today."

My dad was a police officer. He was supposed to do the arresting. How could this happen?

My dad explained that he was being set up by the media and that they were falsely accusing him of stealing narcotics from the police department. Greatly confused, I asked for more details, but none came. My dad was intentionally vague in his explanations because as I would soon discover, the "lies" were all true.

The truth was that my dad had developed an addiction to painkillers due to a number of factors, some of which were his marriage was failing and he had separated from my mom; another relationship was consuming him with guilt; he was worried about me and my sister; his grandfather was ailing with dementia and my dad was responsible for his affairs; and he was struggling with symptoms of PTSD due to an on-duty shooting incident he had survived as a police officer.

The situations were overwhelming, and due to his avoidance of help he turned to masking his pain in a destructive way.

This was a real-life nightmare for a son to hear and a dream come true for the local media. This crooked cop story would fill the local headlines and nightly news as my father awaited his trial.

After hearing the news from my dad, I called Chris, my fraternity brother and friend who currently led us in a weekly Bible study, to pray for me. Chris met me in the parking lot of our favorite Mexican food restaurant. He hugged me, we prayed, and I miraculously felt the peace of God comforting me in my most devastating moment. Chris then told me about an Intervarsity meeting on campus that I could attend for more prayer.

As I sat in the back of the church, I couldn't hear a word the preacher was saying. Instead, I began to flip through my Bible in search of anything that could bring clarity, understanding, or comfort to anyone in my family. God brought me to the Psalms, and the verses brought words of truth to my exact situation. I sent text after text to my dad with these verses, but there was no response. Eventually I received a "thank you," but that was all.

I remembered what God had told me in December: "Matt, this is your last chance; if you do not turn from your sins now you never will, and you'll end up in the place of weeping and gnashing of teeth." God knew that this storm was coming and he knew how I had coped with my problems in the past. God knew that I would resort to drugs and alcohol to hide the pain and medicate away my feelings just as my dad had been doing.

Before Jesus intervened in my life that December, I was becoming more careless than ever with my substance use. I remember a night when I mixed alcohol, cocaine, mushrooms, and marijuana. It was also becoming common practice for me to mix alcohol, cocaine, and ecstasy at parties and then drive myself home … not to mention that I was also involved in the distribution of illegal narcotics. I was living recklessly in ever-increasing measure, and God knew where my path was headed. I sincerely believe that had I not listened to God that night in December, had I chosen to ignore his warning, I would have eventually overdosed, died in a party-related incident or drunk driving accident, or been arrested.

Instead of drinking or popping pills to escape the reality of this situation with my dad, I was able to pray and experience God's peace and comfort. Although the world was shaking all around me, God was sovereignly still. He was holding me in his arms while the waves crashed against me. I was safe. Without him, I would have definitely drowned in the raging waters of this violent storm.

For the first time since my salvation experience I felt the tangible presence of God in my life. I had every reason to panic and worry, but the

Lord gave me peace. He was in control. This situation was out of my hands but tightly bound in his. God knew what he was doing, and I trusted him.

I eventually drove home to comfort my dad in his time of trial. When I arrived, I witnessed for the first time in my life a broken man, ashamed, and sitting alone in a darkened room. Depression, guilt, and shame were written all over his face. It was extremely difficult to sit in that room with my dad.

I had yet to hear the truth from my dad and waited patiently for him to come clean. In a moment of clarity I received the insight from God that I first needed to confess my hidden lifestyle to my dad before he would experience the freedom to share the truth about his.

While standing in the kitchen I made the decision to debunk any misconceptions regarding this "golden boy," and I unwrapped the story of the secret life I had been living since high school. I told my dad about all the drugs I had abused and sold, the lies I had told, the women I had slept with, and the other bits of information I was hoping he would never discover on his own. I explained how God had intervened and pulled me out of the dark pit I had created for myself. I told him that Jesus had taken all of my guilt, shame, and embarrassment about my past life and nailed it to the cross with him, covering those sins in his blood. I continued to explain that I was forgiven and that God was carrying me in his arms through this difficult time, and that he wanted to do the same for my dad.

After sharing this with my dad, I saw tears in his eyes for the first time. He told me about how he was so overwhelmed with his life that he didn't know how to handle it. He admitted to stealing medication from family, friends, and civilians from work because they helped him cope with the issues in his life.

I'm not exactly sure when my dad received Jesus Christ as his personal Lord and Savior, but he eventually gave everything to God, and Jesus saved him. This conversation with my father confirmed the truth found in James 5:16, which promised healing to those who confess their sins to one another. It was freeing to bring my sins into the light and to watch my dad open up about his. We no longer had to hide behind the façade of perfection. Neither of us had to be the "strong one" in the family, but we could instead own our faults and folly and allow God to heal us.

After our conversation I watched as God miraculously provided for my dad throughout the next two years. At the time of my dad's initial arrest he had multiple felony counts against him, which consequently resulted in the loss of his job and the potential loss of his pension, benefits, and hopes of retirement.

Despite the publicity that "crooked cop trials" usually receive, God sheltered my dad from most of the media's wrath. He was charged with one felony that allowed him to attend recovery meetings and public service, which eventually removed the charge from his record. In the end, my dad lost his retirement benefits, but more importantly, God saved his soul.

During the two-year period when my dad was out of a job, God continuously provided for him with odd jobs and spiritual growth. My dad began attending AA recovery meetings, Bible studies, and church. His relationship with my mom began to improve to the point where they would eventually remarry after an affair and seven years of separation. God was working miracles left and right to provide for, restore, and heal my family. My dad was slowly able to regain his dignity, reestablish his faith, and trust in Jesus. This crisis ended up saving our family. God truly does make beautiful things out of dirt.

Sorority Sister

After dealing with my dad's situation, I returned to school. Sonoma was a refuge for me. Since I had come to know Jesus, God had established a lot of healthy support for me in Sonoma. I was now regularly attending church, participating in a Bible study, and visiting the church college group that met for midweek worship.

With a few months of these activities under my belt, I was starting to feel strong enough to venture back into the places from which God had saved me. I had so many friends who needed to hear about Jesus that I could no longer lock myself away in my house. It was time to get out, share Christ with my college buddies, and show them how God was changing my life.

One way that I found effective was to drive others around on the weekends. It was becoming widely known around school that I was willing to play the role of designated driver, and people were definitely taking advantage.

Thankfully, I enjoyed driving my friends around town. It was a free service to them and entertainment for me. That is, until one of my inebriated passengers threw up in the car; that wasn't so fun.

One weekend in the spring, I was invited to a party at a rival fraternity house. The previous summer while working on campus at Sonoma State, I had made friends with Darren Sanchester, who was highly influential in this fraternity. Darren was instrumental in my faith journey for many reasons, and his inviting me to this party was one of them.

On my way to the party, I received a phone call from classmate Julie Johnson. She needed a ride to Darren's party, so I packed my car with Julie and her sorority sisters. On our drive to the party, I told the girls that I could offer my services only until midnight. Church was now top on my weekend priority list, so I couldn't be out too late on Saturday nights.

Julie was shocked to hear that I would be attending church and revealed that she has too was Christian. Julie expressed that she was interested in attending church but had not yet found one while away at college. I asked Julie if she wanted to attend Calvary Chapel with me, and she agreed.

After that first Sunday, Julie started coming to my Bible study, attending church with me, and even carpooling with me most Sundays. Julie and I quickly became close buddies. We often texted prayer requests, shared joys and sorrows, and really began to enjoy one another's company.

One day during class I asked Julie if she wanted to drive with me downtown to feed some homeless people. We drove to the parking garage of the Santa Rosa mall, parked, and headed downtown to find someone we could invite to lunch. We walked the streets of Santa Rosa for almost an hour without finding any homeless people.

What could have turned out to be a disappointing day actually led to a conversation that would once again change the trajectory of my life…

Julie and I had met through the Greek system at school, but as psychology majors, we also shared many classes. Julie once told me about her job and how she counseled mentally ill people at a dual-diagnosis clinic in Santa Rosa. I didn't really understand what a job like this entailed, so Julie told me that she performed treatment plans, facilitated group therapy, distributed medication, and executed intake interviews, along with the many daily house chores required to run the facility.

The way she described her job made me question the validity of her credentialed employer. How could they allow unlicensed staff to perform the duties of licensed clinicians? It didn't make sense. In fact, my critical and often judgmental nature almost prevented me from capitalizing on one of the greatest opportunities of my life.

Thankfully, curiosity overpowered my criticism and I started asking her more questions about her clients and coworkers, and how she got the job. Julie could tell that I was interested and asked if I wanted to interview for an on-call position. I needed a job but was hesitant to accept her offer. Although I was a psychology major, I wasn't all that interested in becoming a counselor. There was no way that I could sit in an office for eight hours a day and listen to other people's problems. I would inevitably fall asleep and get fired.

Julie assured me that it was nothing like I was envisioning. Her "taste and see" approach eventually won me over. I then applied for the job and one week later had an interview with Director Wainwright.

A Hiring at Healing House

I knew that God was involved in the interview process, because I actually got the job. Even though I had no experience, Director Wainwright hired me with a "sink or swim" mentality. I personally believe that everyone in that office expected me to drown, but I prevailed. Even more than that, I fell in love with the job and the people.

Never in a million years had I thought that I could love, serve, and listen to people the way that God was enabling me to at Healing House. My days were now spent living with the poor, helpless, hurting, abandoned, and ostracized. These people were without families, homes, mental stability, safety, love, or food, and we were able to provide for all of their needs.

Many of my coworkers seemed burned out and tired from the long hours, but I often left feeling more energized and alive than when I started. It was a life-giving place for me. I was getting paid to put the Bible into action by demonstrating the love of Jesus to others. God was growing me and teaching me to love with compassion and joy. I couldn't believe how wonderful working for the Lord could be.

Hazing

Initiation is the process of accepting an outsider into an already established group of closely connected people. Initiation rites occur in the military, fraternities, sports teams, and apparently also Healing House.

Part of my daily duties included housecleaning. A coworker of mine asked me to clean the guest bedroom and bathroom, paying special attention to the shower. I wasn't a big fan of cleaning showers. All the soap scum, mildew, and body hair made my skin crawl.

After cleaning the bedroom, I made my way into the bathroom. It smelled horrible. Choking back my vomit, I cleaned the toilet, floors, and sink, but I couldn't get the stench out of the room. I then remembered my coworker's request to "pay special attention to the shower."

Pulling back the curtains, I found it. Right in the middle of the tub. A giant turd. It stared at me right in the face, mocking me. One of our residents had literally squatted over the tub and taken a dump right onto the floor with the toilet just two feet away.

That's right, poop in the bathtub and I was expected to scoop it up.

Most of the hazing I experienced in college included drinking and puking, but this was way worse. I would have much rather endured the hazing of my lacrosse team and fraternity pledge semester than picked up human poop.

My coworkers were dying with laughter. "Welcome to the team, kid."

I never did hear how they initiated Julie, but I can't imagine it had to do with poop.

There was never a dull moment in that house. I learned something new about life, psychology, God, and myself every day.

One of my favorite skills that I picked up while working at Healing House was the game of chess. I learned how to play from a young man with dissociative personality disorder, meaning that he could instantaneously switch between his many personalities without warning. One minute he was Fred the firefighter, the next he was Colonel Smith of the US Army, and then he was a little boy named Charlie. You never knew what to expect or whom you would be talking to. When people ask how I became so good at chess, I often joke that it's easy to become good when you learn how to play against four people at once.

On a side note, I once met a woman who had the split personality of a dead racehorse. We would be sitting in the backyard, she chain-smoking a cigarette and I intently listening to her ramble about memories of times past on the racetrack. I was listening to the stories of a dead racehorse. Talk about a trip!

Healing Hannegan

During the final semester of my senior year in college, I limited my interactions with my fraternity brothers. It wasn't that they were bad people; I just couldn't handle the temptations that I often felt around them. I knew my boundaries well enough and did not want to test the waters of temptation. Eventually I would be strong enough to attend their parties, hang out at the bars, and go places where the "tax collectors and sinners" hung out, but as a baby Christian, I wasn't ready.

This caused me to be selective when choosing the times and places I would interact with certain people. Since I had been MIA for most of the semester, I chose to attend my fraternity's biannual "active social" that the pledge class sponsored.

Every year, the pledges' goal was to raise funds throughout the semester to throw the active brothers in our fraternity a party or event to celebrate our brotherhood. This year our active social included an afternoon of paintball, and I decided to attend.

About halfway through our paintball session, my frat brother Mitch appeared at the paintball facility. His face was red and his eyes were puffy like he had been crying. Mitch was not his usual self, which was noticeable to everyone in the room. It turned out that Mitch had been at the hospital, where he was diagnosed with a terminal heart condition. The doctors said that he had six to twelve months to live. I couldn't believe it. We've all seen movies or heard stories in which people are handed death sentences, but this was my first encounter with someone I cared about.

What do you say to that person?

Surprisingly enough, Mitch walked right up to me and asked if we could talk. I hugged him and agreed. We then walked to a table away from the paintball field. At this point, almost all of my frat friends knew that I had become a Christian, and in times of need people tend to start asking the difficult questions about life, death, heaven, hell, God, and the like.

As Mitch was talking, God told me to pray for him. I had never prayed for anyone like this before, and I felt unprepared and honestly scared. Despite my fears, God relentlessly continued to request that I pray for Mitch.

I tried silencing his voice, but it only grew louder. Since fighting with God was futile, I gave in and asked Mitch if I could pray for him.

Never having done this before and not quite confident that I was doing it correctly, I placed my hand over Mitch's heart and began to pray.

I asked for healing, that God would reject the diagnosis and allow Mitch to live, and that God would close the hole in Mitch's heart that was causing the stress on his body. I also prayed that Jesus would reveal himself to Mitch so that he would come to know the hope of salvation, forgiveness, and eternal life offered by grace through faith in Jesus Christ.

Honestly, I couldn't tell if my prayer worked. I didn't feel anything, see anything, or experience anything that would make me believe that my prayer had been answered.

I've read about healing miracles in the Bible and faithlessly thought that it might still be possible for God to heal people today, but never did I imagine that God would actually heal someone before my eyes and through such a simple prayer.

However, something did happen. A healing miracle happened in Mitch's heart that day. None of us knew it until his birthday the following year and the year after that and every year since our prayer on that paintball field. Five years after that simple prayer, Mitch is still alive and well. The doctors gave him six to twelve months, but God, the healer, the great physician, had other plans.

I'm not sure if Mitch ever became a Christian, and I pray that he reads this book one day, but Mitch is a miracle. Every heartbeat is a reminder of God's grace for Mitch and of God's miraculous healing power for me.

Judgmental Georgia

I have a guilty confession to make.

The main reason I attended church in high school was not God.

It was the girls.

Now, if you knew me back then or were one of my high school pastors, this isn't news to you, but it's true. If it weren't for the girls at church, I would have found an excuse to stay home every Sunday with my dad.

Of the many evidences that God was changing my life, this one was one of the most significant. Now that I was back in church, sincerely seeking after God and becoming a disciple of Jesus Christ, I couldn't care less about chasing the girls in church. They just weren't my focus. In fact, during the first few weeks of following Jesus I read Josh Harris's *I Kissed Dating Goodbye*, a book that completely changed my view of dating. After reading this book, I took a sabbatical from the dating scene. I wanted to know God better, heal from my past mistakes, and stay far from temptation, so I cut what I deemed unnecessary out of my life for a season.

Three months into my season of singleness I was approached by a very bold woman named Georgia at Calvary Chapel. During her introduction, she informed me that she had been watching me since I arrived at church … not just that day, but for the last three months.

I put on my best poker face trying not to look terrified by my pseudo stalker. Georgia informed me that she knew all about guys like me. Later, Georgia would elaborate on what guys like me meant—"womanizing, meathead, frat boy, d-bags."

In church!

Georgia had no shame.

With guns blazing, Georgia continued confronting me with the rumors that were floating around the church about me. Apparently, classmates from college had attended Calvary and were not hesitant to let others know about the "riffraff" they were allowing in their services. Georgia's introduction quickly turned into a warning that she was watching me and that I'd better think twice before dating any of the girls at Calvary.

I can't lie—Georgia was intimidating. She was a tough-looking girl with a chip on her shoulder, but in the spirit of competition I couldn't back down from her unspoken challenge. I was going to befriend this girl and show her that she was wrong about me.

It took a few weeks of conversation at church and outings with the Calvary college group, but I eventually accomplished my goal and befriended Georgia. Oddly enough, we actually became quite close. She still made fun of me and my past, but it was no longer in a threatening or judgmental way. I started to see Georgia like a sister and truly cared for her. She even returned the sentiment and began calling me "bro."

Despite our closeness, Georgia was still guarded and would often say things like, "I know you're going to start dating someone soon, and then you'll totally forget about me. All guys are the same." Apparently Georgia had abandonment issues and walls around her heart the size of Jericho.

Georgia and I developed a unique relationship. It was known in the church that I wasn't interested in dating anyone, yet I spent a great deal of time with her. We would hang out at my house with my roommates, watch movies, spend hours talking on the phone at night, eat meals, and attend church together. My relationship with Georgia was very similar to my relationship with Julie; the only difference was that I might have actually considered dating Julie. Thankfully, I was wise enough to realize at the time that I had no concept of commitment and probably would have ruined my friendship with Julie if I had ever tried moving out of the "friend zone."

Hanging out with Georgia was totally different; it honestly felt like I was hanging out with one of the guys. Sometimes I felt like Georgia's counselor, other times like her brother, and sometimes I had the feeling that Georgia saw me as more than just a friend. In fact, Georgia would often joke about watching the movie *Just Friends*, the Ryan Reynolds movie about being placed in the "friend zone," but our situation was too closely related and I wanted to spare myself from the awkwardness of ever having a "DTR" with Georgia.

A DTR, for those who don't know, is a conversation where you "define the relationship," something that never needed to occur between Georgia and me because our relationship was completely platonic, or so I thought …

One day when I got home from work, my roommates informed me that Georgia had showed up unannounced and was waiting in my bedroom. When a girl "friend" shows up without an invitation to wait in your bedroom (for hours), a talk about boundaries is well deserved.

Having no idea how to handle this situation, I casually walked into my room like everything was normal. Georgia was also sitting on my couch, filing her nails like everything was normal.

This was not normal!

I asked her what she was doing in my bedroom. Georgia said, "Waiting for you—what do you think?"

I was finally coming to terms with the fact that my relationship with Georgia was unhealthy and needed to change. I had no intention of ever dating or pursuing Georgia and needed to make this clear.

Before I could initiate our much-needed boundaries conversation, Georgia began asking me some very pointed questions about the girls in my life.

I was honestly shocked. Shaking my head (in my head) I stared at Georgia in disbelief as she asked about Julie and if I ever planned to ask her out, and if it wasn't Julie, whom I was considering dating … along with a barrage of other questions about my nonexistent love life.

The theme of today's encounter was intrusiveness. I didn't realize it was appropriate to enter someone's house without permission, wait in his bedroom until he arrived home, and then proceed to demand answers to very personal questions.

Although I shouldn't have entertained her questions, against my better judgment I answered anyway:

"No, Georgia, I am not planning on asking anyone out, including Julie. But since you're so curious about my love life …"

What came out of my mouth next shocked both of us.

"If I could marry anyone, anyone in the world, I would marry Alissa Griehshammer."

"Alissa who?" Georgia sarcastically snapped.

"Alissa Griehshammer" I fired back.

"Who is Alissa Griehshammer?" she asked.

"Haven't you ever had a dream guy? Someone you've always wanted to date, but never in a million years thought it would happen?"

I was afraid of Georgia's answer and felt slightly bad for provoking her.

"Well, my dream girl is Alissa Griehshammer. We went to elementary school together. I always wanted to date her but never had the chance. I have no idea where she lives, what she's doing, or if she is even alive, but if I could marry anyone, it would be her."

This must have shocked Georgia, because she was silent, which was awesome. Georgia was never silent. She always had an opinion, always had something to say, and most definitely always had to have the last word, but not today.

I used this silence as an opportunity to tell Georgia that our relationship needed to change. It wasn't right for me to spend so much time with a female I didn't intend to date.

That conversation didn't sit well with Georgia. She left soon after, and our friendship began to unravel.

CHAPTER 4

COME ON, CUPID!

The final straw with Georgia came after I signed up on a dating website. Yes, you read that correctly—a dating website. My coworkers at Healing House insisted that my life was lacking because I was single. After a couple weeks of their persistent badgering, I finally caved and created a profile.

After searching for a few weeks I ended up meeting Jill. We talked nearly every day online during the month of July and eventually made plans to meet.

Our first date went well. At least it wasn't a total disaster. Actually, I'm not quite sure.

Jill invited me back for dinner two nights later, but this time she brought her entire family. Did this mean that she liked me or that she needed three additional opinions to make up her mind? Either way, date two was completely void of privacy. Our party included her father, Joseph; sister, Jocelyn; and brother, Joshua.

As expected, dinner was awkward.

I barely knew Jill, and this seemingly premature family date idea did not provide the atmosphere or opportunity to learn more about her. Instead, Jill's family played "awkwardly stare at the stranger as Dad asks him questions but doesn't allow him to answer." It's a strange game that I don't recommend to anyone.

I'm not joking. Any conversation I attempted to have with Jill was quickly silenced by Joseph. Not only that, but Joseph never let me answer any of his questions either.

Joseph: So, what are your plans now that you have graduated?

Me: Well, that's an interesting question …

Joseph: Joshua, how's your dinner, son?

There was silence at the table as I waited for Joseph to allow me to continue. The opportunity never came. Instead, Joseph asked me another question.

Joseph: So, Matt, what do your parents do for a living?

Me: My dad is a police officer, and my …

Joseph: (To our waiter) Excuse me. Can I have some hot water with lemon?

Waiter: Of course, sir, right away.

The entire dinner went on like that. At one point in the evening I wanted to stop the "conversation" to ask if Joseph was messing with me. I knew Jill's dad was a psychologist and thought that this might be one of his "tests."

I kept looking at Jill for any confirmation of my suspicions like, "Is this normal?" She smiled, nodded her head, and continued eating.

I couldn't wait to get out of there.

After dinner, Joseph drove us all back to his house in Hayward. As the girls and Joshua climbed out of the car, I began to follow them. Before one foot touched the ground, Joseph interrupted my escape and asked if I would accompany him on a walk.

Whom was I dating here, Joseph or Jill?

Thankfully, Jill petitioned, but her father persisted. He seriously wouldn't take no for an answer. Jill told him that she didn't feel like going on a walk, to which Joseph responded, "Good. You weren't invited."

And just like that, my date with Jill ended and my walk with Joseph began.

* * *

It took a few blocks for the edge to wear off, but I eventually began to feel comfortable talking to Joseph. While we were on our walk, he finally allowed me to answer all the questions he had initially asked during dinner.

Although he was asking extremely personal questions, I had a strange peace about answering without any insecurity. Joseph even asked me to share my unabridged, unedited testimony. I, of course, left out many of the dirty details but gave him enough of an outline for him to understand his daughter was dating someone who was truly saved by God's grace.

Strangely enough, my story did not repel him. In fact, Joseph demonstrated empathy and understanding like I had never experienced before.

Apparently, besides the whole sex, drugs, and rock 'n' roll portion of my life, Joseph and I had much in common. Our backgrounds in mental health, Christianity, and education were all quite similar.

We walked around Joseph's neighborhood for almost an hour before heading back to his house. By the time our walk ended, I had honestly forgotten that I was there to see his daughter at all.

Jill met us at the door. The worried look on her face obviously communicated that she wasn't happy with Joseph for hijacking our date night. I assured Jill that he didn't scare me off and that I would like to see her again.

The next day, Jill invited me back for dinner. Once again, the entire family packed into Joseph's SUV as we drove to their favorite family restaurant.

When the waitress arrived, she placed an entire fish in front of me. With eyes intact, this fish glared at me from the plate.

"Have you ever eaten fish eyes?" Joseph asked.

Stomach churning, I replied, "No. I have not eaten fish eyes."

Who eats fish eyes?

Thankfully, they respected my decision to pass on this family delicacy, or Jill would have witnessed me walking out the door. No joke. I don't do fish eyes.

Anyway, after dinner, Joseph asked me to go on another walk.

Jill was not happy.

I was literally spending more time with her dad on these dates than I was with her.

A Walk to Remember

That week, I drove back and forth from Sonoma to Hayward three separate times to go on dates with Jill followed by walks with Joseph. On the third night's walk, Joseph asked me to take a step of faith.

"I believe God has a purpose for bringing you into my life. Pray about it, and let me know if you are interested in being mentored by me."

"What would a mentorship entail?" I asked curiously.

Joseph explained that he felt led by God to train me as an intern in counseling and psychology, and to mentor me in our shared faith.

"Take a step of faith, and meet me back here at my home office on Monday. I have a proposition for you."

Not exactly sure what Joseph was offering, I agreed to spend time in prayer over the weekend before making a decision. Having never been mentored before, I was curious to hear his explanation.

After spending the weekend in prayer without any miraculous confirmations, I decided that it wouldn't hurt to take a step of faith and trust God with the outcome.

That Monday I made the journey back to Joseph's house in Hayward.

In his home office Joseph suggested that I spend three days a week in mentorship with him.

This guy has got to be crazy, I thought. *Three days a week? I would have to quit my job—a job that pays real money, money that I need to get out of debt from my college loans—for a free mentorship?*

Looking over my shoulder at the door, Joseph could sense my hesitation.

"This is more than a mentorship, Matt. This is the opportunity of a lifetime, but it starts with a step of faith."

I thought coming back to his home was my step of faith; what was all this "step of faith" talk about? My inner dialogue was racing a mile a minute. *Who does this guy think he is?*

To keep my interest, Joseph explained that faith in God would take care of my college debt.

Call me doubting Thomas, but that was a lot of money!

"Wait. So I just take a 'step of faith,' start this mentorship with you, and God will miraculously pay off my school debt?" There was obvious uncertainty in my voice.

"God will take care of it and more!" he stated boldly.

His confidence made me curious.

Joseph then began to unpack his idea of mentorship in further detail. While listening, I was reminded of a conversation that Joseph and I had had on our walk the week before when Joseph asked me what I wanted to do with my life. I was hoping for a full-time position with Healing House with the dream of eventually becoming a police officer, but this was all tentative and uncertain.

I had explained to Joseph that my only real plan at the time was to apply for the Peace Corps and trust God to guide me from there. Without a solid plan in place I figured that the Peace Corps would be a great way to serve the Lord, travel the world, defer my school loans, and figure out what to do with the rest of my life.

After hearing my plans, or lack thereof, Joseph had told me that I didn't need the Peace Corps. He said that if I wanted to pay off my school loans, travel the world, and figure out what to do with my life, that I should take this "step of faith."

"Well, what do you think?" Joseph asked, interrupting my flashback.

Laughing nervously, I replied, "I think I have to quit one of my jobs."

I was currently working part-time at two different nonprofit organizations. To take this mentorship with Joseph would require me to quit one of my jobs. I loved my job as a crisis counselor at Healing House and hoped to obtain a full-time position there. The other job had its perks as an overnight counselor for a juvenile transition program, but the opposite sleep schedule, low pay, and short ceiling of promotion made for an easy choice. However, I would miss the paid naps, movie watching, and workout sessions that I was currently enjoying at that job.

"Do you have a passport?" Joseph asked.

"A passport? No, why?"

Joseph smiled. "Better hurry up and apply. We leave for China in three weeks …"

One thing that I would quickly learn about Joseph was that he is both a man of his word and a man of action. I was honestly in shock at how soon I would begin to see fruit from my step of faith. Less than one month after meeting Joseph, I was flying first class to China.

Red Pill or Blue Pill

Before we left for our trip, Joseph's daughter gave me an ultimatum. She said that I could either date her or be mentored by her dad, but that I could not have both. We had been on only a few dates, but unfortunately, none of them was convincing enough to throw away the incredible opportunity I had with Joseph.

I had my whole life to fall in love … easy decision.

Flirtatious Folly

During our trip to China, Joseph revealed his belief that God had a purpose for bringing us together. I'm not a believer in coincidences. I mean, I met the man's daughter on a dating website and ended up in China with him just one month after. There had to be a reason for this unique encounter. I had no idea what that purpose was, but I was enjoying the ride.

After some training in Guangzhou, we flew to Hainan, a tropical island off the southeastern coast of China. In Hainan, it became obvious to Joseph why God had brought me into his life.

While leaving our hotel, we were escorted to a limo by our hostess. She was a lovely young Chinese woman with a smile that I could not ignore. I asked Joseph how to say, "You are beautiful" in Chinese, but Joseph refused to tell me.

When we were seated in our luxurious limo, Joseph asked, "What exactly were you hoping to accomplish by telling a stranger that she was beautiful?"

"I was just trying to be nice."

"You were trying to flirt," Joseph sharply responded.

"True, but what's the harm in that?"

Joseph quickly came to understand that as my mentor, there was much more work to be done than he originally had thought.

The more time we spent together, the more he learned about my past relationships and failed commitments. I told Joseph about a dating book I had read and how I wanted to have a successful marriage one day. I explained that the problem I was currently facing was that I always lost interest after gaining the object of my pursuit and affection. I also told him how I feared failing in my marriage as my parents had, which probably kept me from committing to anyone.

"Is that what you truly want?" Joseph asked. "A marriage that lasts?"

"Of course, more than anything," I replied.

"If that is truly what you want, I have a proposal for you …"

An Offer You Can't Refuse

"If you are serious about growing closer to God, getting out of debt, learning how to commit, becoming a counselor, and having a successful marriage, I will help you accomplish those goals. I am willing to focus my time, effort, and resources to help you, but I need you to be committed to the process."

(I nodded my head for him to continue.)

"If you are willing to sacrifice your dating life and all romantic relationships for the next three years, I will sacrifice the next three years of my life to help you achieve your dreams. Does that sound like something that would interest you?"

What sounded like a scene from *The Godfather* was truly an "offer I couldn't refuse." Granted, I wasn't sold on the whole no-dating thing, but I didn't have any prospects at the time and figured that it wouldn't hurt to see where this train would take me.

Honestly, it wasn't that difficult a decision. I was already reaping the rewards of this relationship, so I knew he meant business. Besides that, what he was asking didn't seem like that big a deal. There would be no dating, but instead I could continue cruising around China while sipping coconut juice on tropical beaches? Sign me up!

Joseph also added that this was a commitment of freewill, meaning that I could walk away at any time … although doing so would consequently cut off all the acquired benefits I was currently enjoying. I was comforted knowing that this commitment had a termination clause allowing me the freedom to choose my path without obligation.

So, as the proposal stood on the table, I could commit to this mentorship and give up my rights to have a romantic relationship for the next three years, or I could walk away like nothing ever happened.

What would you do?

Think about it ...

What if you were promised the opportunity to fulfill your life's purpose, accomplish any task with full financial backing, and glorify God in the process?

What would you sacrifice?

Dating?

Time?

Money?

What is purpose worth to you?

What about healing ...

Or learning to overcome the greatest obstacle to unlocking your potential?

If delaying gratification meant that the payoff would be exponentially better in your future, would you be willing to give up your greatest immediate desire?

As a broke college graduate with no definitive direction in life, I could not afford to pass up this deal. I agreed to the terms and conditions of Joseph's proposal, although I still kept my options open. In other words, I was repeating the pattern of every relationship I had ever experienced in the past; I committed with my mouth but not with my heart.

CHAPTER 5

MARRYING MARIE

It didn't take long after our return from China for me to discover adversity in my newly established commitment journey with Joseph. Adhering to the "no-dating clause" in particular was more difficult than expected. Granted, I didn't do myself any favors by continuing to check my online dating profiles, but I didn't see the problem with window-shopping.

Marie, from San Diego, was the first woman to display an interest in me after I began my no-dating commitment. According to her profile Marie was a strong Christian woman who loved the Lord. Her "about me" section was full of scripture references and quotes from famous Christian writers about life and love. Marie's father was even the pastor of a local church. At first glance, all signs pointed toward pursuing this promising woman of God, so I did.

Marie and I began to communicate through the dating service and Facebook. After only a couple weeks of consistent e-mail exchanges and a few phone calls, Marie made something uncomfortably clear …

She was looking for a commitment.

Not just any commitment, either.

Although she never used these exact words, from our conversations and her interrogative questions, Marie made it clear that she wanted a quick courtship, a short engagement, and a wedding … all within six months.

Even if I had wanted to commit to Marie, I had just started a "commitment journey" with Joseph in which I was supposed to forsake all dating opportunities in order to learn the meaning of the word *commitment*.

I clearly couldn't keep a commitment if I was already considering a dating relationship with a mystery girl from Southern California.

I mean, let's be real. I heard Marie's voice on the phone a few times, but this could easily be another Manti Te'o situation; only God knows if she even existed.

Anyway, I continued conversing with Marie over the course of October, and my relationship with her was becoming obvious to Joseph. I was distracted during our discussions, always looking at my cell phone in meetings, and less interested in talking to Joseph about the meaning of commitment.

One day after Joseph and I had lunch, he boldly confronted me about Marie. Granted, he didn't know her name, but he could tell that I was talking to someone. He asked me if I was still committed to our journey, which made me stop and think how I was going to answer his question.

My delayed response gave Joseph all the information he needed, "Matt, you're not a slave in this commitment. You have the free will to walk away anytime. Just say the word and it's over, *but* if you do want to walk this commitment journey, you have to give 100 percent. You can't have both. If you want to continue with mystery girl, that's fine. It's your decision."

We had just returned from a life-altering trip in China, where I committed to this no-dating journey. Until this point in my life I had never made and kept any commitment of significance, and I really wanted to see where this road would lead. I told Joseph all about Marie and asked him to help me break things off with her. After our conversation in the car, I drafted a letter to Marie asking her forgiveness for leading her on and explaining my inability to commit to her. I never heard from Marie after that.

Lesson Learned

There will always be opposition when we set out to make commitments. One month into my journey, I was already faced with the opportunity to bail. This was the whole reason I was in the commitment journey in the first place. I wanted to become a man of integrity, a man who could keep his word and make promises that he would actually fulfill. I wanted to be married one day and commit my life to one woman. To accomplish this goal, I had to continue climbing my Mount Everest.

Safety Precautions

While driving up any mountain you will find that guardrails have been put in places of potential danger. Slippery slopes, steep cliffs, and rocky roads all require guardrails. The purpose of these guardrails is to keep cars safely on the road. I too needed guardrails in my commitment journey to keep me safely on the road as I climbed my Mount Everest.

Marie may have been the first, but she definitely wouldn't be the last temptation on this journey.

If I was going to successfully make it up this mountain, I desperately needed guardrails to keep me from falling over dangerous ledges. These included canceling all memberships to online dating services, cutting off communication with women I enjoyed flirting with, and installing accountability partners to ensure that I was staying true to the path.

If I intended to learn how to make a commitment without the distraction of dating, but was on a path that included dating websites and casual flirtation with females, I was deceiving myself and would end up at a destination far from where I intended.

Accountability was a huge guardrail for me in this process. If I wanted to learn how to commit, I had to stop being secretive and allow others to have access into my personal life. I would need to give others license to ask questions, poke around, and shine light into dark areas of my life, and accept any discipline or rebukes that would help me stay on track.

Best Birthday Gift Ever

Only one month after breaking things off with Marie, I was already in love.

At Joseph's home office after we returned from China, he asked where I would like to spend my birthday. I was thinking about steak houses, sushi restaurants, and other fine dining establishments. Joseph, on the other hand, had something else in mind.

Looking at a map on his wall, Joseph asked me to pick any country in the world.

I didn't really understand the purpose of this exercise.

"What for?" I asked.

"Pick anywhere on that map, and I'll take you there for your birthday."

I don't know how to communicate the excitement I experienced from hearing his offer.

I remember when I was a kid playing a game with my cousins where we would spin a globe and put a finger randomly on the globe as it spun. Wherever the globe stopped was where we would visit. To actually have the opportunity to make this game a reality was mind-blowing.

The first place that came to my mind was Thailand. And just like that, one month later, we were on a plane flying across the Pacific Ocean to Thailand.

I was in love.

The spicy food, beautiful beaches, Muy Thai fights, tropical trees, and jungle adventuring that included waterfalls, swimming in crystal-blue water, drinking from coconuts, eating exotic fruits, getting traditional Thai bamboo tattoos, getting massages, motor-scootering through the countryside, white-water rafting, ATVing ... we experienced it all.

What more could I have asked for on my birthday?

How about a fresh seafood buffet on the beach with sharks, fish I can't even pronounce, and a Thai sky lantern ceremony to top off the night. Talk about a dream come true.

Not only was I having the time of my life, but it was also in Thailand where we first discussed my going to graduate school. Never in my life had I ever thought about getting a master's degree. I honestly didn't even like school outside of the social scene. The thought of two to three more years was not all that appealing, but my heart changed in Thailand.

After I worked at my first two counseling clinics, God put a love for people who were hurting in my heart. Turning this passion into a career would be a dream come true.

Joseph and I specifically discussed relationship counseling in Thailand, since this was the area where I needed the most work and had the deepest desire to learn and understand. If a master's degree could get me the skills necessary to help people like my parents heal their marriage, I was going back to school.

The dream of becoming a marriage counselor was now engraved on my heart, which I then would engrave on my skin—quite literally.

After seeing so many elephants on our trip, I decided to get one tattooed on my ankle. Elephants are strong yet gentle. They were created by God to bear the burdens of others by helping them carry weight that they cannot carry alone. This is what I wanted to do with my life, and I discovered this passion in Thailand. My tattoo was to commemorate my birthday trip and my newfound desire to become a burden bearer like the elephant.

During this trip, I finally made a decision to go "all in" with Joseph's proposed commitment journey. No longer did I want to waver about the no-dating portion. I wanted to give my all to obtain a life of purpose, overcome my "noncommittal spirit," and learn the skills necessary to become an amazing counselor for Christ. When I arrived home from our trip, I was ready to take things seriously and focus on this process.

Post-Thailand

Accomplishing the goals that Joseph and I discussed in Thailand required focus and dedication. I unfortunately possessed neither of these attributes. Joseph knew this and constantly encouraged me to "plot a piece of land." At the time, I had no idea what this meant. It was all very "Miyagi" to me. Thankfully, he explained what the "wax on/wax off" he was talking about.

In agricultural societies, before land produces any crops and before trees can bear any fruit, the ground has to be prepared. Weeds, thorns, and rocks must be removed; hardened soil must be softened; and clumps of dirt must be broken apart. No matter how many good seeds are planted, or how much water and sunlight are given to a piece of land, nothing will ever grow unless the land is properly prepared. The same must be done to our hearts and minds when we commit to something important. We must clear space and time for positive change and growth to occur.

For me, I needed to make space in my schedule that could accommodate the toilsome days and late nights of studying and mentorship. I needed to prepare my heart to cut out some old habits so that I could integrate new healthier ones.

There were places I needed to stop visiting, people I needed to stop wasting time with, and good activities that needed to go so the best ones could take root in my life. I needed to make room in my heart and mind to receive the seeds of wisdom that would be planted through my graduate school studies, time in the word with God, and mentorship with Joseph. I also needed to clean house—a spiritual "spring cleaning," if you will. This required some sweat and tears to clear the land that would one day grow a harvest of knowledge, wisdom, and righteousness for my future.

Unfortunately, the force of my noncommittal spirit was still strong. I had the head knowledge of commitment, but that hadn't yet reached my heart.

A Christmas Gift from My Creator

The anniversary of my conversation with the Messiah was quickly approaching. It had now been one year since I started following Jesus, and I wanted to commemorate this monumental day. Taking shrooms was out of the question, but I could still spend the evening listening to reggae music and watching *Planet Earth*.

Unfortunately for me, I didn't have the *Planet Earth* DVD set and my dad's fiftieth birthday/retirement party was scheduled for the same night. Slightly disappointed, I accepted the fact that it was not God's will for me to sit on a couch all night and think about my last mushroom adventure. Instead, I would be spending the evening with my dad's friends, family, and coworkers at his silver-and-black Raider-themed birthday bash.

As a member of the family, I was one of the first to arrive. Our private party suite was decked out in silver-and-black Raiders awesomeness. There were pictures of my dad in his SWAT gear with guns, helicopters, and grenades plastered all over the walls. AC/DC played in the background, and it all set the stage for a party of epic proportions.

While I was scanning the room, something caught my eye.

On the back wall, a projector screen was showing a movie. Now, with all the testosterone flowing through this party, you would think that *Die Hard* or *Terminator* would be playing, but no ... there were giraffes, lions, and zebras running around what looked like Africa.

What the heck was the Discovery Channel doing on at my dad's party?

The more I stared at the wall, the more confused I became. Then reality punched me in the face. This was *Planet Earth*!

I approached the DJ who was in charge of the entertainment to confirm my suspicion. Sure enough, I was right. "Why are you guys playing *Planet Earth* at a grown man's birthday party? Did my dad ask for this?" I asked.

The DJ replied, "Honestly, I don't know. I just found this DVD today in the office and thought it would be cool to play. It wasn't planned at all. You want me to turn it off?"

"No, no," I said. "Please keep it going; you have no idea what this means to me."

I could have started crying in the middle of that party.

It was one year to the day since my encounter with Jesus, and he surprised me with *Planet Earth*! I hadn't told anyone that I was hoping to watch this before today; in fact, I hadn't even asked God for it. He just knew.

This was definitely one of those mind-blowing moments that just reaffirmed faith in God for me. God loves us so much that he pays attention to the small details in our lives even when we don't ask. How amazing is this God!

Surviving Winter

After my dad's party, I received a message on social media.

Her name was Winter. We had known each other since middle school through our church's youth group, but the last time I spoke to Winter was during my senior year in high school.

We had always been flirtatious from a distance, but Winter lived forty-five minutes away, which made our relationship unrealistic at the time. Despite the distance, we made plans to attend a high school football game together.

On the day of the game I got nervous and backed out. I texted Winter an hour before I was scheduled to pick her up. I lied and made up an excuse as to why I couldn't go to the game. Suffice it to say, our distant flirtatious relationship was now dead.

Now, five years later, Winter had found me on Facebook. We began to rekindle our friendship just in time for her visit home from Southern California for the holidays. Without Joseph's knowledge, I made plans with Winter to meet for coffee.

Our date went well … so much so that after our initial coffee date, Winter asked me out to dinner. I accepted her invitation and continued down a path that led toward a romantic relationship with Winter and away from the commitment journey with Joseph.

Once again I became secretive around Joseph and distracted during our discussions.

Winter returned to school in Southern California, and we continued talking. I ignored the fact that Winter was currently living the life that God had saved me from just one year before.

Physical beauty will make a man do really dumb things.

Years later I would hear a sermon from my pastor, Mark, who coined the phrase, "She may be hot, but so is hell." Where was Mark when I needed him?

Anyway, the lure of forbidden fruit had me considering some really questionable ideas. For instance, I had a long holiday weekend ahead, which I saw as the perfect opportunity to make a road trip with my roommate to visit some friends in Southern California. That was what I told Joseph, anyway.

It's interesting how quickly temptation leads to compromise, which then leads to lies. My real plans did in fact include a road trip, but they also included a weekend with Winter, her sorority girls, a concert at the House of Blues in Hollywood, a pit stop to visit an old flame from college, and a lot of other temptations.

I was currently clean and sober from all substances and had abstained from sex for over a year, but I now wanted to throw myself back into the lion's den with hopes that I wouldn't be eaten alive. Real smart.

Thankfully, Joseph wasn't sold on my story. Something didn't add up for him, and he made a special trip from Hayward to Sonoma just to check his math.

While sitting in my room, Joseph again asked me about the details of my trip. I omitted the truth, and Joseph could see straight through my lies. With a disappointed look on his face, Joseph confronted me. I denied his accusations, but Joseph continued, "I know you are being dishonest about your trip."

I folded.

Under pressure, with my integrity on the line, I caved. Omitting the truth was one thing; telling a bald-faced lie, I just couldn't do.

I told Joseph about visiting Winter and how I planned to stay at her grandma's house for the weekend. Joseph then, as expected, tried to convince me not to visit Southern California.

My pride then kicked in. I wasn't going to let him tell me what to do. Joseph was not my dad, and he was not God. He couldn't stop me from going.

Hearing my hard heart, Joseph pulled out his trump card. "I knew you were not being truthful with me because God gave me a dream about this last night."

The God card always wins.

Silent with anticipation I awaited his next words.

Joseph described dreaming of being in a room with a beautiful, feminine, angelic figure. She moved around the room with fluidity and was dressed with luxurious adornments. As the figure floated past Joseph, he could sense something cold and demonic about the nature of this creature. Like a wolf in sheep's clothing, this angelic figure was only covering up the evil inside. Joseph said he was terrified of the angel woman. "She exhibited a powerfully strong force from within her. This demon was a deceitful creature who came to destroy." He also mentioned my presence in the room but that he couldn't find me. I was lost in the room with this dangerous creature on the prowl around me.

Joseph reported waking up from his dream with a deep unsettling feeling in his spirit and high anxiety about my trip to Southern California. Joseph reported that in the dream the Lord revealed that I was being deceitful and instructed him to let go of me and the commitment journey.

This reminded me of when Paul in 1 Corinthians 5:5 instructed the Corinthian church to hand a man over to Satan so that he would be saved from his sin. The idea is that the person will be tormented by the devil until he repents and runs back to God. Maybe this was what God had instructed Joseph to do by "letting me go."

After describing his dream, Joseph explained how the Bible characterizes demons as those who parade around as angels of light with the intentions to steal, kill, and destroy. "Beauty is fleeting, and charm is deceptive," he told me. "Do not trust the beauty of the mysterious Winter. As beautiful as she is, she is a monster inside. Do not trust this woman."

This should have been enough to thwart my plans, but it took a bribe from Joseph for me to finally give in and abandon my trip. Joseph offered an all-expenses-paid snowboarding trip to Tahoe with my friends if I chose not to visit Southern California. I finally broke and accepted his bribe. In return, as promised, Joseph paid for my gas, hotel, sushi dinner, and snowboarding tickets for me and two friends.

Before leaving for Tahoe, I wrote Winter a letter explaining that we could no longer see one another and that I would not be visiting her over the weekend. Like in the letter to Marie, I apologized for leading her on.

The trip to Tahoe helped me forget about Winter and how mad she was about my letter. I was also able to refocus on my commitment journey with Joseph and get back on track.

Like a Thief in the Night

Since the option of dating was off the table, I planned to spend Valentine's Day snowboarding in Tahoe with Joseph. In all my years of snowboarding, I had never spent more days on the slopes than during my first year in the commitment journey with Joseph. He had just paid for me and two friends to snowboard in Tahoe, and now here we were again. Joseph didn't even ski, but instead he used these weekends away to train me in counseling after I returned from the slopes.

Honestly, I had no real intention of doing much more than snowboard on this trip, but since Joseph was offering to foot the bill, I went along with his training proposal.

Before we left for Tahoe on Friday morning, my Facebook status stated, "Enjoying the abundant life through the blessings of Jesus Christ … Boarding in Tahoe till Monday. God is good, all the time."

I tried to place God in a box by stating my plans for the weekend, but God can't bless us inside of a box; he needs to be free.

Friday went as planned; I woke up early at my best friend Chris's house in Sacramento and drove to Sierra-at-Tahoe in record time, arriving just before the lifts opened. I snowboarded all day by myself, taking breaks whenever I wanted, waiting for no one, and enjoying my music and time alone. It was the perfect day—the sun was shining, I was never too hot or cold, and the lines were nonexistent.

At the end of my day I drove into South Lake Tahoe, where I planned to meet Joseph at our hotel. I took my suitcase and laptop into the hotel lobby, leaving my snowboarding equipment in the car.

Once we settled into our suite, which included spectacular views of the Sierras and the frosty blue lake, Joseph made reservations at 19th Kitchen, the best and most pretentious restaurant in Tahoe. My dinner included a New York steak, lobster mashed potatoes, and lobster chowder, totaling a whopping eighty dollars, not to mention my twenty-dollar glass of cabernet. Our dinner cost over two hundred dollars, but the time spent and conversation with my mentor were priceless.

After dinner I was exhausted from snowboarding and went to bed early. The next day Joseph and I spent the entire morning talking at the hotel. Our counseling time continued through breakfast and into the afternoon. Before I knew it, the afternoon was gone. Tired from our day of training, I was ready to revitalize myself at the gym.

I needed my gym shoes from the trunk of my car, which was parked in the hotel garage, so I ran down to retrieve them. As I approached the car, I realized that my back left window had been shattered, but being naïve, I hadn't yet thought of burglary. I was even more confused when it appeared as though nothing had been taken from my car, but upon further examination I discovered that my snowboard was missing. In its place was a business card from the security staff reporting that they had found my car in this condition around nine o'clock that morning.

My initial reactions were confusion and shock, as I had never been the victim of a crime before. After calming myself, I assessed the situation to see if anything else had been taken.

To my surprise I found that my wallet and an envelope holding five hundred dollars cash and other important documents were still in the car. This burglar knew exactly what he wanted and wasted no time searching for the hidden treasures that I had unknowingly left in my vehicle.

Once the police report had been filed and the insurance company had been informed, Joseph and I decided not to let this incident spoil our weekend vacation. Gym shoes in hand, I decided it was time to work out any lingering frustrations.

While I was at the gym, God gave Joseph a revelation about my recent misfortune and told him that he wanted to see if I would still be living the "abundant life" without snowboarding this weekend.

This was significant because before I left for Tahoe, multiple friends of mine had commented on my Facebook page about how "blessed" I was to have a free all-inclusive snowboarding vacation for Valentine's Day.

God wanted to test if my joy would remain in him even in my current circumstances. He wanted to teach me that happiness is circumstantial, but true fulfillment and joy come from him alone. As we would soon discover, God did not allow this burglary to punish us but instead to bless us.

After this incident, I gave up my dreams of snowboarding again on our trip and God displayed his faithfulness and rewarded me for trusting in him. Any hint of disappointment was gone, replaced with total peace and acceptance of God's plan for the weekend. I was now completely open to his will and was actually excited to see what God had in store for us.

Earlier in the morning before this incident, I was reading the book of Ecclesiastes about how everything in life is meaningless. The author argued that since none of us can take anything with us when we die, the pursuit of wealth, possessions, wisdom, power, and pleasure are all meaningless, a "chasing after the wind."

The words from this book began to resonate with me as I thought about my current situation. My snowboarding equipment was now gone, but so what? God was still here, he loved me, and would never leave me.

I was good without my gear. My uncircumstantial joy was in Jesus, not in snowboarding.

After my workout, Joseph and I spent the remainder of the day discussing the complexities of my life in a revealing counseling session. It was in this session that I was also able to confront the core issues of my noncommittal spirit and discover how my insecurities caused me to create a false self that was preventing me from experiencing intimacy in my friendships and relationships. I was discovering the root of these issues and how to overcome them.

It was also in Tahoe, talking to Joseph instead of snowboarding, where I decided to go "all in" again with the no-dating portion of our commitment journey. Although I had agreed in the past, I didn't truly understand the importance of this part and withheld my full commitment. No longer would I walk halfheartedly in this journey. While staring at the snowcapped Sierras I was ready to climb my Mount Everest, having fully counted the cost of consecrating my life to the Lord. As a sign of my consecration, Joseph gave me a ring to wear as a constant reminder.

Catching More Than a Cold

One of the greatest lessons I learned from my mentor was that wisdom is not taught but caught. Joseph rarely ever took a classroom approach to our mentorship. Instead, he walked with me through life, modeling the lessons he was hoping I would learn by witnessing his example.

In Philippians 2:3, Paul commanded followers of Jesus to "do nothing out of selfish ambition or vain conceit. Rather, in humility value others above yourselves." This is a completely countercultural way of thinking, but Joseph constantly modeled it for me.

Every year, Joseph conducted counseling seminars in different countries around the world. While planning his spring tour, Joseph put his own interests aside and considered something that would bless me instead.

Knowing that my family originated in Italy, Joseph planned a trip to Rome and brought me along for the experience. Not only that, but a few weeks earlier, Joseph had caught me on my laptop in his home office browsing the best snowboard resorts in the world.

"So, which resort has the best snowboarding?" Joseph asked.

"I dunno. Probably somewhere in Switzerland."

"Pick one."

"Oh, yeah? Just pick one, huh?" I sarcastically replied.

"Yeah, pick one and I'll take you during my next trip."

Like with my birthday trip to Thailand, my mind was blown once again.

I chose Verbier, a resort in the Swiss Alps, and two months later we were on a plane to Europe.

Our first stop was Rome. We toured the Colosseum, visited Vatican City, ate fresh pizza and gelato every day, and still managed to find time for some mentoring along the way. After a successful three-day visit in Rome, we took a train to Verbier, Switzerland, to experience the best backcountry snowboarding the world has to offer.

Natural High

Not since college was I as high as I was in Switzerland. I was so high on this mountain, there literally wasn't a single tree in sight. All I could see for miles and miles were white mammoth-sized mountains. I then spent the next three days exploring the monster mountain in Verbier.

Flippin' Out

Hands down, the highlight of my trip was the snowboard competition. The Swiss watch company Swatch held "best trick" competitions every weekend where free lift tickets, watches, and snowboards were offered to the winners.

I'd never been in a snowboard competition before, but this one had a slight twist. Swatch provided an airbag to practice your tricks before the competition. I entered the contest, learned how to throw a double backflip in about three hours, and took third place in the competition. My prize included an extra day on the slopes while Joseph met with his contacts in Geneva. Talk about a mountaintop experience!

God's Gifts to All

No matter where in the world I traveled with Joseph, he always managed to find a Japanese restaurant. Thankfully, this time, Joseph's knack for noodles actually saved our trip to Switzerland.

No joke, the food in Switzerland was terrible … come on, Swiss people!

In all fairness, Switzerland could have had the best food in the world and Joseph would have still found a Japanese restaurant to eat at instead.

On the second to last night of our trip at our new Japanese food hideout, Joseph told me about the "gifts of the Holy Spirit." Having attended only nondenominational churches in my first year of following Jesus, I'd never heard about God giving gifts to people other than that of his son Jesus.

Joseph explained all the different gifts and told me that after dinner we could pray for me to receive them. He described the gifts of prophecy, miracles, healing, speaking in tongues, and spiritual discernment. In my mind, these gifts were like spiritual superpowers, and who wouldn't want superpowers? I wanted one of these gifts from God, so we went back to our hotel after dinner and prayed.

It was literally four hours later, and nothing. I hadn't known what to expect, but after praying for four straight hours I figured something miraculous would happen. Nothing did, and I went to bed.

The next day we received a report that a volcano had erupted in Iceland. The eruption was so large that the ash literally blacked out the sky, stopping all western air travel. This volcanic eruption would potentially strand us in Europe for the next week. Talk about mountain-moving prayer!

By God's grace and Joseph's high-class flight status, we were trapped in Germany for only three hours before catching a flight home. There was always adventure to be enjoyed with Joseph, and after arriving home from Europe I was more committed to our journey than ever.

CHAPTER 6

A ROADRUNNER ROMANCE

Her name was Alissa Griehshammer. We shared Mr. Fields's third-grade classroom together at Walnut Grove Elementary School. Alissa was beautiful but intimidating. She was a gorgeous little girl who ran around the playground in pigtails and with fearless athleticism. When the other girls were playing hopscotch and braiding hair, Alissa was dominating the boys in foursquare, kickball, and even football.

Although we shared the same classroom, I never actually talked to Alissa. Unfortunately, the other boys didn't seem to have that problem. I become jealous of the boys at school and realized that I wasn't only afraid of Alissa, I was also in love.

My first crush.

It took the rest of the year to build enough courage to talk with Alissa. On the last day of school, before the summer vacation, I was finally prepared to talk to her. I anticipated the final school bell's ring all day long. When it finally sounded, Alissa Marie Griehshammer was nowhere to be found. After searching the parking lot and playground, I made the long walk across the walnut grove with my tail tucked tightly between my legs. Disappointed at this missed opportunity, I kept my secret crush hidden in my heart.

After a long summer, I was excited to return to Walnut Grove Elementary School with hopes of sharing a fourth-grade classroom with Alissa Griehshammer as I had the previous year.

I soon discovered that this was not God's plan.

Further disappointment soon struck as I witnessed my secret love walking closely next to fifth-grader Mark Port. Alissa was in a fourth-/fifth-grade split class that year, and my hope of love was quickly slipping away.

How could I ever compete with a fifth-grader? They were so much older and more respected; it just made sense that Alissa would desire a more mature man.

From that point forward, Alissa Griehshammer became a dream. Although I never forgot about my third-grade love, I lost sight of her after elementary school.

Over the subsequent years of middle school, high school, and college, the gorgeous girl from third grade made sporadic cameo appearances in my life. I would sometimes hear her name mentioned in passing, but I never had the opportunity to talk with her.

Since sharing a third-grade classroom, Alissa and I had only two personal encounters, and neither time resulted in any conversation. There were one time at the gym and another over Christmas break in college …

I needed a Christmas gift for my mom and knew that she loved books and trinkets from the local Christian bookstore. My dad accompanied me on this shopping expedition as we blindly navigated the unfamiliar aisles of books that neither of us would ever read. Failing to find anything, I decided to buy a gift certificate instead.

Immediately, I recognized Alissa at the cash register.

Did she remember me? I mean, we'd never actually exchanged words before. Would she remember sharing a classroom all those years ago?

It didn't really matter—a beautiful godly girl like her would never go for a womanizing frat boy like me. And she shouldn't have.

I was fully aware of her angelic reputation, and I wanted nothing to do with potentially ruining that. I sincerely respected Alissa, which was unusual for me. Instead of adopting the standard "conquest" attitude, I understood that I had no business talking to her, much less making eye contact.

Trying to avoid a potentially awkward situation, I made small talk with my dad instead of engaging in the conversation I desperately desired to have with Alissa. After we paid, I sheepishly thanked her and walked out of the store, once again with my tail between my legs.

One year later, in 2008, I had my encounter with Jesus. Nine months after that, I met Joseph and found myself under his mentorship. In the spring of 2010 I was traveling the world, preparing for graduate school, advancing in my career, and growing in my faith, and I was fully committed to the journey with Joseph.

In other words, I was content.

Paul was right when he wrote, "Godliness with contentment is great gain" (1 Timothy 6:6). I finally had peace. Granted, there were times when I wished that I had a free Friday night to spend with friends, but I understood that this time was an investment. I knew that there would be a return on my investment, so I let my Friday nights go without a fight.

The Lord knows I would have rather been enjoying a beer with some buddies or playing video games at home with my best friend, Steve, but no, I spent every Friday night and Saturday afternoon with my mentor. I was truly invested. No one else knew or understood why or what I was doing all those weekends in Hayward with Joseph, but I was confident that God had a purpose and I was determined to discover it.

Fate or Facebook?

I don't know what it is about social media, but God really does seem to work through it in mysterious ways.

Just when I start to feel comfortable and confident about my path, a test arises, an unforeseen event occurs, my world is shaken or stirred, and I find myself in the middle of chaos.

During the spring of 2010, I received an unexpected Facebook notification. To my surprise, I had a photo comment from none other than Alissa Griehshammer.

At this point fourteen years had passed since we shared that third-grade classroom, and now here she was commenting on my Facebook profile. I didn't even know that she knew who I was.

Apparently, Alissa had become curious about me when I started talking to Joseph's daughter Jill at the end of the previous summer. When

I first started talking to Jill, she reached out to Alissa hoping that Alissa had some dirt on me, since we were both from Pleasanton. Alissa didn't, so she sent me a Facebook request sometime in August of 2009.

I didn't think twice about Alissa's request, because I was currently pursuing Jill. Had this occurred nine months prior, before I started following Jesus, I may have considered talking to both Alissa and Jill at the same time. But I now had the Holy Spirit, who helped me overcome my womanizing ways.

Alissa commented on a picture of my family. She recognized my mom, who frequented the bookstore where Alissa worked.

Our interaction was brief. Only a few comments were exchanged, and weirdly enough I knew that pursuing any sort of relationship—friendship or otherwise—was out of the question at the time. I figured we hadn't had any interaction in fourteen years; what was the rush of starting anything now?

That's when I knew that the Holy Spirit was at work in me. I finally had an open door to converse with Alissa Griehshammer, and I let it go without a fight.

Monumental Maryland

Months later I visited my aunt and uncle in Maryland. They gave me a tour of the Washington DC mall, which provided plenty of prime photo opportunities. After arriving home I posted my photos for the world to see. Again, to my surprise, I received another photo comment from Alissa. This time she wasn't so subtle.

Under a picture of me and my aunt Lori, Alissa posted, "You're kinda presh."

Did I read that correctly?

"Presh," for those not in the know of current lingo, is shorthand for precious.

Alissa Griehshammer thought that I was precious. When did this happen?

As excited as I was about the possible implications of her comment, I quickly remembered my commitment journey. I had already gone down this road twice before and knew where it ended. Joseph would find out, ask if I was still committed, and then convince me to break it off.

But this was Alissa Griehshammer!

The battle began.

Conflicted, I brought my concerns to the Lord. "God, I know what I'm currently committed to and where these interactions have taken me in the past, but this is Alissa Griehshammer. Surely there is an exception clause somewhere, right?"

I sincerely prayed to God asking for wisdom and guidance. I had wanted this opportunity for years, and it was finally here. What was I supposed to do?

"God help me!" I cried.

Never having made such a request in the past, I boldly asked God for confirmation. I prayed for a sign as to whether I should pursue Alissa or let her comment go without a reply.

That very night I had a dream.

In my dream, Alissa and I were on a camping trip together with our families. During the camping trip Alissa and I took a walk along a riverbank. While we were holding hands, Alissa turned to me and said, "We will be together one day."

I woke up with excitement and praised God. I literally had asked God the day before about receiving confirmation, and that night I had the dream.

The question on my mind was simple: "What now?"

So I received confirmation; what was I supposed to do with that? Was I supposed to ask her out?

The dream hadn't said we would be together right now; it had said "one day." What was I supposed to do today?

Apprehensive about my next move, I responded to Alissa anyway, and we began a flirtatious exchange of "likes" and "comments" through Facebook. Unsure if this was breaking my covenant with Joseph, I continued in secrecy. I figured that it was easier to ask for forgiveness than permission, and I rationalized that my dream had given me the "go ahead" to at least start a friendship with the girl.

I began to anticipate her comments on my page and grew increasingly excited about our exchanges. Not only was I talking to my third-grade crush, but the element of secrecy made our interactions all the more exciting.

I started to think about messaging Alissa personally using the newly added instant messaging feature on Facebook. As with anything else, I sought God in prayer for permission. "Lord, I know that I'm in this commitment journey; I understand that. However, I'm confused about the dream. Can I talk to her and continue to build a relationship with her? I need a sign, Lord. I don't want to move ahead unless you are involved. God, please guide me."

My prayers were sincere. Honestly, if God had told me not to talk with Alissa until my commitment journey was over, I would have obeyed, but that didn't happen.

The next day, while talking to some friends on instant messenger, I noticed that Alissa was online. I wanted to message her but didn't know if I should. Instead, I prayed, "Lord, I would love to chat live with your daughter. Could you give me a sign? Something … anything?"

Almost immediately after praying, and for the first time ever, I received an instant message from Alissa.

Prayer answered.

Earlier that day I had posted a status about my upcoming trip to Haiti with my church. Alissa was curious to hear some details about this trip because she too was interested in going.

I don't think I'd ever been that nervous in my entire life. Just reading her simple introduction made my heart tremble. My hands began to shake as I felt the adrenaline surging through my veins. Someone must have cranked the thermostat to "Sahara Desert," because I was now also sweating profusely.

It was one of those conversations where immediately afterward you sort of black out and forget everything that was just talked about. All I knew was that our line of communication was now open.

That night I had another conversation with the Lord. "Okay, God, I'm really excited about this whole Alissa situation and the confirmations that you have blessed me with, but what should I do from here? Am I allowed to ask her out, or is that out of the question?"

Let's recap: I asked for a sign and was given a dream; I asked for another sign, and Alissa instant messaged me. Did this mean that I had a green light, or was I mixing the signals? I went to bed that night hoping for some answers.

The next day, as was customary, I checked my e-mail. Another message from Alissa! This time the tone was different. Instead of the simple flirtation that I was learning to love, Alissa cut straight to the point. "Hey, Matt, it's been fun getting to know you a little bit online, but would you be okay getting together for coffee sometime so we can talk in person?"

In the words of Jeff Foxworthy, "There's your sign."

Really, God? That clear, huh? I prayed for specific confirmation about asking Alissa out on a date, and before I could even make a move, my sign was already waiting in the mail room.

Invitation accepted.

This was serious. I was actually about to go on a date with Alissa Griehshammer. Just when the reality was starting to settle in, I thought more about the commitment journey.

Who was Joseph to play God? Ever since Joseph first proposed the no-dating commitment, I had been hesitant to accept for this exact reason. What if God chose to send my wife during the commitment journey— what then? Would I have to say, "Sorry, God, our plans are more important than yours"? I was pretty sure it didn't work like that.

This was my struggle throughout the entire commitment journey. I wanted to meet the woman I would marry, but I also wanted to learn how to commit to that woman so that I would be able to keep her for life without my noncommittal spirit getting in the way. Ultimately, God would have the final say, and "What God has joined together, let no one separate" (Mark 10:9).

Despite the covenant, I was convinced that God had given me enough confirmation to go ahead with the coffee date.

The Hacienda Hangout

Alissa and I made plans to meet at a local coffee shop in Dublin.

Nervously waiting outside for Alissa to arrive, I prayed for the confidence to pull off this coffee conversation. "Lord, I've been waiting fourteen years for this opportunity. Please don't let me mess this up!

The thought of your daughter brings my heart rate up to "Cheetah" on the treadmill. Calm me down, Father. I need your peace. Please give me the words to speak, a calming sense of confidence, and plenty of conversational points. This is all you, Holy Spirit."

Now fully prayed up, I was ready for Alissa Griehshammer.

If she was at all nervous, I couldn't tell. Alissa's approach to my coffee table was cool, calm, and confident. So much swagger. To my surprise, the moment we made our initial contact, the conversation flowed effortlessly. Although an angel in form, Alissa was the most down-to-earth girl I had ever met.

We spent the next three hours laughing, swapping stories, and sharing testimonies between the coffee shop and adjacent bookstore.

I couldn't have been more joyful. Never had I dreamed that it would be so easy and fun to reconnect with my third-grade crush.

For the first time ever, I was left with a peace that encouraged me to trust God completely with a relationship. I wasn't worried about the next date or other potential guys in Alissa's life. The outcome was wholly in his hands, and I felt free. There was no need to manipulate, lie, or try to make Alissa think I was anyone other than myself. I had the freedom to tell her the truth and trust that God would make things work out if she was in fact part of his plan for my life.

Somehow, this strategy worked.

After our initial date, my relationship with Alissa quickly evolved. We spent our weekends together at the movies, attending church, and hanging out late at night at diners. Alissa and I enjoyed playing video games together, making s'mores in her backyard, taking walks along the freeway near her parents' house, and discussing possible ministry ideas at the local bagel shop.

One of our favorite activities was talking in the car. We would sit in my car for hours talking about life, love, God … anything and everything really. Those conversations almost always ended in prayer where we constantly lifted our relationship to the Lord asking for his wisdom and guidance. Although we were growing in love and adoration toward one another, we wanted God's blessing above all else.

Luckily, Joseph hadn't noticed my latest distraction. He was too busy planning a trip to Israel, where he would spend the next two weeks with his family. I knew Joseph wouldn't be happy to hear the news about me and Alissa, but I couldn't care less. I finally had the desire of my heart, the girl of my dreams.

After only two weeks, I knew that I was falling in love with Alissa Griehshammer—not just the idea of the girl from third grade, but Alissa Marie Griehshammer as she was now. She was perfect for me, and I wanted her to be my girlfriend. However, up until this point, Alissa had no idea that I was even on a commitment journey. If we were going to have a lasting relationship founded upon trust and truth, she needed to know.

A "Grown-Ups" Conversation

It was a Saturday night, a night when my best friends from Bible study were having a guy's night out at the movies. The founder of our Bible study would be moving to Oregon for his job, and this was his farewell get-together.

Despite the circumstances, I invited Alissa to join us. I had already gone to lunch with all the guys earlier that day and figured they wouldn't mind if she tagged along for a movie.

Since I was already at the movie theater plaza with the guys, Alissa planned to meet me there. The movie was about to start, and Alissa was nowhere to be found. The guys waited as long as they could, but they eventually left me to reserve our seats.

Alissa didn't show up for another almost thirty minutes. The movie had surely begun without us. Once Alissa arrived, I texted the guys asking where they were seated. No answer.

We walked into the theater with the movie already playing and surprisingly could not locate my friends. The only available seats were in the front row. Not a good start. I hated the front row. Not only that, but my friends probably thought that I had bailed on them for Alissa.

Honestly speaking, the movie was terrible. It was probably the single worst movie I had ever paid to watch in my life. Alissa and I kept looking at each other with "Are you kidding me?" expressions.

The movie ended thirty minutes after we took our seats. This was either the shortest movie of all time, or we had walked into the wrong theater.

It turned out that we had walked into the wrong theater.

Alissa and I were less than impressed with the poor acting, lame jokes, and childish humor of the *Grown Ups* crew, so we decided to wait for my friends at the Mexican restaurant next door.

Looking back, I find it funny to see how God weaves everything together for his purposes and our good. Sitting in the movie theater hadn't given us any time to talk, but the restaurant did. Instead of sitting through another hour of *Grown Ups*, Alissa and I were able to discuss Joseph and the commitment journey over some appetizers and dessert.

I explained that I had made a commitment not to date anyone for the next two years, but that I had prayed for wisdom, guidance, and permission to pursue Alissa and felt that God had given me the green light. I apologized for not telling her sooner, which she quickly forgave. I then asked if she would support me in telling Joseph about our relationship. Alissa confirmed her support by praying with me for courage and boldness to tell Joseph the truth. Did I mention that Alissa was a blessing from God?

Parking Lot Proposal

The next day was a Sunday. I wanted to check out Alissa's church, which was apparently more charismatic than what I was used to. My interest in experiencing a charismatic church had been piqued two weeks before when Alissa and I discussed her "baptism in the Holy Spirit." Although I had been exposed to the gifts of the Holy Spirit in Switzerland by Joseph, I had never met anyone until Alissa who actually had the gift of speaking in tongues.

Reportedly, while in church as a teenager, Alissa was prayed over for the baptism of the Holy Spirit. While people were laying hands on her in prayer, Alissa momentarily blacked out. When she came to a few moments later, she found herself crying out to God in an unknown language. She described a burning sensation covering her body while she was speaking in this angelic language, which she now calls her "prayer language."

I had been seeking the baptism of the Holy Spirit, namely the gift of tongues, for the last few months since my trip to Europe, and I figured that attending her church might provide that opportunity.

On Sunday morning before driving to Alissa's church, we attended a prayer service at Cornerstone Fellowship, my home church. The congregation at my church prayed for all of the teams flying to Haiti during the summer, which included me and my two best friends, Joel and Steve. After the church prayed for God's protection, provision, and presence on our trip, Alissa and I drove up the hill to Valley Christian Church in Dublin.

I'm not sure what I was expecting to happen, but nothing out of the ordinary did. I guess I had hoped for an opportunity to receive the baptism of the Holy Spirit, but the opportunity never came. Strangely enough, I wasn't as disappointed as expected. That probably had to do with Alissa. It was hard for me not to experience joy in her presence. As we walked out of the church and into the parking lot, I knew that the time had come. Alissa and I needed to have a DTR.

Alissa was a gem, too precious to leave anything to chance. It was time to ask Alissa Griehshammer to be my girlfriend.

This may not seem like a big deal, but for me, I was basically telling Alissa that she was the girl I wanted to marry. She already knew that dating was out of the question for me at this point in my life. I was only interested in courtship, and courting Alissa meant that we were serious about our relationship and would move from friends toward marriage. This was not a question of, "Are you the right person for me?" This was, "You are someone I would like to spend the rest of my life with. Let's intentionally work toward that goal."

Intense, I know.

So, before breaking off my commitment journey with Joseph, I asked Alissa if she was willing to commit to being my girlfriend. She accepted my invitation, and just like that, we were an official couple. The day was Sunday, June 27, 2010.

Nuclear Warfare

I now had a legitimate situation on my hands. Joseph needed to know. Without his knowledge or consent, I had made a decision to break our previously established covenant.

Joseph would be returning home in just three days, and I needed to tell him the truth. This may sound simple, but this was no easy task. Twice before, we had gone through this same situation, and each time he had said the same thing. "Matt, we made a covenant. You have free will to stay in or bail out, but you cannot have both. The choice is yours."

In my mind, this situation was completely different from the previous two times. I hadn't sought out a relationship with Alissa. In fact, even though I wanted to talk with Alissa, I knew that it went against the covenant, so I let her initial advance go for three months. Then, after Alissa continued to place herself in my path, I brought the situation before the Lord and received sign after sign pointing me to pursue her. This was clearly God's doing, which would obviously make Joseph excited to hear about it.

I was confident that Joseph would understand that God had interfered with the commitment journey by fulfilling his will over ours. God's plan for my marriage was much greater than Joseph's plan for my marriage. This conversation should be a piece of cake.

Honestly, even if the conversation went sour, I had already made my decision. Asking Alissa to be my girlfriend and making it public on Facebook was my formal resignation. I was no longer asking for permission; I was simply stating a fact. I was in love, God had brought her into my life, and the commitment journey was over.

The day before Joseph returned home from Israel he called me from overseas. I hadn't spoken to Joseph on the phone all week. We checked in with seemingly ceremonial small talk and eventually discussed plans for his arrival. After finishing official business, we moved into personal news. I eagerly told Joseph that I had a surprise for him. I honestly thought he would be excited for me.

Instead, he offered the familiar question. "Are you still committed, Matt?"

I hated this question because he asked it often with intent to dig around for any signs of a guilty conscience. It was a manipulative maneuver but effective nonetheless.

I dodged the question alluding once again to my "dream" surprise. I told Joseph that God had spoken loud and clear to me about our commitment journey and that I was excited to share my personal revelation with him when he returned. Joseph was apprehensive at best and quickly ended the phone conversation.

On Wednesday, June 30, 2010, Joseph returned from Israel.

That afternoon, as planned, I headed over to Hayward to meet Joseph for dinner. On the drive to Joseph's house, Alissa and I prayed on the phone. I remember that after our prayer, I was thinking about Jesus's parable the pearl of great price.

A farmer found a priceless pearl on some property. To prevent anyone from claiming the pearl, he buried it in the ground. The farmer then sold everything he had to buy the piece of property containing the precious pearl.

Alissa was that pearl, and I was ready to give up everything to have her.

Chevy's Shutdown

To my surprise, Joseph and I would not be dining alone. Joseph's son, Joshua would also be joining us. Naturally, this would postpone the Alissa conversation. I tried my best to make small talk in hopes of avoiding the secret of my new relationship, and this made for an awkward evening. My strategy was to deflect all conversation by instead asking Joseph to talk about Israel.

The plan failed.

It failed not because of my inability to avoid his questioning but because Joshua had his own confession to make. Ironically, as I was sitting across from Joseph pretending to listen and instead rehearsing my lines for the big conversation, Joshua began to speak.

As the words started to spill from Joshua's mouth, my jaw dropped. I could not believe what I was hearing …

Joshua, a sophomore in high school, was forbidden, by his father, to date anyone until college. Joseph wanted to ensure that Joshua's priorities were straight and that he was focusing on what truly mattered (to Joseph): school, basketball, and success.

Joshua, like me, had a confession to make. There in front of my eyes, I watched a conversation unfold that was identical to the one I had intended to have with Joseph later in the evening. Almost the same words I had planned to use were now spoken by Joshua, and the same reaction I had dreaded from Joseph soon followed.

Joshua's attempted rebellion was immediately met with forceful resistance. Joseph refused to entertain Joshua's desire to date. Despite Joshua's attempt to bring God into the conversation, Joseph would not listen. In Joseph's opinion, Joshua was not ready for a relationship, he could not handle it, and Bridgette, Joshua's new girlfriend, would only lead him away from his goals.

"No. Not happening. Not until college."

Conversation over.

Really? I would have to reenact that? Why didn't I just tape Joshua s' convo and put it on repeat for Joseph; that would have been a lot easier.

When we got back to his house after dinner, it was time for round two. Joseph started venting to me about the conversation that had taken place with Joshua. I just sat there listening and waiting for the perfect place to tie our dinner conversation into my revelation about Alissa. There was no perfect time, just awkwardness

"So, you're not going to believe this, but …"

I told Joseph everything about the last month and how Alissa and I were now dating.

The man was stunned. I couldn't tell if his expression was one of doubt, disbelief, or defeat, but he could not believe that I would put him through the same conversation twice in one night.

It was an uphill battle from the beginning, but I stuck to my guns. Honestly, it was hard for Joseph to argue against God's involvement with the dreams and confirmations. However, as Joseph would explain, he was mainly upset that I kept my relationship a secret from the beginning. He felt betrayed, which was completely understandable.

After expressing his disappointment, Joseph let me know that he could not in good conscience support my decision to date Alissa. He believed that although God may have brought Alissa into my life, we still had a covenant to complete.

The next morning Joseph reported that he hadn't slept all night. He said there was no peace in his heart about my decision to date Alissa, but if I wanted to start seeing her as a friend he was willing to compromise his principles by allowing me to continue on the commitment journey.

I knew that this wouldn't work, because we were already more than friends—we were "Facebook official."

Lunch Date Devastation

The following day was difficult. I could feel the tension between us caused by Joseph's lack of support for my relationship with Alissa. I also knew that my time of mentorship was coming to an end. Despite the circumstances, I invited Alissa to meet for lunch near Joseph's home.

At lunch, Alissa asked me about my conversation with Joseph. After I reported all that had happened, Alissa had a worried look on her face as though she weren't convinced that I was planning to stay with her. I assured Alissa that it didn't matter what Joseph said; there was no way that I was going to leave her.

Our lunch ended, and Alissa drove home.

I then returned to Joseph's house, where the tension in the air could have been cut with a knife. As I feared would happen, Joseph spent the next two hours presenting his case as to why I needed to break up with Alissa. Joseph was initially met with my hardened heart and unrelenting spirit, but as he continued talking, something extremely overwhelming and unexpected occurred.

I could feel them in the corners of my eyes. I fought them as long as possible with clenched fists, but eventually the floodgates were opened. Uncontrollable tears came flowing from my face. I'm not sure what pushed me over the edge, but I was suddenly convinced that I was supposed to break up with Alissa.

Wait … What?

How I went from promising Alissa at lunch that I would never leave her to feeling completely convicted about ending our relationship, I do not know. At the time I wasn't sure if Joseph was just a master manipulator, as my family would all tell me, or if this truly was God's will for my life. The only thing I knew for sure was that my will was broken and that I needed to talk with Alissa.

I drove straight from Hayward to Alissa's house in Pleasanton. We met in my car, where I described my conversation with Joseph. Alissa asked what I planned to do.

I was once again at a crossroad. The decision before me was one I had made two times before: continue on the commitment journey or begin a new relationship.

Just seeing Alissa's face was enough for me to reconsider the conviction that had hit me so strongly at Joseph's house just hours before. I panicked. Crying alone was one thing; watching Alissa cry was a whole new ball game.

I told her not to worry. I wasn't going anywhere.

The next day Joseph tried to reason with me again about Alissa, but I was unwavering. There was no way I was willing to let her go without a fight, not this time.

Joseph could sense the sincerity of my stubbornness and realized that I had no intention of letting go. Instead of walking away from our mentorship, Joseph made another proposal. He said that he was willing to continue in our covenant if I was willing to spend the weekend with him to gain proper perspective on our commitment journey.

This felt like a trap.

In my heart I knew Joseph would attempt to use this weekend to break us apart, but for some reason I accepted his offer.

I was starting to second-guess myself and my convictions. Maybe I was blinded by Alissa. Maybe I wasn't hearing clearly from God. Maybe my selfishness and emotions had gotten the best of me.

I was once again swayed by my inability to commit.

Maybe time away from Alissa to clear my head was exactly what I needed.

I wasn't sure.

After apprehensively accepting Joseph's proposal, I contacted Alissa. I could sense the confusion and pain in her voice as I explained that I couldn't spend time with her this weekend as we had previously planned. Rightfully so, she didn't understand why it was a good idea to spend time with the man whose goal was to split us apart.

Honestly, neither did I, but I went ahead and spent the weekend at Joseph's house anyway.

Killer Silence

During the day on Saturday, Joseph and I went for a drive. He wanted to talk about our commitment journey—specifically, all that had happened in the last ten months since we met.

After climbing into his car, I realized that I had left my phone in the house. I decided to leave it, assuming that our drive wouldn't take very long.

When I returned several hours later, I found multiple missed calls and texts from both my mom and Alissa.

My heart broke after listening to my mom's voice mail …

"Matt, if you don't want to respond to my calls or texts, that's fine, but to leave the woman you claim to love in the dark is not okay. She is worried sick about you and does not understand why you aren't speaking to her this weekend. Be a man and talk to her."

The words cut deeply and sparked a raging fire in my heart. I went from fine to furious in a matter of seconds, with Joseph as the target. This weekend of "proper perspective" was hurting the woman I loved and endangering our relationship.

Now short of breath and shaking, I told Joseph that due to an emergency I needed to leave right away. Having just returned from our car ride together, he was confused and hurt by my sudden turnaround.

"What's going on?" he asked. "I thought you were staying until Sunday?"

"No. I can't stay here any longer. I'm sorry; I need to leave. There is a family emergency."

I lied and he knew it.

Joseph tried to reason with me once more, but I was unwilling to listen. My hatred toward him and the rage inside me grew with every word that he spoke.

"Joseph, I need to go now! I am going to explode and do not want you to get hurt."

He tried to comfort me by placing his hand on my shoulder, but I shrugged away violently and stormed out of the house.

I immediately called Alissa and apologized for keeping her in the dark. She graciously forgave me as I explained the turmoil I was experiencing.

Alissa could sense the urgency in my voice as I told her that I was on my way to see her from Joseph's house.

The Prayer

Too embarrassed to see her parents, I called Alissa upon arrival asking if she would come outside. I was sure her parents hated me for putting their daughter through such an emotional roller coaster.

When Alissa opened the front door, I didn't say a word but immediately wrapped my arms tightly around her as though letting go would mean losing Alissa forever.

"You're shaking," she said.

"I know. I'm sorry. I just hate being in this situation and putting you through this."

We then went to my car and talked about the weekend and my conversations with Joseph. We were weighing our options and looking to God for direction. In desperation, we prayed, "Lord, we want to honor you with this relationship. We both love you and each other, and we want to seek your will for our relationship. You know the situation we are faced with, Lord, and we pray that you will give us a clear answer as to what we should do. Should we continue in this relationship and trust that you will make it work, or should we wait until I finish the commitment journey?"

It was a simple request, really. "God, should we continue or wait?"

That was our prayer on the night of July 3, 2010.

Alissa and I had already agreed that we would spend the Fourth of July together, and we decided to begin our day at church. Little did we know that the Lord already had his answer prepared for us.

Independence Day

I arrived at Alissa's house early the next morning and from the moment she climbed into my car I noticed an unfamiliar tension between us. Undoubtedly, my indecisiveness about the commitment journey, our prayer from the night before, and the uncertainty of our relationship added some extra stress to our current situation.

I was also unsure how to act toward Alissa while waiting for God's answer to our prayer. Should we continue as boyfriend and girlfriend like nothing was hindering us, or should we reserve our affections until we received a conclusive answer? I didn't know what to do, and it was quite obvious to Alissa.

Once inside the auditorium we took our seats. Shortly after we sat down, the worship band began to play. It was hard to concentrate during worship, with all of the unanswered questions in my mind. I should have been focusing on God, who could have brought me peace, but I instead chose to stew in my anxiety.

When worship ended, the lights dimmed.

Silence filled the room …

Tick. Tock.

…

Tick. Tock.

…

Tick. Tock.

…

Tick. Tock … (Silence)

The sounds of a ticking clock played over the loudspeaker as the projector displayed a watch on the screens above us. The caption below the clock read, "Don't you just hate waiting?"

God thinks he's funny.

Wouldn't you know it? The morning's message was titled, "Waiting."

No joke, the entire message was about God's intended purpose behind patience and waiting. Alissa and I sat in the Cornerstone sanctuary in complete shock that the Lord had so clearly answered our prayers.

There was an eerie and awkward silence between us after that. We just sat there, waiting for the message to end, wondering what "waiting" looked like in our relationship.

Alissa's body language was signaling for some kind of assurance that we were still okay. Unable to comfort her, I sat silently still.

I desperately wanted to hold her hand, but I knew it was wrong. I couldn't give her any false hope. We had asked for a sign the night before and had received our answer. I wasn't foolish enough to pretend otherwise.

The silence continued between us as we walked out of the auditorium.

"So, what did you think about the sermon?" Alissa asked.

My silence spoke volumes.

We continued from the auditorium into the courtyard where my friends Joel, Steve, and John were waiting. They looked at me and tried not to laugh at the obvious awkwardness.

Alissa went to the bathroom while I cried out to my friends. They comforted me and asked what I was going to do. I told them that I had received my answer, and they gave an understanding nod.

Alissa returned to my side and gave a defeated look as if to say, "Let's get out of here so you can break up with me already."

Not wanting to ruin the holiday, Alissa and I decided to enjoy our day together before discussing the implications of the morning's message.

For lunch, we drove to Half Moon Bay, where we had a family picnic with Alissa's parents at the beach. After the picnic we headed to my parents' house for a barbecue. It was all very American. Honestly, it felt like a reenactment from one of my favorite childhood movies, *The Sandlot*. Alissa and I sat in lawn chairs on my parents' street corner, listening to "America the Beautiful" while fireworks lit up the Fourth of July sky. We held hands (against my better judgment), cuddled under a warm blanket, and enjoyed what would most likely be our last night together.

When the fireworks were finished, I drove Alissa home. At the door to her house she asked for an answer. "Can you at least tell me what direction you're leaning?"

I couldn't find the courage to tell her the truth. "I had a really good time with you today. Can we talk about this in the morning?"

Coward.

Denny's and the Garden of Eden

Morning arrived sooner than expected, and I was still uncertain about how I was going to communicate my feelings to Alissa. Before I could collect my thoughts, I received a text message from Joseph. He asked me to meet him for breakfast so we could discuss what had happened over the weekend.

I was hesitant but felt supernaturally compelled to comply.

Joseph and I met at Denny's on Monday, July 5.

As it turned out, Joseph drove to Denny's in Pleasanton in faith that I would accept his breakfast invitation, and had it not been for the "wait" message at church, I wouldn't have agreed to see him.

Upon my arrival, Joseph explained that he had received a revelation the previous evening about our commitment journey. In this revelation God showed him the Garden of Eden and how our current circumstances correlated to the experience of Adam and Eve. Joseph explained that in our commitment journey, I could have anything I wanted from the garden, but like Adam and Eve, I was instructed to avoid the forbidden fruit.

Despite all of the blessings, privileges, amenities, and accommodations, the forbidden fruit was still more enticing. As consistent with the rest of my life, I wanted what I could not have. Although the commitment had an expiration date, I simply could not wait and wanted the fruit in my timing, not God's. Joseph would later explain that one of the many purposes of this journey was to ensure that once I obtained the fruit, I would be able to enjoy it for a lifetime.

After Joseph's revelation, I explained to him what had happened at church the morning before. Although it was painful for me to admit, I agreed that the wait message was confirmation of our commitment journey. Joseph also encouraged me that God understood my commitment and knew the desires of my heart. If Alissa was supposed to be my wife,

God would bless our marriage through my obedience, but I needed to let her go now and wait expectantly with faith.

After our breakfast, I called Alissa. We discussed the wait message from Sunday morning and how it had confirmed our prayer from Saturday night. Alissa agreed that we should wait, but she was unsure how this waiting period would look and for how long it would last. We discussed my covenant and how I had agreed not to pursue a romantic relationship for the next two years. She then suggested that we step back from our relationship to remain friends instead, but in my heart I knew that was impossible. I wouldn't be able to go backward with Alissa. More time spent with her would only increase my love and desire for her.

I knew the only way for me to finish my commitment journey was to completely cut ties with Alissa. There was no room for double-mindedness. If I wanted to fully consecrate myself to this commitment journey, I needed to make a difficult decision. As painful as it was, Alissa and I broke up on Monday, July 5, 2010.

Alissa assured me that although she did not desire to separate, she respected my decision and would wait for me to finish my covenant.

She truly was a woman of faith.

I honestly believed that God would bring us back together at some point in the future, but hearing her express the desire to wait for me confirmed that.

What had the potential to be the most painful conversation of my life, turned out to be a joy-filled and peaceful experience that surpassed all understanding.

Although there was pain, I also had hope. I had a faithful Father and a godly girl, so no matter what the outcome, I felt relief knowing that it was in his hands.

Before ending our final phone call, we both expressed our feelings for one another and our sadness in having to part ways. However, we also rejoiced in God's faithfulness for answering our prayers in such a miraculous fashion.

What an amazing God we serve.

After I hung up the phone, my journey of faith, hope, and trust continued.

CHAPTER 7

THE HEALING PROCESS

The healing process began on July 6, 2010.

Although I knew that breaking up with Alissa was the right thing to do, it still hurt like heck.

There were sleepless nights and countless tears. I remember many commutes home from work when those tears would nearly blind me. I seriously had to consider pulling off the freeway a few times to prevent a car accident.

Everything seemed to remind me of her; I couldn't escape.

One song in particular, John Waller's "While I'm Waiting," absolutely wrecked me. I would sing this song at the top of my lungs while snot and tears flowed from my face:

> While I'm waiting, I will serve you.
> While I'm waiting, I will worship.
> While I'm waiting, I will not fade.
> I'll be running the race, even while I wait.

The pain of losing Alissa was way too great to waste, a truth that motivated me to stay committed while on my journey.

The following excerpt came from my journal a few days after I broke up with Alissa:

> July, 7, 2010: One thing I know for certain, I will not suffer in vain. As painful as this trial is, I refuse to stray

from the path set before me. If I detour from the road assigned to me, I will have suffered for nothing. I will not falter; I refuse to stumble. The cost is too great. My love for God, his love for me, my love for Alissa, and my desire to glorify his name with whatever ministry he calls me to will forever deter me from falling away. I know what is required of me; I have counted the cost. This decision was not made in haste; it was a call too deafening to deny.

I now know that God does not waste pain. Instead, "In all things God works for the good of those who love him, who have been called according to his purpose" (Romans 8:28). Through this process I learned to ask in any painful circumstance or situation, "What is God doing in this situation? How can I grow from this?" I've learned that God's goal is to teach us to reflect the image of his Son, Jesus. I've learned to praise him in the storm, trusting that he is refining me in the fire. I've learned to have faith that God is God and God is good despite my circumstances. I've learned to praise God through the pain.

Malachi and the Mango Tree

After a few weeks I would be able to put these words into practice as I headed down to Haiti on a missions trip.

To aid in the disaster relief effort from the earthquake of 2010, I joined a team from my local church that flew down to Port au Prince, Haiti, to help rebuild the city. My team focused on a girls' orphanage that had been completely demolished by the earthquake.

Spending time with the Haitian kids brought indescribable joy to my heart. It was the healing experience that I needed to overcome my recent heartbreak and to focus on the Lord's work. Seeing how happy these orphans were despite their circumstances also really helped change my perspective on life.

During our trip, we stayed at a run-down Haitian hotel and took a utility truck to and from the orphanage. For our meals, we had an amazing chef who cooked us authentic Haitian food for breakfast, lunch, and dinner. Although we had enough food and ate like kings, the kids around us barely had enough to survive.

We were commanded not to feed the orphans, which broke all of our hearts. While we were eating fish, chicken, plantains, grits, and other Haitian delights, the kids usually ate the same mixture of rice and beans, with the occasional piece of fruit from their mango tree every day.

One delicacy available to these kids at the orphanage came from the sugarcane fields. While we were repairing the broken walls of the orphanage, fieldworkers were busy in the hot Haitian sun cutting down sugarcane so the kids could have more space to play. However, once the sugarcane stalks had been removed from the field, the kids would no longer have access to this delicious treat.

I remember sitting in the sugarcane fields full from supper while many of the kids were still hungry from the short supply of food. As I sat watching the kids play at a distance, a little boy named Malachi came walking up to me with a proud look on his face. In his hand was the largest, most succulent piece of sugarcane available in the field. Although I was still full from dinner and he was probably hungry from the lack of food, Malachi extended his tiny arms to offer the coveted sugarcane to me.

This little boy was willing to sacrifice what everyone else wanted, to instead serve me. Once again my heart was broken. How could I live my life so selfishly while having such an abundance while this little boy was willing, without hesitation, to offer me his first and his best?

I saw Jesus shine through Malachi that day. He laid down his desires for mine and served me out of the love and kindness in his heart.

While on our missions trip we were blessed with the opportunity to visit a Haitian beach resort with the orphans. We splashed in the water, played soccer, and walked the shoreline looking for seashells. The beauty of the beach made me think about Alissa.

Against my better judgment I decided to bring her some shells home from the Haitian seashore as souvenirs. The night I got home from Haiti, I snuck over to Alissa's house past midnight and placed a seashell on her truck. The shell was stuffed with a poem which was written on a Haitian dollar.

Do I regret giving Alissa this gift?

No.

Did it complicate and aggravate our waiting period?

Absolutely.

A few days after Alissa received my gift, she returned the favor.

Upon arriving home from work one day in July I found a Valentine in my mailbox. The card was from Pixar's "The Incredibles," which stated, "As long as you're here, I won't disappear."

After our brief exchange of gifts, Alissa and I once again cut off all communication.

Kona Conundrum

At the beginning of the summer, before Joseph left for Israel in June, we had planned to spend a week in Kona, Hawaii. Coincidentally, Alissa and her family would also be vacationing in Kona during the same week.

After our breakup in early July, I was both anxious and hopeful about our shared vacations in Kona. Would we run into each other? How would I handle such an encounter? What would Joseph do? How would Alissa react?

To ensure the possibility of a rendezvous, I kept this information hidden from Joseph knowing that he would inevitably change our itinerary to prevent such a meeting.

Strangely enough, just weeks after Alissa and I had severed ties, Joseph decided that he would rather vacation in Maui.

Situations such as these demolish my belief in coincidence and strengthen my trust in divine intervention. God knew the anxiety in my heart about potentially running into Alissa while in Hawaii. Yet, without revealing to Joseph that we would be on the same island as Alissa and her family, he altered our plans.

I was both relieved and disappointed at this discovery. I was relieved that God had alleviated my stress, worry, and anxiety, but disappointed that I would not see Alissa. God knew my heart and provided accordingly; I am truly thankful for my Jesus!

Enlisting in the Army

Prior to our vacation I had another dream.

In my dream, I was driving with my friends to the airport where we would be flying to Hawaii. However, on the way to the airport we decided to meet with an army recruiter. This detour was never part of the original plan, but we were all suddenly very excited about joining the army. None of us had ever discussed this possibility in the past, but at the moment we were impassioned with the idea. While meeting with the recruiter we all signed our names on the dotted line.

Moments after I made this commitment, the reality of my decision settled upon my heart like a ton of bricks. I was supposed to vacation in Hawaii, but instead I had committed to the military; what was I thinking? Not only would I miss my awesome vacation, but how would I finish my master's degree program?

Frightened by the reality of my decision, I approached the recruiter to ask for clarification on the details of our agreement. I told the recruiter my predicament by explaining that I was currently registered for graduate school. She looked at me sternly and stated that I should have counted the cost before enlisting in the military.

After waking from this dream, I was plagued with thoughts of my impulsivity and how I often made commitments that I later regretted and could not fulfill. I desperately needed to eliminate my noncommittal spirit.

Until this cycle was broken, I would continue to follow my passions into commitments that would remain unfulfilled. With my marriage, career, and ministry in the near future, I would have to learn to commit or prepare myself for a life of disappointment, pain, and regret.

Winning the Lottery

Upon our arrival at the airport, Joseph and I checked our bags and walked toward the boarding area. As we approached our gate, I unexpectedly heard my name over the loudspeaker. "Matthew Jones to the customer service counter. Matthew Jones to the customer service counter."

Apparently, Joseph had requested a first-class upgrade for our five-hour flight to the Aloha State, and sure enough, by lottery, we were selected.

First-Class Conviction

Flying first class is quite the luxurious experience: warm nuts, champagne, cushy reclining seats, and personal service that exceeded expectations.

While reclining comfortably in my seat, I began my preferred onboard activity of people watching. As people filed to their seats, one particular couple caught my attention. There was an older gentleman with long dark hair and tan skin who was accompanied by a beautiful young black woman. They were quite affectionate with one another, partaking in PDA as if they were the only ones on the aircraft. As I watched this couple with curiosity, I realized that I recognized this man.

Joseph nudged me and asked why I was staring, to which I responded, "Do you know who that is?"

Not up to date on his pop culture, Joseph replied, "No, why do you care?"

I whispered quietly trying to contain my excitement, "That's Carlos Santana!"

"Carlos who?" he replied.

"Carlos Santana! He's one of the greatest guitarists of all time!"

Joseph responded, "Well, are you going to talk to him or just stare?"

In my heart I wanted to have a conversation with the guy, but he was clearly enjoying himself and I didn't want to disturb him. I also did not want to cause a commotion. Maybe people were oblivious to his presence, and if I made a big deal out of it, others would bombard him with requests for pictures and autographs as well. Joseph knew my inner dialogue and decided to curb my distracted mind. He grabbed the book I was reading and crawled quietly up to Carlos. Handing him my book, Joseph asked Carlos to sign an autograph for me. As Carlos looked back, he smiled and waved, to which I politely responded with congruence.

Sure enough, after this request, the seal of confidentiality was broken and crowds of people surrounded Carlos asking for autographs and pictures. I was satisfied with my autograph and courtesy acknowledgment, so I contentedly watched the chaos continue from my seat.

When Joseph returned to his seat, he had a mischievous smile on his face. When I asked what was up, he stated, "You know there is no such thing as coincidence, right?"

Joseph continued to explain that God had a purpose for placing us in first class and for establishing this divine appointment with Carlos Santana. Joseph then reminded me of the previous Christmas when he had gifted me with a brand-new acoustic guitar. His recollection continued to depict my passionate excitement for this new pursuit and how badly I wanted to take lessons to master the art of guitar. He then asked where my passion for the guitar had gone. Truth be told, I had given up on guitar lessons after a two-month trial. I knew where Joseph was headed with his analogy, and I immediately hardened my heart.

As my mentor, Joseph took every opportunity to integrate life lessons into our journey together. I was often resistant toward his attempts to interject truth into my life, but I was never successful at shutting him out.

It is true when they say that nothing in life is free. Although I never paid for these vacations monetarily, I was always forced to pay attention to Joseph's life lessons. I can recall many times when I would hope and silently beg God to allow me to enjoy one trip without any theological, spiritual, or psychological interventions. However, this was my price to pay.

Rough life, right?

Joseph's interventions always came at uncomfortable times and always concluded with conviction. I knew that God was giving Joseph insight because he knew things about my inner processes and thoughts that only God could know. The only suitable explanation for these interventions was the involvement of the Holy Spirit.

As my spidey senses tingled, I knew that Joseph's mentor moment had arrived. It was time to pay the piper, and boy, was it an emotionally taxing event. Referencing Revelation 2:4 from the Bible, Joseph pointed out that I had "lost my first love."

Consistent with my noncommittal spirit, Joseph once again witnessed as my passion flared up only to be extinguished by my inability to follow through with a commitment. I so badly wanted to play the guitar, but once

I received the guitar and began lessons, the novelty of my dream ended, leaving my guitar in the closet to collect dust. Unfortunately, this was the pattern in my life.

I was also reminded of the previous winter when I had expressed my desire to take up the sport of snowblading, which was a hybrid between snowboarding and skiing. After watching countless online videos of snowbladers on YouTube and browsing online catalogs and magazines, I was hooked. All I could think about was how awesome it would be to have a pair of snowblades so I could fly down the mountain like the professionals.

While I was on my computer at Joseph's house, he could tell that I was distracted. He finally asked what was so interesting, so I excitedly explained all about my new passion for snowblading. Joseph reminded me that I had just spent six hundred dollars on new snowboarding equipment at the end of the last snow season, but this did not diminish my desire at all.

Instead of focusing on what I already had, I decided to chase after the next big thing. Although I loved snowboarding and had been riding for over ten years, I lost sight of my love to instead chase the enticing venture of snowblading. The joy I once found in snowboarding faded as the fresh excitement of snowblading consumed my mind. After a few days of continued talk about snowblades, Joseph finally broke down and offered to help me purchase the equipment. My heart nearly burst out of my chest as the realization of this dream was materializing before my eyes.

Since I purchased my snowblades four years ago, I have ridden them one time. My snowblades now sit in my closet collecting dust next to my guitar. Once again, I had obtained the object of my affection, but my passion was quickly extinguished by a failure to commit. The only thing that remained from my passionate pursuit of these snowblades was the sense of guilt and stupidity for wasting four hundred dollars. This was once again a direct effect of my noncommittal spirit.

The catch-and-release curse was in full effect. I would strive to obtain my passion, but the moment I realized the work required to cultivate that passion, I would give up. Joseph helped me see that this is what happens in many relationships. People enjoy their current situation until something better comes along. They leave their original love in pursuit of their newly acquired desire only to discover that once the "new car smell" wears off, they are no better off than they were in their last relationship. Problems will surface; work, dedication, and commitment are required, and people feel that the grass will be greener elsewhere.

Consequently, the individual continues to look for a relationship that provides instant gratification without the coinciding commitment. The unsatisfied individual will continue to cycle through relationships until he or she realizes that all worthwhile endeavors require effort, dedication, and commitment. Without these crucial elements, satisfaction in relationships will never be sustained.

I was beginning to better understand the reason behind this commitment journey. Joseph knew that I loved Alissa, but he also understood that our relationship would crash and burn with the current condition of my heart. I needed to break free from this pattern of unfulfilled passions and desires. If I wanted to have a lasting marriage, effective ministry, and successful career, I would have to overcome this giant obstacle, my Mount Everest.

Tidal Waves of Passion

It's interesting how God can use nature to speak to us in powerful ways— Moses and the burning bush, Noah and the flood, Jonah and the fish, or the Israelites in the desert. I too learned a powerful lesson about commitment in nature while boogey boarding at Maui's Big Beach.

While cruising the coastline on my rental scooter, I saw a variety of pearly white sand beaches, pristine blue water, and best of all, monster waves!

Despite the beauty of Maui's Big Beach, this palm tree paradise presented some dangers that required serious consideration. The waves at Big Beach were large and powerful. Signs warned surfers and other water sports participants of the potential dangers of playing in and around the ocean. At this particular beach, visitors were warned about the strong current and "shore breakers," which were large waves that crashed directly on the sand of the shore.

The waves at Big Beach were known to swallow swimmers whole, only to spit them back onto the shore with broken vertebrae, dislocated limbs, and the occasional fatality. In other words, death or serious injury awaited anyone who carelessly entered the ocean without first counting the costs of the dangers ahead.

Despite the warning signs and horror stories from the lifeguard on duty, I continued on toward the shoreline. Warm water and big breakers were my motivation for visiting Hawaii in the first place; I wasn't going to let "safety" steal my fun.

After testing the waters I grabbed my boogey board and headed into the surf. The waves formed quickly and crashed thunderously onto the shore. It didn't take long for me to realize that these waves were fierce and demanding of my respect.

As the opening set approached, I paddled as quickly as possible to position myself in the perfect place to catch one. The oncoming wave pulled me backward and elevated my boogey board to the top of its crest. I remember that as I sat on the top of this wave, I felt the force of the ocean pulling my boogey board directly toward the ocean floor. It took all of my strength to avoid nose-diving into the sand. Had I not focused all of my energy and strength into the task at hand, I could have easily ended up in a wheelchair. However, I pulled into the barrel of my first wave and surfed safely to shore.

As I was lying on my board, I could hear the sound of an approaching wave. Before I could react, I was overtaken by a backbreaking surge of water that crashed over my body. I was immediately swept off my board and thrown around in circles like a T-shirt on tumble dry. The wave then smashed me on the ocean floor and rolled me in the sand until I came to a complete stop.

Now sandy, sore, and embarrassed, I sat on the beach thanking God for sparing my life. Before I could stand to my feet, another wave pummeled me to the ground and I was surrounded again by furious white foam. This time I was able to stab my feet into the sand before the wave could flatten me like a pancake.

As the water retreated back into the ocean, I ran up onto the beach. The lifeguards then called everyone out of the water as a precaution due to the unusually large sets that were now crashing on the shoreline.

This was a truly humbling experience as I realized that I was powerless against a force of nature beyond my control. I found out quickly that the warning signs posted at this beach were not for decoration.

My experience at Big Beach helped me understand the danger of distractions. If I had allowed the beauty of the beach, barbecues, and bikini-clad women to take my focus off the waves in front of me, I could have suffered some serious consequences.

With my back to the ocean, I was vulnerable to any wave pummeling me without warning. The same goes for our commitments. If we take our eyes off our goals, we can be swallowed up by a multitude of distractions and temptations. The distractions may look good at first, but they eventually leave us rolling around in the sand with a busted back, broken dreams, and unfulfilled goals.

Getting distracted in your marriage could end in a costly affair. Forsaking time with your children could result in the loss of those relationships or damage to their emotional well-being. Wasting free time instead of investing in a business idea, fitness goal, or hobby postpones our success and satisfaction. Choosing to spend your nights partying instead of studying may result in irreparable damage to your GPA. Some consequences are obviously worse than others, but you get the idea.

Not only does commitment demand our full attention to avoid distraction and temptation, but it also requires strength and endurance to persevere when the waves in the commitment are larger than expected. We cannot predict our temptations and trials. Some may absolutely catch us by surprise, but we must read the signs and count the cost before diving into the waters of commitment.

Ultimately, before making a commitment, we must count the costs of our decision, be prepared for trials and temptations, and endure the strong currents and overpowering waves that try to throw us off our path. Our best chance at surviving the waves that arise is facing them head-on, focusing all of our attention on the task at hand.

Although he was not the greatest role model, I admire the words of Tony Montana in *Scarface* when he said, "All I've got in this life is my balls and my word, and I don't break either of 'em for nobody."

I want to be that kind of a man. Not the cocaine-selling, arms-dealing drug lord portrayed in *Scarface*, but a man who is known for keeping his word even when it hurts, a dependable man who will suffer great pain to protect his integrity. The Bible says, "A good name is more desirable than great riches" (Proverbs 22:1) and "Lord, who may dwell in your sacred tent? The one who keeps an oath even when it hurts" (Psalm 15:1, 4). That is my ultimate goal—becoming a man of integrity who, like Jesus, follows through on his commitments, keeps his promises, and is true to his word.

CHAPTER 8

FORGETTING YOUR
FACE IN THE MIRROR

August 15, 2010

Hawaii provided the perfect environment to recalibrate my perspective on the commitment journey.

With graduate school just weeks away, I couldn't afford to have any distractions. Skating through my master's program was not an option; I would need to consecrate myself completely to reach this mountainous goal.

I had always skated by in school. I rarely had bad grades, but they were never exceptional either. I simply did what was required of me—no more, no less. Most of the time I figured out how teachers operated in class and found ways to get As without breaking much of a sweat. This usually required late-night cramming sessions days before the test, with a nonexistent retention rate. I could pass the exam with an A on Tuesday and forget the topic of the test on Wednesday.

Grad school had to be different. I wasn't just doing this for me; I wanted to accomplish something for God's glory.

Coming from a broken home, I desperately wanted to help restore broken relationships and hurting families. God created us for relationships, yet most of us haven't figured out how to successfully utilize God's most precious gift of selfless and sacrificial love. I wanted to help people learn how to love, forgive, heal, and communicate, and I knew this degree program would equip me to provide such services.

The week before my grad school orientation, I received an unexpected voice mail. After an entire summer without communication, Alissa had decided to contact me. She expressed her need to talk with me and requested that I call her back as soon as possible.

Considering that we had cut all ties of communication back in July, I figured that there must have been some kind of emergency for Alissa to call me like this. On the other hand, even if there was no emergency, I didn't want to rudely ignore her message as if I had never received it. Knowing Alissa, it took a great amount of courage and prayer to leave that voice mail.

I called her back to discover that Alissa wanted to discuss the potential of starting a platonic friendship. She was still unclear about the ramifications of the "wait message" and believed that it was okay to have a friendship.

In my mind I thought, *God wouldn't forbid two believers from being friends, right? Besides, we haven't spoken in nearly two months; the flame from our summer fling has surely died down by now.*

To keep the fire at bay, we decided to talk only once a week. We had hoped to keep this boundary on our communication until I completed my graduate program and finished the commitment journey with Joseph.

This boundary didn't last long, as our "friendship" quickly sparked into a full-blown forest fire. Instead of talking weekly, we began talking daily. If it wasn't a phone call, we were texting; and if we weren't texting, we were playing games against each other on our phones. I was in love with Alissa Marie Griehshammer, and it was quite obvious to Joseph.

For the fourth time since I'd started the commitment journey, my heart was once again divided and distracted.

It didn't take long for Joseph to confront me in his usual fashion. "Are you still committed, Matt?"

I lied and told him that I was.

At the time, I rationalized that a friendship with Alissa did not compromise the commitment journey.

Instead of confronting the lie, Joseph distanced himself from me.

Our limited interactions were now filled with tension and lectures about "total commitment." Joseph would often tell me that I would never see God's plan or experience his blessings from this commitment journey if my heart was divided. He said it was like having my feet in two boats; eventually my legs would split, and I would either hop completely into one boat or fall into the ocean.

He was right—my heart and mind were completely divided. What made things more difficult was that everyone else in my life was telling me that Joseph was manipulative and controlling. They did not understand that I had signed up for a commitment journey, one where I pledged to remain single and forsake other relationships for a total commitment.

A relationship with Alissa, no matter how seemingly ideal and desirable, was in direct opposition to the commitment I had made before God. It just makes sense that I would experience a test like this. I don't know why I was so surprised that opposition was coming after a decision I had made to honor God.

Opposition and Confusion (September 2010)

From the very beginning of my relationship with Joseph, I experienced resistance from my family and friends. They didn't understand why I spent every Wednesday, Friday, and Saturday with him. They didn't understand why I committed to singleness for three years. They didn't understand the purpose of the commitment journey.

To them I was just a puppet, doing and saying whatever Joseph asked. The travel, perks, and money were all considered carrots being dangled in front of my face to keep me under Joseph's control.

However, I realized that opposition from family and friends was my price to pay.

Joseph reminded me that I wasn't on this journey for my family and friends; I was on this journey for God. Then I remembered that Jesus promised pain and persecution for following him.

The words from Jesus should have brought comfort, but they brought only more confusion.

My mind was in constant tension between two opposing pieces of scripture—"Honor your father and mother" (Matthew 15:4), who were both telling me to leave the commitment journey, and Jesus's words "You must be willing to leave father and mother to follow me" (Luke 14:26).

My parents and Joseph were believers, yet they were offering contradictory advice on God's will, blessings, and plan for my life.

This was an incredibly confusing time with inordinate implications. Following Joseph's advice meant disregarding my parents and losing Alissa, while following my parents' advice meant breaking an oath before God while getting to keep Alissa.

Ultimately, this decision was much larger than my parents, Joseph, or Alissa, and I realized I needed to figure out what it meant to follow Jesus under the current circumstances.

Based on scripture, I knew that following Jesus would take me down the narrow path of most resistance. The easy decision was rarely the right one. In light of this revelation, I understood that following Jesus would bring pain and persecution, but the questions remained, was I following Jesus by staying in this journey with Joseph? Or did I make a rash vow that should have never been made in the first place?

All the people in my camp (family and friends) were convinced that Joseph had questionable motives and morals. They were concerned that I was being lured into a trap, that this man had ulterior motives and unhealthy intentions for our relationship.

These were the voices, opinions, and concerns of my closest family and friends. Couple these with my desire for Alissa and the unwavering support from family and friends of our relationship, and I too began questioning Joseph.

Finding objectivity was an extremely difficult challenge. No one in my camp knew anything concrete about Joseph other than what I told them. None of my family or friends had any evidence to support their accusations, yet Joseph was on trial. His integrity, his motives, our overseas travel … everything was under their review.

Had this man been brought into my life by God or by Satan? If Joseph was from God, I needed to stay the course and keep my commitment, but if he was an evil man with ill intent, I needed to leave my job immediately and pursue a life with Alissa instead. There was seemingly no middle ground.

Out of all the advice my friends and family had to offer, Alissa spoke the most truth during this time. She encouraged me to seek answers from God and God alone. Only he could shine the light of his truth into my current darkness and confusion.

She was right—no one else had the appropriate contextual understanding or divine wisdom to decipher God's sovereign will. I needed to seek God alone.

One of my favorite pastors told me that if we want to hear from God, we need to read what he has already written. Since I desperately wanted to hear from the Lord, I scavenged his word high and low.

After many tears and desperate pleas for answers, my search for truth brought me to the story of Jephthah from the book of Judges.

A Sorrowful Sacrifice

Jephthah was made the commander of the army of Gilead. His mission was to defeat the Ammonite king. Before battle, Jephthah promised that if God would grant him victory over his enemies, he would offer a special thanksgiving sacrifice. Jephthah promised to sacrifice the first thing to greet him on his return home.

Jephthah defeated the Ammonite king and returned home to fulfill his promise to God.

I imagine that Jephthah envisioned his dog, sheep, cat, or goat coming out to greet him; however, as the story unfolds …

> When Jephthah returned home to Mizpah, his daughter came out to meet him, playing on a tambourine and dancing for joy. She was his one and only child; he had no other sons or daughters.
>
> When he saw her, he tore his clothes in anguish. "Oh, my daughter!" he cried out. "You have completely destroyed

me! You've brought disaster on me! For *I have made a vow to the* LORD, *and I cannot take it back.*"

... and he did to her as he had vowed (Judges 11).

Jephthah made a promise to the Lord and had to fulfill his vow despite the heavy cost.

Granted, I didn't have to kill Alissa, but it felt like I had to let her die in my heart to obey the promise I had made before God.

I had made a covenant and needed to fulfill it, but my heart was still hardened toward the conviction God was so clearly bringing to my attention. This hardness of heart caused me much pain throughout the following weeks. Although I knew what the Lord had impressed upon my heart, I still had others telling me that I needed to flee from Joseph.

In this time of rebellion, I was brought to yet another convicting piece of scripture from 2 Timothy 4:3: "For the time will come when people will not put up with sound doctrine. Instead, to suit their own desires, they will gather around them a great number of teachers to say what their itching ears want to hear."

Anyone who heard that my mentor was preventing me from dating a beautiful, godly girl who loves Jesus would tell me to run for the hills. Who in their right mind would think it wise for a grown man to spend most of his free time isolated from friends and family, to instead spend time with an older man who would not condone dating during this season?

Without the context of my past relationship history and my present covenantal promise, the situation just sounded crazy.

I knew that, which brought all the more truth to 2 Timothy 4:3. I knew that people would think it was crazy for me to stay in a covenant with Joseph and not date Alissa. I wanted affirmation and confirmation to leave the journey, and I found people who would provide exactly that. Although I had people telling me what I wanted to hear, I still felt no peace. Leaving felt like walking away from God's plan and purpose.

My itching ears desperately wanted to hear that Joseph was bad, Alissa was good, and I should leave the commitment journey and pursue the girl of my dreams. Instead of listening to God and the lessons he was teaching me through his word, I surrounded myself with people who would tell me what I wanted to hear, which resulted in a great deal of pain, as running away from the Lord usually does.

Season of Suffering

During the month of September, Joseph knew that my heart was no longer invested in the commitment journey and I knew the practical implications of my decision to either stay or leave.

Was I ready to throw everything away: the mentorship, travel, luxuries, promises? Was I really ready to walk away?

For two weeks I could not sleep and felt exhausted. My eyes felt heavy, and my chest felt compressed. Fatigue does not even begin to describe the lethargy I experienced in this time of confusion and chaos. If I slept at all, I would often wake up more tired than when I went to sleep. I felt like a slave to this commitment and wanted to leave. There was a thousand-pound weight on my back that I desperately wanted freedom from.

There were actually times during the month of September when I contemplated suicide. The pressure to make this life-altering decision was absolutely crushing me.

This decision was eating away at my soul and especially affected my family. I would sit in the living room with my dad in silence as the elephant in the room trampled our relationship. I felt so alone in a house filled with family. I would come home from work, go straight to my room, and lie on my bed praying and asking God for relief, guidance, and direction, but they never came.

I felt like no one understood the pain and pressure I was experiencing. The worst part was that I couldn't talk to anyone about it. Even when I was able to talk with others, I only left feeling more confused.

Talking to my family, friends, and Alissa made me feel resentment and bitterness toward Joseph. Talking to Joseph made me feel convicted about my need for the commitment journey. It was a vicious cycle. I couldn't cut off my family, and I didn't feel the freedom to cut Joseph out of my life, even though I asked God to take him away from me on many occasions.

There had to be a middle ground, but I couldn't seem to find it. My parents and Alissa hated Joseph and did not want to hear about him.

Joseph constantly tried convincing me that the commitment journey was the best thing for me, my future marriage, and my ministry. He often explained that no one else could ever fully understand our journey, because no one else had been walking the journey for the last twelve months. So, he maintained, asking the opinions of others would only further confuse me.

When God Remains Anonymous

There were countless times during this year when I questioned Joseph's role in my life, and then I would experience an uncanny coincidence that would confirm that he was from God. For instance, I am very particular about my food and beverage selections, but I had never consumed an energy drink in front of Joseph. Yet one day he randomly brought me a care package with my favorite flavors of energy drink and gum.

The following week I started having car trouble and began to feel anxious about finding a mechanic. The next day Joseph called me to his home, and there sitting at the kitchen table was Fredrick, a family friend who happened to own an auto mechanic shop. Joseph didn't know my car needed repair, but God provided what I needed through him anyway.

Another day I had run out of protein powder, and when I arrived at Joseph's home I found he had purchased me my favorite bottle of protein powder, which he had never seen me use before or heard me talk about. How he knew, I'll never know, but it was as if God was directly communicating my needs to Joseph and he was responding by providing those needs at the perfect time.

One of the biggest confirmations came after I had just left Joseph's home after a two-hour lecture about the importance of our journey together. I was extremely frustrated to have spent two additional hours talking with Joseph about a topic that we had discussed a million times before.

Talk about beating a dead horse. This horse was not only dead but buried, resurrected, beaten again, buried again, resurrected again, and beaten over and over again.

I was tired of talking about our commitment journey, and I was ready to leave.

I remember being so mad at Joseph that I changed his name in my phone to "Mother Goose." He had no idea that I had changed his name, but I was so tired of seeing his stupid name pop up on my caller ID screen that I had to change it to something that would make me laugh instead of cringe.

Later in the evening I received a text message from Mother Goose. I nearly dropped my phone when I opened his message. There before my eyes was a picture of a goose. Joseph texted me a picture of the geese on the grass across from his house. In shock, I asked Joseph why he sent me the picture. He casually explained that he had seen those geese outside his bedroom window for almost twenty years and had never had the desire to photograph them, but God told him to take the picture and send it to me.

Really? The same day that I change Joseph's name to Mother Goose, he "randomly" sends me a photo of a goose.

Coincidence?

Maybe.

God yelling at me to wake up? Most probably.

These may seem like insignificant examples and one could say that I was reading too much into them, but these incidences occurred consistently throughout our relationship. There were just too many to count; how could they be anything other than confirmation from the Almighty?

Time and time again I questioned, and time after time I was answered.

According to Jesus, you will know a tree by its fruit. Good fruit cannot come from bad trees, and bad fruit cannot come from good trees. What fruit was being produced from my commitment journey with Joseph?

Let's see: I was growing closer to God, serving in my church, participating in a men's Bible study group, unlearning negative thought patterns and behaviors through the mentorship, and learning how to commit so that I could glorify God through my relationships. Not only that, but my relationship with my family was improving; I was beginning graduate school, quickly paying off my undergraduate debt, and traveling the world; and I had many godly friends and accountability buddies helping me stay true to my faith.

Yet all of this was discarded because I couldn't have one thing. All of the good fruit was tossed in the garbage because the tree was growing apples, not apple pies. I was once again focused on the 20 percent when the other 80 percent was amazing.

Commitments will often be tested by the 80/20 principle. It is a common occurrence for people to overlook the 80 percent of what they have, to instead pursue the 20 percent they don't.

Many men have thrown away marriages because someone in their office offered the 20 percent that their spouse lacked.

We have all seen people justify abandoning careers, goals, and family for another enticing opportunity.

What many people, including me, fail to realize is clinging to the 20 percent almost always means losing the 80 percent.

Is it worth the loss? Count the cost in your commitment and decide for yourself.

Deciphering the Source Code

I wanted concrete answers and a revelation from God. I needed to know which path to take. Prayer was the most effective and efficient way for me to obtain guidance from God, so I added the prayers of others to my own cries for help.

I remember specifically asking my mom to pray for answers on my behalf even though I knew how she felt about the situation. God must have been laughing when I made this request. I can only imagine him saying, "My son, you have so little faith. I can speak to you just fine. The problem isn't that I'm not speaking; the problem is that you don't want to listen. My words aren't in your plan. Your stubborn heart is deceptive. You are looking for others to bring you words that you want to hear, instead of being obedient to what I'm already telling you."

A few days after asking my mom to pray, I received a phone call from her. She instructed me to meet her and my dad at Emil Villa's, a restaurant where my sister used to work.

I really didn't know what to feel or expect, but I figured that God had answered her prayers since she seemed so urgent about the meeting. I dropped everything I was doing to hear this revelation from my mom.

When I got to the restaurant, my parents were sitting expectantly at the breakfast table. My mom told me that she felt that God had revealed a message and some scripture through her prayers.

In an attempt to describe Joseph, my parents opened up the Bible to the book of Psalms, where they read, "His speech is smoother than butter, yet war is in his heart; his words are more soothing than oil, yet they are drawn swords" (Psalm 55:21).

My parents were convinced that Joseph was enticing me with material possessions and promises of a bright future and world travel, but that his heart was evil and deceitful. They were convinced that he had ulterior motives for asking me to join this commitment journey.

I love my parents dearly and understand that they were sincerely concerned for me. They wanted to protect me and were doing their best to understand this situation.

But what if my parents were wrong?

Would the consequence of obeying them be disobeying God?

I would like to think that I will always choose obedience to God over obedience to anyone else, but I could not decipher what was true in this situation. All of their arguments for why this was a bad situation made complete sense; however, Proverbs 3:5 tells us, "Trust in the Lord with all your heart and lean not on your own understanding. In all your ways submit to him and he will make your paths straight."

There was something I just could not reconcile when hearing my parents' words. Although the whole world would look at my relationship with Joseph and say, "Something is not right about that situation," I felt no peace about leaving the commitment journey.

Please believe me when I tell you that I *begged* God to release me from the covenant. I cried and I pleaded for his permission to walk away from the commitment journey. I asked God to take Joseph away from me or make him walk away, but it never happened. I never felt the freedom to leave. I never felt peace about giving up. Something in my spirit was telling me to stay.

I thought that breakfast with my parents would bring me peace, but it only brought more turmoil. I felt that staying in my commitment journey would hurt my parents now more than ever. Staying on this path would communicate to them that I didn't value their opinion and didn't believe that they were hearing from God correctly.

I never told my parents this, but as they showed me the passage from Psalm 55, I couldn't help but notice the verse above that read, "My companion attacks his friends; *he violates his covenant*" (Psalm 55:20).

There was that word again.

It was so clear. My parents, bless their hearts, were using a scripture to show me the intentions and motives in Joseph's heart, yet they were actually revealing my own heart. I was the one breaking the covenant. I was the one attacking my companion by slandering his character and allowing others to do the same.

God brought my mom this scripture but not for the purpose she had hoped it would accomplish.

Once again I was cut to the heart. I knew what God was saying and understood the implications, but I wasn't ready to deal with the consequences.

Ever Hearing, Never Listening

God's will for me was becoming increasingly clearer; however, there was one problem.

I wasn't willing to obey.

I had a hard heart that was fearful of losing the one thing I wanted, Alissa. I still believed the message on the Fourth of July was applicable; I just didn't believe that it required me to completely cut her out of my life like Joseph insisted.

I would once again have to make a choice: commitment journey or relationship with Alissa.

It wasn't fair. I wanted both.

Besides, cutting off all communication was Joseph's opinion, not God's command. The message from church had said, "wait," not "never talk." I had a hard time believing that I was committing any type of sin by continuing my communication with Alissa.

Why couldn't we work on a friendship during this two-year commitment time? Let's be real … by the time I completed the commitment journey, Alissa and I would have established a solid friendship that would be beneficial for our future relationship. I mean, all good marriages are firmly founded in friendship, right?

I didn't know what to do. Should I listen to Joseph and completely cut off communication with Alissa, or should I listen to my parents, friends, and loved ones, who were telling me that I could have both?

Breakdown at Bethany

I continued talking with Alissa throughout the month of September. The more time I spent talking to Alissa and my family, the stronger case I developed against Joseph. Because I was now spending most of my time with Alissa and my family, time with Joseph suffered and our relationship deteriorated.

The tension in our meetings continued to rise as I hardened my heart toward Joseph and refused to listen to him. I would blatantly ignore him, which turned our tension into hostility.

I remember leaving work early one day to attend a night class at Bethany University. On my drive to Santa Cruz I reached the end of my rope. I could not handle the stress anymore. I needed help. I needed counseling, or I was going to do something drastic. I called my mom asking for the contact information for a pastoral counselor at our church. She gladly provided the information for Pastor Alex.

From the Heart of Mount Everest: A Journal Entry

My heart cries out in desperation that the Lord would allow my parents, peers, and friends to understand my struggle. It is an indescribably painful feeling to know that you are following the call of Christ but having no support from those nearest and dearest to you. I do not blame them for their ignorance; how could they understand the personal conviction I have received from the Lord? I do not expect them to, which is why I feel so alone on this journey along the narrow path. When you are called by Christ, you are required to drop everything you are doing, pick up your cross, and follow Him.

I know that my parents love me and desire only the best for me, but this is a journey that I must walk alone. Not alone in the sense that I am the only one on the journey because I am certain that the Lord is holding my hand, but alone in the sense that the wisdom of the world will never comprehend what the Lord requires of them until they are personally called.

Help me, Lord!

The Straw That Broke Commitment's Back

On the brink of a total breakdown, I contacted Pastor Alex for counseling.

When asked why I wanted to schedule our counseling appointment, I explained to Pastor Alex that I felt enslaved in my relationship with my mentor.

Having no understanding or context surrounding Joseph and our commitment journey, Pastor Alex encouraged me to be completely transparent about our relationship.

I told him everything: how we met, what I committed to, what I was prohibited from doing, and what we did during our time of mentorship together.

Pastor Alex offered his wisdom and counsel regarding the purpose of discipleship and how Jesus mentored his followers. He also helped me to examine my relationship with Joseph to identify any areas that did not match Jesus's style of discipleship.

Pastor Alex then echoed the concerns of everyone in my camp that it was absurd for another man to keep me from dating a godly girl unless God himself gave the directions. This obviously wasn't new information, but it was enough to push me toward pursuing Alissa again.

Not only were my parents, friends, other family members, and Alissa telling me that I shouldn't be involved in the no-dating portion of the commitment, but now my pastor was also on board.

It was time to jump ship.

Pastor Alex encouraged me to discuss my convictions with Joseph, and he prepared my heart for any reaction or retaliation that this conversation could cause. Basically, my pastor prepared me to lose everything, but I was surprisingly at peace with this.

I was finally free.

CHAPTER 9

LET FREEDOM RING

Before having any conversation with Joseph, I was already planning to communicate my newly discovered sense of freedom with Alissa.

Previously hindered by my no-dating commitment, I never had had the freedom to tell Alissa how I truly felt, but after my counseling session, I couldn't keep the truth to myself.

When I got home from counseling, I made the call.

The moment Alissa picked up the phone, I was finally able to fully express my feelings for her. "I love you!" I gushed.

Taken by surprise, Alissa paused momentarily before responding with a relieved, "I love you too!"

Alissa asked about my counseling conversation, so I excitedly explained all that had transpired and how I felt complete freedom and total peace. She then asked if I planned to quit my mentorship. I told her that I would have a meeting with Joseph tomorrow when I would take my stand and gladly accept any ensuing consequences.

Victory Speech

As I prepared to talk with Joseph, I was reminded and encouraged by a piece of scripture that my dad had pointed out at the Emil Villas revelation breakfast:

> My son, if you have shaken hands in pledge, are trapped
> by what you have said, and ensnared by the words of

your mouth, do this, my son, to free yourself, since you have fallen into your neighbor's hand. Go to the point of exhaustion and give your neighbor no rest! Allow no sleep to your eyes, no slumber to your eyelids. Free yourself, like a gazelle from the hand of the hunter, like a bird from the snare of the fowler (Proverbs 6:1–5).

I was already experiencing the lack of sleep, exhaustion, fatigue, heaviness, and enslavement. It was time to reclaim my freedom.

When my moment had finally arrived, I boldly entered Joseph's house. He curiously inquired about the purpose behind the meeting I had so adamantly requested. I told him all about my conversation with Pastor Alex and how our commitment journey consequently needed to change.

By the defeated look on his face I could tell there was pain, but he kept his composure. Joseph ended our meeting and let me leave without much of a fight.

Feeling empowered and free, I called Alissa on my drive home.

"It's done," I told her. "I'm coming to see you in SoCal."

Last-Ditch Effort

Right around the time when Joseph found out about my trip to Southern California, I received an invitation to attend his health club. I begrudgingly accepted his invitation with the understanding that Joseph intended to thwart my plans to visit Alissa.

I have to tip my hat—the guy was persistent.

The moment I received his invitation I experienced a flashback from the previous summer on Fourth of July weekend when he asked me to cancel my plans with Alissa to instead "regain proper perspective on our commitment journey."

To protect myself from repeating the past I ignored Joseph throughout the entire workout. We literally did not exchange a word until our painfully awkward two hours at the gym came to an abrupt end.

As we were walking out of the gym, Joseph looked at me with disappointment in his eyes.

As angry as I felt toward Joseph, my heart softened just enough to apologetically offer the only words we would exchange all day. "I'm sorry to have put you through this. You knew I was a selfish person."

He walked over to me and gave me a hug good-bye, and we parted ways.

I don't know how I could have treated someone so hatefully who had done nothing but show me love and sacrifice everything he had to bless me.

God's grace is incredible. Why he didn't strike me dead for treating his son Joseph so poorly, I don't know. Looking back, I realize this was exactly the reason why I was in the commitment journey in the first place—my history of using people for my personal benefit, breaking promises, burning bridges, and walking away from commitments that I couldn't keep.

Uncovering Hidden Idols

I guess Pastor Mark Driscoll was right; when we idolize people, we often demonize them as well. While in the commitment journey with Joseph I often correlated and confused God's will and Joseph's will, along with God's blessings and Joseph's blessings. I would do and say things to please and appease Joseph believing that God's blessings were intimately connected with him.

Because I sought Joseph's blessings at times more than God's, I also demonized Joseph and was able to passionately hate him when he seemingly let me down or disappointed me. However, Joseph was not God; he was simply a vessel that God used for his purposes. I believe our relationship could have been much better had I grasped this concept sooner.

In my mind, Joseph was the only thing standing in the way of my relationship with Alissa. What I didn't realize was that he was not standing alone …

The City of Angels

The following weekend I took the BART train from Pleasanton to San Francisco. It was finally happening. I was taking my first step of freedom toward a life with Alissa, away from a life with Joseph and the commitment journey. It felt like a dream. Leaving my worries in Northern California to escape for a weekend with the woman of my dreams honestly didn't feel real.

After an hour-long flight, I exited the airport in Los Angeles. Alissa picked me up curbside at LAX in her bright red Toyota Tacoma pickup truck. We drove to her house before heading to dinner at the Cheesecake Factory. We spent the evening together watching movies, talking, and sitting in her hot tub. Later that evening Alissa dropped me off at my sister's apartment, where I couch surfed for the weekend.

The next day Alissa and I attended church, enjoyed Huntington Beach, and then walked Karl, my sister's dog, around Balboa Island.

Later that evening Alissa and I sat in her truck and, as requested, I explained my relationship with Joseph. I was able to explain to her how he came into my life at a time when I did not have a good relationship with my dad and how God was using him to teach me about commitment.

Alissa showed signs of understanding and expressed that she felt more peace about the purpose of my relationship with Joseph now that she had a glimpse of our complex history. The timing made sense for me and Joseph to connect under the given circumstances. Granted, she still didn't like the commitment journey and how it limited our relationship, but she ended the weekend feeling more comfortable about it all, which was a total blessing and an answer to prayer.

The next day Alissa took me back to the airport. It was an amazing weekend with the girl of my dreams, but it was now time to return to reality.

Friends and Fried Chicken

I arrived at the LAX airport around three thirty for my 4:45 flight. I said my good-byes to Alissa and headed toward the self-check-in counter at the airline kiosk. While checking my itinerary I discovered that my flight had been delayed until six o'clock. Although I had a reading assignment to complete for grad school, I was not looking forward to this flight delay.

I sat in the airport lobby at gate 42b waiting to board my flight home to San Francisco. I tried reading, but was distracted by a cute little four-year-old girl who was playing with a cardboard cutout of a puppy and a bunny. Seriously, who in their right mind could get any work done under those conditions?

So, against all odds, I attempted to concentrate by putting in my earbuds. This strategy seemed to work until I realized that my phone was about to die. I needed to use my phone at the BART station in Pleasanton to call my dad, so I walked over to the cell phone charging station.

While standing near the charging station, I met an ex-military man who was ranting and raving about his new passion for Zumba workout classes. The guy was entertaining, so I stuck around to listen to his ridiculous stories. During the conversation I also met a hairstylist from the Bay Area who joined my conversation with Zumba man. Instead of doing my homework, I ended up spending my layover chopping it up with these two interesting and somewhat odd individuals.

When the airline attendant finally announced the initial boarding call of my flight, the three of us said our good-byes and went our separate ways.

As I was walking toward the boarding gate, I could hear a woman's obnoxiously loud voice behind me. I turned around to see an African American woman rushing toward the boarding gate complaining about her overpriced lunch of fried chicken and beer.

I couldn't help but laugh as I remembered the words of the great comedian Dave Chappelle: "People always see the divisions in our foods. Just because I eat chicken and watermelon, they think that's something wrong with me. Let me tell you something; if you don't like chicken and watermelon, something is wrong with *you*. Where are all these people that don't like chicken and watermelon? I'm sick of hearing how bad it is; it's great! I'm waiting for chicken to approach me to do a commercial. I'll do it for free chicken! It's the least I can do."

Laughing my way to the podium I waited in line to board the aircraft.

Prophets on a Plane!

After the attendant ripped my ticket, my mind then shifted to the potential ministry opportunity that awaited me at my seat. I usually asked the Lord to use me to share the gospel with my neighbors during long flights. I never know how the flight will unfold or whom he desires me to minister to, but I try to make myself available if the Lord should call me to share my faith in his son Jesus.

As I approached my seat, I noticed that a middle-aged Asian woman was sitting in the window seat of my row. My thoughts began to race on how I would share my faith with this woman.

Before I could finish these thoughts, I noticed that the hairstylist from the cell phone charging station was sitting one seat ahead of me. This brought a sense of relief knowing that I had already established rapport with someone in my general vicinity.

My new friend turned around and jokingly asked me not to kick her chair. I agreed with a smile as any anxiety about this flight quickly flew out the window.

Then, unexpectedly, the loud woman from the terminal walked up to my row. I thought to myself, *God would place this woman next to me.*

Sure enough, the woman I had just stereotyped would be sitting with me for the next ninety minutes. God clearly has a sense of humor.

The woman then introduced herself as Jenette and asked if I wanted her to swap seats with the woman in front of me. I thanked Jenette for the kind offer but assured her that it wasn't necessary. Jenette then continued to joke, "You sure? I can set ya'll up if you're feeling that?"

I let out an obviously uncomfortable chuckle, which ended Jenette's playful matchmaking banter.

As Jenette was placing her luggage in the overhead compartment, I saw a book on her chair titled, *Living in the Victory of Jesus.*

I was both surprised and delighted to discover that Jenette was a Christian. I told Jenette that I liked the title of her book, so she offered it to me. I thanked her but respectfully declined.

After sitting down, Jenette unexpectedly blurted out her boundaries. "If we are going to sit next to one another for an hour, we need to clarify a few things; there will be no snoring or drooling, and if you do drool, you had better not drool on me!"

Smiling awkwardly, I assured Jenette that I had some reading to finish and most likely wouldn't be sleeping on the flight.

Intrigued, Jenette asked what I was reading.

I showed her the cover of my *Christian Counseling Ethics* book. She asked what I was doing with a counseling book, and I explained that I was a graduate school student in pursuit of a master's degree in clinical psychology.

"So you're a counselor?" Jenette asked excitedly. "Do you want to practice on me?"

I couldn't tell if she was serious, but I agreed to counsel her anyway.

In our "counseling session" Jenette told me that she felt guilty for setting boundaries with her controlling mother and how control issues ran in her family. She expressed concern for how to raise her own children and how she didn't want to repeat the cycle of unhealthy control that her family tried to impose on her.

Jenette then changed the direction of our conversation by discussing her faith, the church, and her spiritual gifts. Jenette told me that God had given her the gift of prophecy and spiritual discernment. She explained that she could see through people and see what they were hiding, their intentions, and their motives.

I nervously wondered what God was revealing to her about me. Did she know about the chicken jokes?

Jenette gave the example of walking into a church and being able to see that some men were addicted to pornography, or were child molesters or wife beaters, as well as wives who were enablers and other such things. She explained that God had given her the ability to see the sins of people as if they were wearing them like a cloak. According to Jenette, these sins were available for her to see so that she could expose them to the light.

Like the prophets of the Old Testament, Jenette was charged with the duty to speak on behalf of God. He would give her words to speak: prophecies, revelations, judgments, etc., and it was her job to faithfully share these words with whomever God directed them toward. Jenette also explained that she would experience suffering and other consequences if she was disobedient and didn't speak as the Lord had commanded.

Hearing Jenette's story reminded me of Jonah, who had been charged by God to prophesy against the city of Nineveh. Instead of fulfilling his duty, Jonah ran from God. He boarded a ship to sail far from the city God had called him to.

Jonah's disobedience to God brought a sudden and literal storm in the waters where he was sailing. Jonah's crew soon learned that his disobedience had caused the storm and that throwing him into the water would calm the raging sea. The ship's crew threw him overboard, and he was then swallowed by a whale.

For skeptics like myself, Jenette's story sounds far-fetched, but according to the Bible, God has historically charged prophets like Jenette in the past and has also brought severe consequences for their disobedience.

Now, I know this may sound like a raw deal for Jenette, being a prophet and all, but she was also promised God's blessings for her faithfulness. She explained that God had blessed her with two beautiful children and a thriving hairstyling business, which she also used to glorify God by telling her clients about Jesus.

Suffice it to say, she had my complete attention. I was practically mesmerized by the power and authority from which she spoke. Her testimony was incredible, and the prophetic gift that she professed astonished me.

As a believer in divine appointments, I'm sure it was no coincidence that I was sitting next to a prophet from God. But what was the purpose of our meeting? I began to pray silently.

"Are you ready?" Jenette asked.

"Ready for what?" I replied.

"Well, you're wondering why God has me sitting here next to you, right?"

Honestly speaking, I was terrified. I simply sat there with fear and trembling wondering what God would say to me through Jenette. I'm almost always afraid God is going to tell me something that I don't want to hear, mostly because I have a difficult time being obedient.

After praying, I repositioned my body toward Jenette. She sat still staring at the ceiling making a facial expression as if she were popping her ears or cracking her jaw.

"So … Are you ready?" Jenette asked once again.

I nodded my head.

"There is a man named Ron in your life. Ron is trying to influence some decisions in your life that he knows nothing about. You have found favor in the Lord; continue walking in the path set before you. Cherish your favor; do not be ashamed of it. No one in your camp will understand the path you are walking, but it is a path of blessings."

Whaaaaaaaaaaat? I thought to myself as I stared intensely into Jenette's eyes. My dad's name is Ron! And everything that Jenette said about him was true. Yes, my dad loved me. Yes, he wanted the best for his son, but he didn't understand my situation and continuously discouraged me from following Joseph in the commitment journey. This was craaaaaaaazy.

Jenette continued, "There are questions about integrity in this situation, correct?"

I was astonished again because there were in fact issues regarding integrity in my relationship with Joseph. Outside observers considered our relationship strange. As was previously mentioned, some believed that Joseph had ulterior, impure motives for his kindness toward me. But Jenette encouraged me to continue walking this path because it was ordained by the Lord, even though no one in my social circle—friends or family—would understand my current situation. She comforted me by saying that God was pleased with me, and she encouraged me to share my story with others with the confidence that God would give me the words to say.

Jenette was adamant about her next point. "Do not let your perceived inadequacy distract you from God's sufficiency; he will supply everything that you need. He will bring you the right words at the right time; you need only be faithful to write them down."

As I would later learn, present-day prophets usually echoed confirmation more than providing fresh revelations. Joseph had been encouraging me to write about our journey from the beginning, but now I was hearing confirmation that this was a directive from God.

Jenette's words served as a wonderful reminder and motivator when I became discouraged about my writing. This isn't my story, and it's not for my glory; it's always been about God.

Once the plane landed safely in San Francisco, everyone around me was eager to get off. Not me, though. I could have sat with Jenette for hours if the flight attendants had allowed it. I had so many questions!

It was now my turn to grab the luggage above my seat. With backpack in hand, I waited to walk down the aisle. I could hear Jenette shuffling her belongings behind me. As we both stood still in foot traffic, I heard Jenette say, "Oh yeah ..." as if she had forgotten something. "That girl you spent the weekend with ... you're going to marry her."

What?

There was a pause as I stood frozen trying to collect myself.

Had I heard that correctly?

Jenette continued collecting her things and carrying on as though nothing life-altering had just happened.

Let me get this straight. She was telling me, that the Lord was telling her, that I was going to marry Alissa Grieshhammer? That the woman I've had a crush on since third grade will one day be my wife?

I was ready to go ballistic.

If you've ever watched a World Cup soccer game, you will understand the emotions coursing through my veins. I wanted to tear off my shirt in the middle of the aircraft screaming, "GOOOAAALLL!" Yeah. I was that excited.

I could not believe it, and at the same time I did. Whether it was the Holy Spirit or Jenette's calming sense of confidence, I had childlike faith that what Jenette had spoken was truth.

Hoping to receive clarity, I told Jenette about our dating history, including the "wait" message we had received in July. Jenette began with a disclaimer that she did not receive any revelation from the Lord regarding the "wait" message, but that according to scripture, it was better for me to marry Alissa than to "burn with passion" over her as stated in 1 Corinthians 7:9. Jenette continued explaining that God had a plan that was bigger than I could ever imagine and that I needed to trust in him and be obedient to him in this journey.

The aisle was finally clear, so Jenette and I exited the plane.

With many questions in mind, I had hoped that Jenette would entertain me for a little while longer. I scouted some empty chairs in the airport terminal and asked Jenette if we could pray together. As we sat down to pray, I placed my hand on her knee and she placed her hand on top of mine. We prayed together thanking God for speaking to me through Jenette.

For the last two weeks, I had been desperately seeking the Lord and asking him to speak to me regarding my relationships with both Joseph and Alissa. Lacking faith, I had requested that the Lord's answer be abundantly clear. God answered my prayer by sending a prophetess on an airplane to deliver his message. There was no second-guessing this one; I had all the confirmation I needed.

After we had finished praying, Jenette told me something striking. She revealed to me that I had received the gift of healing through the laying on of hands. She explained how she could feel the Spirit moving through me as we prayed together and that the Lord wanted me to know about my giftedness.

I then remembered praying for my fraternity brother who was healed of his "terminal" heart condition. Okay, God. I see you.

This night could not get any better. For months I had been praying for God to reveal my spiritual gifting, and in one fell swoop he had answered all of my prayers.

Jenette solemnly explained that I was to use my gifting only if I felt led by the Holy Spirit. She admonished me with the instructions that if I were to try and lay my hands on anyone without the Spirit's guidance, that I myself would become afflicted.

Finally, before departing, Jenette reminded and encouraged me. "Matt, never allow your perceived inability to cloud the effectiveness of your God-given gifts and talents."

I hugged Jenette good-bye and thanked her for obediently ministering to me as instructed by the Lord. Glowing with excitement and bursting with joy I headed toward the airport shuttle.

Before boarding the BART train home I called Alissa. Lacking all self-control I told her everything …

A Frantic Phone Call

Alissa initially received the news of my airplane prophecy with great joy and thankfulness.

Later that night, however, her feelings changed. Alissa called me crying on the phone.

"What's wrong, Liss?" I asked.

Through tears, Alissa explained that she was struggling in her faith. She felt distant from God and had her doubts about the prophecy. It was hard to believe that God would want me to stay in my mentorship with Joseph. This, along with the prophecy that Alissa and I would one day marry, was all very heavy and a lot to process.

I didn't know how to respond, so we instead prayed for understanding and direction. Alissa had many questions and prayed that God would provide the answers.

Feeling separated from God is one of the worst feelings in the human experience. It was this experience that made Jesus cry out on the cross, "My God, My God, why have you forsaken me?" (Matthew 27:46).

Alissa was reading her Bible every day, praying, and going to chapel, and she felt she was honoring God in her relationship with me; however, there was a gap. She did not feel God's presence, and she couldn't figure out why.

After praying with Alissa for God's comfort, peace, and clarity, I went to bed.

The next morning, I woke up to a text from Alissa asking me to check my e-mail. Apparently, just after midnight, Alissa had composed the following:

> I hope this doesn't wake you and that you get it in the morning, but I had to tell you. God answered me. I wrote down a bunch of doubts and fears and questions in my journal about whether or not I should believe that lady and "Where are you, God? I'm feeling dry kind of stuff" ... Well, that verse that talks about dry bones came into my head, so I went to the concordance in my Bible to look up *bones*. But *believe* randomly caught my eye, so I looked

up the first verse it referenced, which was *2 Chronicles 20:20*. Check this out; it says, "Believe in the Lord your God, and you shall be established; believe His prophets, and you shall prosper." *Prophets.* And it had already been underlined by the previous owner of the Bible … and the commentary said something like, be open to God speaking through godly men and women; test it against scripture, and take it to him in prayer.

I wasn't even looking for anything about prophets and that's where he brought me. He answered all my doubts, questions, and fears with one verse. Still trippin' me out. Thank you for praying! God is faithful to answer"

I cannot communicate the joy I felt while reading this e-mail. God is so faithful to answer our prayers, even when we doubt his word. Hours after praying that God would speak to Alissa and confirm in her what was spoken to me, I received this e-mail. You can imagine the excitement I felt knowing that God was active and moving in this situation—not only in me but in Alissa as well. This was no longer a storybook God or dogmatic faith; I was in the moment, experiencing God and his prophets, as well as his promises, words, and truth. I may have had my questions, doubts, and concerns, but God was answering all of them and making sure that Alissa heard the same answers too.

My experience on the airplane once again confirmed the reality of God's power and presence. It was also a wake-up call that he was trying to get my attention. I was convinced that the message provided on that plane was God's voice speaking truth through his prophet Jenette.

After receiving Alissa's e-mail, I contacted Jenette. She had to know what God was doing!

I asked if she was willing to meet for coffee or lunch on Sunday. Jenette declined my offer but instead invited me to her church, Lily of the Valley, in Oakland. I wouldn't have cared if Jenette had wanted to meet at the zoo; I was in!

As usual, I spent Friday evening and Saturday morning at Joseph's house. Expecting that he would discourage me from talking to Jenette,

I made no attempt to inform Joseph about my Sunday morning meeting. Interestingly enough, Joseph very specifically and quite unusually asked about my Sunday morning plans.

I couldn't lie to him, so I confessed my plans with Jenette after church.

Before I left Joseph's house, he warned me that although Jenette may be a prophet, she is not a counselor or translator of God's word. Joseph was suggesting that I should not meet with her unless she had another prophetic message to share. He explained that if I asked her questions about her prophetic words, she might misinterpret the message, since she was only a messenger, not an interpreter.

I understood what he was trying to say but had no intention of changing my plans. I wanted to explain to Jenette what the prophecy meant to me by providing her with some background information on the conflict with which I was currently confronted.

Lily of the Valley

I woke up on Sunday morning with anxiety and fear in my heart. I was honestly afraid of visiting Jenette's church. There is something about the unknown that has always frightened me.

Compounding my discomfort and anxiety, my dad began to increase my worries. There was no hiding the fact that he disapproved of my visit to this church. Although the church wasn't in the worst part of Oakland, it was still in Oakland, and my dad despised Oakland. Having been a police officer for nearly thirty years had hardened his heart and instilled a sense of reverent fear toward the place, which is understandable given its exceptionally high homicide rate.

Instead of dwelling on these fears, I gave them to the Lord. On the drive to Oakland, I sent Alissa a message explaining my anxiety and asking her to pray for me. She comforted me and offered kind words of encouragement and assurance that everything would be okay and that God was watching over me. Alissa also expressed a comical disappointment in not being able to attend Jenette's church with me.

Alissa and her family had grown up listening to soul music, watching *Sister Act*, and attending a variety of gospel churches, so this multicultural love had been ingrained in her since childhood. The combination of prayer and comic relief had me feeling a sense of peace as I drove down I-880 toward Oakland.

As I pulled into the empty parking lot of the church, I realized that I was early. Sitting in my car, I called Jenette. She picked up the phone explaining in a hurried manner that she was still at home getting ready. In the background, I could hear her children running around frantically. I sensed that Jenette wouldn't be at the church for a while, so I remained in the car to weigh my options. After praying and seeking encouragement to venture into the church alone, I did exactly that.

A bit nervous and apprehensive, I stepped out of my car and headed toward the church. Curiously enough, as I got closer, my nervousness lessened and I felt a sense of calmness and confidence that I can only attribute to the Holy Spirit. As I neared the door, I was greeted by an older black gentlemen who kindly extended a welcoming hand. Although I was clearly the minority in their congregation, the hospitality and warm welcome I received from the Lily of the Valley Church made me feel at home. I took a seat in the back left side of the church as I examined my surroundings.

Charismatic is an understatement when describing what was going on around me. People were singing, flailing their arms, jumping around, dancing, waving flags, screaming, speaking in tongues, and celebrating the Lord's greatness. Despite the evident love of the Lord, I once again felt incredibly awkward and uncomfortable. I was alone in a foreign environment where I knew no one and could not relate to the charismatic style of worship. Isolated and intimidated, I eyed the exit.

Before I could gather my belongings to leave the church, Jenette suddenly appeared. She wasn't alone, either. Her children, Princess and Providence, were with her. I felt instantaneous relief. I could finally relax now that I knew at least one person.

Jenette's daughters were adorable. With pigtails and braids they jumped around singing songs to the Lord. My seat selection was apparently restrictive to the girls, so Jenette motioned for us to move across the room. We found a spot on the right side of the church near an aisle so the girls could worship and dance freely. Watching them celebrate God's goodness brought me a tremendous amount of joy.

Worship soon ended, and the bishop took the stage. He was a large black man with a powerful voice. The moment he started speaking, the bishop had my undivided attention.

His sermon spoke of the eagle. Like the prophet, an eagle has vision. Not only do eagles have excellent vision, but they are focused. The bishop exhorted us all to keep our eyes on the prize and not to get distracted.

Distractions and prophets ... this sermon was starting to hit a little too close to home.

I tried writing off his words as mere coincidence. Could God have tailored that sermon specifically for my situation? Sure, but it was general enough to disregard.

Then it happened.

The bishop opened his Bible and began to read, "Believe in the Lord your God and you will be able to stand firm. Believe in his prophets and you will succeed."

Wait.

I'd heard this passage before. That's ...

"2 Chronicles 20:20," referenced the bishop.

No *way*!

Of all the verses the bishop could have chosen, he'd selected Alissa's confirmation verse from Tuesday night.

Did he know? Was he also a prophet? Was this some sort of conspiracy set up by Joseph to convince me to stay on the commitment journey?

Once again, I sat frozen in awe of the Lord. This was no joke. God was speaking.

First he sent me a prophet. Then he brought Alissa to 2 Chronicles 20:20, encouraging her to believe in the prophecy. Then, just to hammer his point home, God sent me to a church where the bishop would reiterate Alissa's original confirmation.

Mind.

Blown.

I've heard the word *coincidence* defined as times when God remains anonymous. Here, however, he wasn't being all that discreet. Helen Keller could have called God out on this one.

I immediately texted Alissa, "You're never going to believe what the pastor is preaching on this morning?!"

"What?" she replied.

"Would you believe me if I told you, 2 Chronicles 20:20?"

"No. Way."

"I know, right? That was my reaction!"

"Are you kidding me?" Alissa lost it.

Before we could finish our text conversation, the bishop interrupted with his final exhortation. "If you want to hear God's voice, look at what he has already written for you."

Simple yet profound.

At the end of his sermon the bishop stepped in front of the pulpit, raised the microphone to his lips, pointed directly at me in the back of the chapel, and said, "Son, please stand up."

Sensing my hesitation, the bishop repeated, "Son, please stand up. I have a word from God to share with you."

Are you kidding me?

As if I didn't stand out enough being the only brother from another mother, the bishop wanted me to stand up in front of the whole congregation? I did not sign up for this!

I looked at Jenette for some assurance.

"What you lookin' at me for? Stand up!"

With all eyes now on me, I stood up.

After clearing his throat, the bishop said, "Son, when you switched sides of the room this morning during worship, you caught my eye. At that moment the Lord gave me something to share with you."

Really? I thought to myself. *Twice in one week?*

He continued, "You are at a crossroad. The Lord wants you to know that he is going to answer all of your questions this week in his word. He will bring peace and clarity. Keep searching his scripture to hear his voice."

The bishop then moved on with the program like nothing had happened. No one else was given a prophecy. No one else was called out in front of the congregation. That was it.

Feeling fearful and confused I took my seat.

Jenette took one look at me, and we both started laughing.

I'm not sure about hers, but mine was a nervous laugh. God wasn't playing. This was no joke. He was trying to get something through my thick skull, and apparently this took two prophets to accomplish.

After the prophecy, the bishop asked all first-time visitors to stand up. I was thinking to myself, *Oh, no. What now? This is just too much!*

I was handed the mic and asked to introduce myself. "Hi, my name is Matt Jones, and I am from Pleasanton as a first-time visitor; thank you all for having me!"

And thank you for calling me out in front of everyone! (I wanted to say that one but restrained myself.)

"Who invited you here, Son?" asked the bishop.

I pointed to Jenette, who then grabbed the mic. Standing up, Jenette proceeded to tell the whole congregation about our experience on the plane. "We met in Los Angeles on the airplane home, and while sitting next to Matthew, the Lord gave me his business with names and everything. I prophesied to him and then brought him here."

I couldn't tell who was more shocked—me, the bishop, or the congregation. Jenette then handed the mic back to the bishop, and church ended.

As people were fellowshipping in the sanctuary, I couldn't help but sense all eyes on me. I was feeling enough excitement as it was and didn't need the added pressure of explaining my situation to the whole congregation. Avoiding any conversation, I quickly exited the building.

After thanking Jenette for the invitation, I walked straight to my car. *This prophecy stuff is exhausting*, I thought as I sat waiting for traffic to clear. Texting Alissa, I told her all about the service and the second prophecy.

Although receiving such prophecy may seem exciting, I was honestly a little scared. God had already confirmed that Alissa and I would marry one day and that the current situation I was in with Joseph was God's blessing. What did he want to tell me next?

I began to pray, almost desperately, that the Lord would make his answer crystal clear. I didn't want to guess or "lean on my own understanding" (Proverbs 3:5) to interpret his message: "Lord, please give me clarity to understand your will, whatever it may be."

My expectations for God's answer were quite high, and reasonably so; twice in seven days I had been given a prophecy. I had read about prophets in scripture and heard stories about them from others in the church, but never had I experienced them for myself. My eyes were once again open to the wonders and reality of God, a feeling I experienced with fear and trembling.

I finally understood what it meant to fear the Lord. He was becoming so real to me that it was almost scary. With my newfound understanding that my Heavenly Father was in fact alive and moving in my life, I continued my search to hear his voice.

Awaiting Prophetic Confirmation

On Sunday night after the second prophecy, I had my buddies Wes and Steve over to play video games. While waiting for Steve to arrive, Wes and I caught up from the last week. I told him all about the prophecies, scriptural confirmations, and my current expectations for the Lord to speak.

Wes suggested that if I was looking to hear the voice of God, I should seek him through prayer and fasting. I was not closed to the idea of fasting, but I chose to hold off until Wednesday to try it.

Anticipating God's voice was stressful. What would it sound like? What would he say? How do you prepare yourself to hear the voice of God? Would it be like a blazing fire or sound like a quiet whisper? Both were biblical. I didn't really know what to expect.

A Weighty Word

To reduce this stress, I went to the only place that seemed to bring relief—the gym. While sitting in the parking lot at 24 Hour Fitness, I felt a familiar notion, a prompting from God.

It wasn't a physical touch or an audible voice, but I could feel a heaviness inside me that would not allow me to leave the car. As I sat still in my sandy-beige Nissan Sentra, I could sense the Holy Spirit's conviction.

The Holy Spirit always seems to convict me at times and in ways that seem inconvenient or uncomfortable, and this was definitely one of those times. I wasn't ready for a revelation or some heart-wrenching truth; I just wanted to work out!

God is obviously much stronger and more convincing than even my most selfish desires, and this was no exception. I could sense that the Holy Spirit wanted me to read my devotional before I entered the fitness center. On the passenger's seat sat the *WWJD Today?* devotional, a recently rediscovered gift from my mom when I was in high school. After years of sitting in my closet collecting dust, it was now beckoning me to reopen it and read.

As I picked up the book, thoughts of my relationship with Alissa raced through my mind. I hadn't even cracked the cover, and I could already sense what God was communicating. He wanted me to walk away from my relationship with Alissa.

The last dog-eared page was titled, "Behind Bars." This chapter told the story of John the Baptist in prison from Luke 3. I read the familiar story but didn't understand how John's imprisonment correlated with my relationship with Alissa.

Trusting that God had a purpose for bringing me to this passage, I continued reading the "life application" section:

> In Today's passage, John the Baptist was going through the test of his life ... You must remember that God will test your faith as you get closer to Him. He's not being mean. He just wants you to see for yourself how strong your faith really is. When you study at school, you don't get away with just telling the teacher that you studied. You have to take a test and prove it. God is letting you prove your faith. When bad things happen, consider them a test. Keep your eyes on God and not the circumstances. Have you ever had something happen to you didn't seem fair? Can you think of one thing God may have been trying to teach you during that time? Ask God to help you endure and pass whatever test He may send your way. Remember that no test lasts forever. After a little while, it will be over, and your faith will be stronger (B. Shipman, 1998).

"The test of my life." Really, God?

I mean, I guess that makes sense. You gave me a command, "wait," and then followed it with a promise, "You will one day marry Alissa." Then you confirmed that promise with scripture and then sent another prophet with a promise of peace and clarity.

The command was seemingly clear, but I was missing the promised peace. So I prayed, "If you are seriously calling me to give up Alissa while I wait to finish the commitment journey, I am going to need peace!"

Why God let me talk to him like that, I have no clue. I definitely deserved his backhand for my entitled attitude.

Waiting is hard, and delaying gratification sucks! I wanted her now! As I continued to complain about my lack of peace, Pastor Matt's words from the Fourth of July sermon invaded my mind: "Sometimes what God wants to do in us while we wait is more important than what we are waiting for."

What could be more important than my marriage to Alissa? Doesn't the Bible say, "The man who finds a wife finds what is good"? (Proverbs 18:22)

I've found her; let's get this show on the road!

Rick Warren, arguably the most influential pastor in the world, once preached that every promise comes with a process. I had my promise, and I was now faced with the process. If I wanted to receive God's promise, I needed to endure his process. Thankfully, the devotional assured me that "no test lasts forever, after a while the test will be complete and your faith will be stronger because of it."

I set the book down with the burden of truth resting heavily upon my heart. I needed to let Alissa go.

It wasn't the thought of temporarily losing Alissa that upset me. Deep down I did trust that God would fulfill his promise. What kept me from letting go was the heartbreak that I wanted to spare Alissa.

Weighing my options, I looked down at the tattoo on my wrist. "There is no greater love than this; that a man lay down his life for his friend" (John 15:13). I knew in that moment that God was calling me to lay down my current desire for Alissa to demonstrate my love and trust in him. If this was truly God's plan for my life, the most loving thing I could do for Alissa was to let her go.

The Spirit's voice was loud and clear. "Matt, if you truly love me and trust me, you will obey me."

I climbed out of the car, still selfishly and disobediently holding onto my relationship Alissa. "I hear you, Lord. I have clarity, but I'm lacking peace."

The fact that God didn't strike me dead for my disobedience is a testimony to his patience and grace.

Luuuke, I AM Your Father.

The sense of turmoil from my devotional experience continued into the next day at work. I was anxious, stressed, and all-around exhausted!

During my lunch break on Wednesday I called Alissa, and from the moment she answered the phone, I could tell that she had something on her mind. I inquired about my suspicion, and she exclaimed with great excitement that God had confirmed Sunday's prophecy to her. Alissa explained that she had earlier received a text message from a girl she hadn't spoken to in months.

All too coincidentally, Alissa's friend had sent her a verse from Luke stating, "Blessed is she who has believed what the Lord has said to her will be accomplished."

Are you seeerious? Another confirmation?

God was unrelenting!

My inner skeptic had to see it to believe it, so I asked for the reference to the passage. Alissa explained that according to her text message, the passage came from Luke 1:72.

There was an awkward silence between us as we searched for the passage. We both found Luke 1:72, but there was no mention of the verse that Alissa's friend had texted. Did she make a mistake? Luke 1:72 said, "[R]emember his holy covenant, the oath he swore to our Father."

Alissa was confused as to why her friend would so incorrectly reference this verse and what significance, if any, this scripture held. While Alissa was distracted looking for the real verse, I too was preoccupied …

As it turned out, Alissa's friend had meant to quote the scripture correctly as Luke 1:45, but this was no accident. Although Alissa did not see any significance from the accidentally cited Luke 1:72, I knew exactly what God was trying to say.

The key words in this incorrectly referenced passage were "holy covenant" and "oath he swore." I do not believe there was any coincidence that this verse contained those key phrases. The actual scripture that was sent in the text message was meant for Alissa; however, I believe the verse citation was meant for me.

The purpose of Luke 1:45 was to tell Alissa that she would be blessed if she would believe that God would fulfill what he had promised through prophecy. Luke 1:72 was sent to remind me of the covenant I had made, the oath I had sworn to Joseph before God. It was all too clear that God was saying, "Matt, you will have Alissa, but you must first complete the covenant you made with Joseph before I will give her to you. Have faith. You are not alone in this. See, I am making this known to Alissa as well."

The awesomeness of God seriously blows my mind. Despite my disobedience, he continuously and patiently pursued me. The word *grace* began to take on new heights. No way did I deserve such blatant confirmations, yet he freely provided them—not only to me but to Alissa as well!

Feeling the freedom to finally address the conviction about our relationship, I told Alissa what God was speaking to my heart. We discussed the prophecy and confirmations, and how they were intimately connected to the "wait" message from July. Thankfully, Alissa understood that in order for me to honor the commitment journey, we needed to reevaluate our relationship.

As promised, I finally felt peace. God is so faithful to provide. Although I prayed for Alissa to understand my situation, the Thomas in me doubted it would ever happen—and now it was here. Alissa not only understood but supported me.

Déjà Vu

Alissa had planned to come home during the upcoming weekend for her father's birthday. Before she arrived, Alissa and I agreed to discuss our relationship and the boundaries that would need to exist to allow me to finish my covenant journey with Joseph. However, with this potentially being the last weekend we would spend together, we wanted to take full advantage and not allow this inevitable conversation to rain on our parade. We were revisiting July 4th weekend all over again!

Starving for Direction

To prepare for the upcoming weekend I decided to fast.

For those who are not familiar with the concept of fasting, it is the abstinence from food for a dedicated period of time. Jesus said that men cannot survive on bread alone; they must feast on the word of God (Matthew 4:4). During a fast, you can exchange food for time in prayer and time in the scriptures. Hunger pangs are supposed to remind us that we need God more than food. They also remind us where our food comes from. Fasting is basically a time of intentionally seeking God through dependence on him and desperation for him.

For a guy who rarely fasts, things were going well. To my surprise, I actually had more energy, focus, and joy during my fast than on regular days. Weird how that works.

When hunger pangs were present, I prayed for God's wisdom, words, and favor for my conversation with Alissa over the weekend. Although I knew what God wanted me to do, I had no idea what to say. Ultimately, I wanted both of us to experience peace and joy during our weekend together despite the outcome.

Since Jesus commanded us to feast on the word of God, I continued my fast after work by reading my Bible. It seemed appropriate to study the story of when Jesus fasted, so I opened up to Luke 4. In this section of scripture, Jesus was led into the desert by the Holy Spirit to be tempted. That's right—the Holy Spirit led Jesus into the desert to be tempted. As the story reads, Jesus fasted for forty days and nights.

Thankfully, the Bible then lets us in on a secret: "Jesus was hungry" (Luke 4:2).

The devil knew this and tempted Jesus to turn stones into bread to prove that he was the son of God. Jesus replied with the familiar, "Man does not live on bread alone ..." (Deuteronomy 8:3).

I finished the temptation sequence and moved on to the commentary: "The Holy Spirit does not always lead us beside 'quiet and still waters'. Jesus was led into the desert for a long and difficult time of testing and He may also lead us into difficult times" (Zondervan, 1984).

It seemed apparent that the Holy Spirit was preparing my heart for a difficult time of testing. I continued reading:

> Sometimes what we are tempted to do isn't wrong in itself. Turning stones into bread wasn't necessarily bad. The sin was not in the act, but in the reason behind it. The devil was trying to get Jesus to take a shortcut, to solve Jesus' immediate problems at the expense of his long range goals, to seek comfort in the sacrifice of his discipline. Satan often works that way, persuading us to take action—even right action, for the wrong reason or at the wrong time (Zondervan, 1984).

It's true what the Bible says about God's word being sharper than any double-edged sword. I was once again cut to the heart with conviction. God was clearly communicating to me that there was nothing wrong with wanting a relationship with Alissa, but at this time and in this season, it was wrong.

The time of testing was evident. The voices of temptation were all around me: "I don't understand why you can't pursue Alissa. She is a Christian woman who loves God, you both have solid boundaries, and you want to please the Lord in your relationship. What is wrong with that?"

Nothing! Except the timing of course. The commentary continued: "The fact that something is not wrong in itself does not mean that it is good for you at a given time. Many people sin by attempting to fulfill desires outside of God's will or ahead of his time table" (Zondervan, 1984).

It's comical how clearly God communicates with us at times. Mark Twain hit the nail of the head: "It ain't those parts of the Bible that I don't understand that bother me, it is the parts that I do understand."

I understood and, like Mr. Twain, I was bothered.

When Bible Roulette Blows Up in Your Face

It was now the Friday before Alissa arrived home for the weekend. As was my routine, I spent the morning in God's word. Unintentionally, I opened my Bible directly to Ecclesiastes 5:4–7. When I glanced down to see where my finger had landed, I read three small words:

Fulfill.

Your.

Vow.

Had I read that correctly?

Fulfill my vow?

There was little room for interpretation.

The passage continued, "When you make a vow to God, do not delay in fulfilling it. He has no pleasure in fools …"

God does not waste words. Not only was he telling me to stop delaying obedience, but he was also making it clear that my current actions were foolish and he "does not take pleasure in fools."

Ouch! God wasn't pulling any punches, and he wasn't done either: "It is better not to vow, than to make a vow and not fulfill it. Do not let your mouth lead you into sin. And do not protest to the temple messenger, 'My vow was a mistake.'"

The thought that my vow was a mistake had definitely crossed my mind, and it had also crossed the lips of many of my friends and family. God was clearly stating that revoking a vow made to him was a sin, and here I was trying to wiggle my way out of the vow.

Conviction accomplished.

"Matt, the vow was not a mistake. Stop complaining and fulfill it. Do not be foolish! Once you fulfill your vow, you can pursue Alissa, but not now!"

As was promised in the prophecy, I now had both clarity and peace. God had faithfully removed all the guesswork and laid it out plainly on a platinum platter. I knew what needed to be done, what had to be said, and when I needed to say it. I was now ready for the weekend.

Cave Dwellers

As planned, Alissa and I spent Saturday together in celebration of her father's birthday. We went to her brother's football game and then to their favorite family Mexican restaurant to celebrate her father's special day. After dinner, we all had frozen yogurt and watched a movie together.

Knowing that this was the last weekend to indulge in our time together made this a bittersweet occasion. We decided not to discuss the boundaries we had hoped to negotiate until Sunday evening. Since this would be our last weekend together, we didn't want to ruin the moment.

Sound familiar?

The next morning (Sunday), I drove to Alissa's home to pick her up for breakfast before church. We had a delicious breakfast at the Rising Loafer, a quaint little restaurant in downtown Pleasanton.

We tried our best to ignore the elephant at the table (our boundaries conversation), and we both agreed to save that for later because we just wanted to enjoy our last day together.

Upon arriving at church, we discovered that Matt Van Cleave would be teaching the sermon. My heart became uneasy because this was the same pastor who had delivered the "wait" message in July.

Coincidence?

As I sat down, I prayed that the Holy Spirit would remove all distractions from my mind and open my heart to receive the day's message. I was also praying that the Holy Spirit would speak to us and prepare our hearts for the conversation that would later take place.

Be careful what you wish for …

Matt's sermon was about King David's experience while hiding in a cave: "God does his best work in caves … We will all experience a season of cave dwelling. A time in life where loved ones are stripped away. The cave is where we discover that God is enough … The cave is where God resurrects dead things. Jesus spent some time in a cave. After his death on the cross, Jesus was placed in a cave. Three days later Jesus rose from his grave and exited the cave. The cave is a place of transformation."

Alissa and I both walked away from Sunday's sermon with the same understanding that God was leading us to the cave. Matt's message only further confirmed that God was clearly calling us to isolation from one another. Like David, we would be stripped away from our loved ones to instead grow closer to God.

After church, Alissa and I parted ways for the day. She had a wedding to attend before we could reconnect to discuss the details of our upcoming cave adventure. Thankfully, the abundant confirmations from the previous week had prepared both of our hearts for what was on the horizon. Honestly, God's presence was almost palpable as he extinguished the anxiety between us. Despite the momentary sadness, we knew that this was not the end. God would fulfill his promise to us; we both trusted in his faithfulness.

October Boundaries

One of my favorite memories from my childhood from the month of October was my annual viewing of Disney's Halloween special. Before engaging in our dreaded boundaries discussion I shared this infamous October tradition with Alissa. After watching, Alissa and I decided it was time to stop procrastinating and discuss the terms of our relationship.

We were in agreement that we could not pursue a romantic relationship at this time. What we did not understand was how to move forward from there.

We did understand, however, that our attempts at remaining "just friends" had failed miserably in the past. To prevent another relapse, we established the following guidelines:

1. One phone call per month (because we clearly couldn't handle one per week)
2. No Facebook interaction
3. Giving holiday cards was okay, but no family engagements or get-togethers
4. We could attend Christmas and Easter church services together
5. Calls or texts in cases of emergency were acceptable

After writing our boundaries in my prayer journal, for accountability purposes, I escorted Alissa to her car. Although we were both sad, there was a sense of excitement in the air. We knew that God had his hand on our relationship and that he was going to bring his promise to fruition. We were also excited to discover God's plan for the next two years, as there was an inevitable purpose behind this waiting period.

While saying our good-byes, we joked about entering our caves so that God could work in our hearts. However, this wasn't a joke, because that was exactly what God intended. It was important for us to remember that "In all things God works for the good of those who love him, who have been called according to his purpose" (Romans 8:28). Even the pain of separation was intended for our good, not to harm us.

After we embraced for a final time, Alissa climbed into her red Toyota pickup and drove home. As the brake lights of her truck escaped my view, I headed back toward the house. Once the reality of our journey settled in, I was met with the long-awaited "peace that surpasses all understanding" (Philippians 4:7, paraphrase). What God had promised in his prophecy had come to completion; my heart was at rest. With our boundaries in place, we could enter our individual caves with confidence knowing that we were pursuing God's will for our lives.

Compromise: The Commitment Killer

As expected, trials and temptations came as Alissa and I attempted to honor our boundaries. Just weeks after our boundaries conversation, Alissa's favorite baseball team, the Giants, won the World Series.

According to our agreement, texting was not allowed. It took every ounce of patience and strength that I could muster from the Lord to keep me from contacting her with congratulations.

The next test came in November on my birthday. According to our agreement, cards were allowed on birthdays. Abiding by the rules, Alissa sent me a birthday card. Not only did Alissa send me a card, but she also purchased football tickets for me and my friends to see the Oakland Raiders play their division rivals, the Kansas City Chiefs.

The seats were perfect, and the game came down to a final field goal in overtime. I had never been to a more entertaining, exciting sporting event in my life. The only thing missing was the one who had made it all possible.

Being the saint that she is, Alissa expressed her desire to attend the game with me in her card, while also communicating her understanding and acceptance of our current situation.

Our next test came on Thanksgiving. Our families were sorely disappointed that we had set such strict and "ridiculous" boundaries on our relationship, and they applied ample pressure to try and make us break. "Matt, why can't you come over for dinner?" Alissa's mom texted.

"I can't, Mama G. I'm sorry. Alissa and I made an agreement."

"Well, she really wants you here. It's just one dinner. Can't you at least stop by? Maybe your parents can come?"

Since I couldn't come over for dinner, I instead made Alissa an elaborate Thanksgiving card.

Tom was a handmade turkey whose feathers each expressed an attribute of Alissa's that I was thankful for. In Haitian fashion, I snuck over to Alissa's house after midnight and left the turkey on her doorstep. Although I didn't necessarily cross any boundaries with my card, I was dangerously close. The feathers communicated much more than friendship.

Further deterioration of our boundaries ensued in the month of December ...

The Snowball Effect

As usual, Joseph took his annual vacation with his family overseas for Christmas. With my source of accountability across the world and familial pressures encouraging me to bend the rules for the holidays, my resistance toward temptation became weaker and weaker.

To honor our boundaries, we decided not to speak on the phone during the month of December. Instead we attended the Cornerstone Christmas Eve service together. After Christmas service, my family tradition included Christmas Eve dinner at my grandmother's house. Although our boundaries clearly stated that we were not to spend the holidays with each other's families, we decided to compromise on these rules for Christmas. We also both broke the card rule and purchased presents for one another instead.

We were on a slippery slope.

Like a snowball, our compromises continued to build momentum. First it was Christmas Eve with my family; then it turned into Christmas Day with her family. Then we continued to allow compromise to kill our commitment by blowing off our boundaries for yet another day.

Where had my conviction gone? I was reminded of a quote from *Saving Silverman*: "Dude, if you got the nachos stuck together, that's one nacho." I mean, spending three consecutive days together wasn't all that bad. Technically we just spent the one holiday together ... no big deal, right?

The following day was a Sunday. We attended church together, had a sushi lunch, and then cuddled on my parents' couch while watching TV. Knowing that this was our final day before getting back on track with our boundaries, Alissa and I spent the entire evening together as well. After dinner with her parents and a few rounds of Michael Jackson's dance experience on Nintendo Wii, Alissa and I called it a night.

New Year's Eve 2010

After Christmas, Alissa and I established that we would once again cut all communication until our monthly phone call in January. That's right—no New Year's.

This was torture!

I ended up spending the evening with my best friend, Steve, instead. We held a Bible study that night to kick off the New Year.

More than anything, I wanted 2011 to be the year of the "great commission" in my life. I wanted to be more bold and courageous in my faith than ever before. People needed to hear the gospel. There were simply too many lost and hurting people for me to remain silent about Jesus.

To accomplish this task Steve and I spent intentional time seeking God through prayer and Bible study. After spending time with God, we concluded the evening with a Madden 2010 football tournament while eating Chinese food.

And yes, I refrained from contacting Alissa all night.

CHAPTER 10

A CATASTROPHIC CONFESSION

The following weekend I drove up to Tahoe with Joseph. He planned to work in the hotel while I snowboarded with some buddies from my Bible study. As we drove through the mountains, Joseph asked about my Christmas vacation. He had recently returned from overseas and had yet to inquire about my holiday, so this was an expected conversation. In response, I offered short, superficial answers, intentionally omitting the time I spent with Alissa.

There was noticeable tension in the car, as Joseph could sense that something wasn't right with me because I had made every attempt to derail his efforts to discover my whereabouts and activities during his absence. Sensing my avoidance, Joseph left the subject alone.

After checking into our hotel, we drove to downtown South Lake Tahoe for dinner. Joseph wanted Italian food, so we found a hole-in-the-wall Italian diner right off the main highway. The dining room was small. There were tiny tables packed tightly together with a quiet ambiance that made it difficult to have a confidential conversation.

While we were at dinner, Joseph once again asked about how I had spent the holidays. I was initially perplexed as to why we were replicating our recent car conversation, but my superficial answers apparently triggered red flags in Joseph's mind. He proceeded with his interrogations in the confidence that if he were direct enough in his questioning, I would come clean.

147

Sure enough, this strategy worked.

One way I have found assurance in my salvation is that I can feel and see evidence that the Holy Spirit is working in my heart. Although I was once a master manipulator, diabolical deceiver, and frivolous fibber, I can no longer tell a bald-faced lie. Anytime I am asked a direct question, despite how painful the answer may be, I submit to the truth and come clean. I could no longer hide the truth, because I knew that my sin would eventually be found out.

After I admitted to spending the holidays with Alissa, Joseph was quiet. He sat in his chair pushing the leaves of his salad aimlessly around the bowl with his fork. With a disgusted look on his face he broke the silence. "Absolutely detestable. I have just lost my appetite. Your self-deception is disgusting. It's sad, really; the only person you are fooling is yourself!"

I must have been the only customer in the restaurant who was not completely shocked by Joseph's reaction. Knowing that this conversation was inevitable, I had prepared myself for the worst. He continued berating me as I sat there calmly eating my pasta. I could hear what he was saying, but I wasn't listening.

According to Joseph, I was lying to myself thinking that I could talk to Alissa once a month, share Christmas with our families together, and still claim that I was not pursuing a romantic relationship. He continued to explain that the foundation of our commitment was that I would spend the next two years focusing on discovering God's intended purpose and ministry for my life. The other stipulation of our commitment was that I had to forsake the pursuit of any romantic relationship, as it would pose a distraction from our goals. He also reminded me that we had finalized our commitment journey in the presence of the Lord, asking him to bless our covenant as we sought to honor Him.

In a defeated tone Joseph stated that, although I could still finish the two-year journey, our commitment would be broken and incomplete. In essence, Joseph was telling me that continuing a "friendship" with Alissa would nullify our agreement and significantly reduce any blessings that I would have received if I had committed to this journey wholeheartedly without any reservations.

I understood what Joseph was trying to say, but I felt that he was wrong to postulate that I would not be blessed if I decided to continue my relationship with Alissa.

To clarify, Joseph explained that there was a definite distinction between accomplishment and blessing. Could I finish my master's degree and become a counselor while keeping my relationship with Alissa and ignoring the covenant I had made with God? Sure, but would I be blessed?

That was the question that brought conviction.

The night ended with me hardening my heart toward Joseph and the conviction of the Holy Spirit. After dinner, we drove back to our hotel room in silence.

In my mind there was nothing that Joseph could say to pull me away from Alissa. In fact, I was hoping that he would walk away from our commitment so that I could pursue Alissa with a clear conscience.

Breakups are always easier when the other person leaves. It takes the responsibility off your back and onto the other person for quitting. Unfortunately, Joseph had more patience than a sloth and wasn't going anywhere!

My phone broke the silence as we entered our hotel room. Steve, my best friend, found himself in a stressful situation with the girl he was dating. I asked Joseph if he would be willing to talk with Steve about this, and they ended up connecting on the phone for a lengthy counseling session.

I was pleased that Stephen was having relationship problems so that Joseph would be distracted from our conversation at dinner and my relationship with Alissa. After he finished the conversation with Steve, we ended the evening without further discussion.

A "Bear Beach" of a Breakfast

As I awoke the next morning, I could hear the sound of Joseph flipping through the pages of a book. I assumed he was reading the Bible, as was his daily routine. I tried to fall back asleep to avoid conversing with him. I could sense that Joseph was going to try to convince me once more to give up my relationship with Alissa and recommit to our journey. I tried my very best to avoid him and slept as long as possible.

Resentment filled my heart as I remained in bed. I lay there perplexed as to how I could harbor such negative emotions toward a man who consistently displayed so much love and generosity toward me. Although I realized that I needed to give these feelings up to the Lord, I still wanted to avoid Joseph, so I slowly rolled over to grab my Bible. I knew that if he saw me reading the Bible, he wouldn't dare interrupt my fellowship with the Lord. As expected, I didn't hear a word from him as I began to read.

That's a great motive for studying God's word, I know.

Continuing to read, I noticed myself becoming distracted by Joseph's morning worship. He had his eyes closed, arms lifted, praising God saying, "Thank you, Jesus. Thank you, God. Praise the Lord Jesus. Praise Jesus!" I knew the devil was attacking me, because I felt nothing but hatred toward Joseph for praising Jesus. I don't know if it was the way he pronounced his "*s*'s" or the fact that I could feel that he had a deeper connection to God than I did, but I could not help but despise this man.

I'm sure God was really proud of me, reading his Holy Word while harboring hatred for one of his children.

As we both concluded our Bible studies, we exchanged "good mornings" and prepared for breakfast. While in the milieu of the hotel room, Joseph continued to praise God and informed me that God had given him a revelation.

My heart always jumped whenever Joseph reported receiving a revelation from God, because it usually had to do with me and how I needed to change. He continued by saying that he could not wait to share what God had placed on his heart and that we were in for a great breakfast conversation.

Yeah, right. Another conversation with Joseph about Alissa and our journey. Just how I wanted to spend my morning.

When we pulled up to the Bear Beach Café, Joseph took out his camera and wanted to take pictures of us together with Lake Tahoe in the background. The last thing I wanted to do was share a photo op with Joseph. I could feel the enemy's presence as I began to hate every movement that Joseph made. Every word that came out of his mouth made me angrier and angrier.

When we sat down at our table, Joseph asked me what I hoped to accomplish in the upcoming year. He wanted to know the goals for my education and work, and the personal commitment that we had made.

I was extremely frustrated with this line of questioning because he had asked me the same things two nights prior. I knew where this conversation was headed, and I did not want to go there.

While flipping through the menu I could sense that Joseph was preparing for a lecture. I was guessing that it pertained to my failure to commit, which consequently resulted in the brokenness of our covenant, because we had been in this same situation countless other times.

Again, I was sincerely hoping that Joseph would use this breakfast to admit defeat and end the commitment journey. As he had stated many times in the past, this was a mutual commitment. Either one of us could choose to walk away at any time. I was internally pleading for him to walk away, but that wasn't where this conversation was headed.

Joseph smiled at me and said that he was excited to share what God had revealed to him. Nothing but hatred flowed through my veins. In my head I was thinking, *Joseph, I already know what you're going to say, and I don't want to hear it.*

Despite my subconscious pleading, he began talking and I began ignoring him once again. I resented every word, every breath that came from his mouth, as I could sense him slowly and overtly moving the conversation toward my relationship with Alissa.

"Don't touch that!" I wanted to scream. "Talk about anything you want, but leave Alissa out of this!" I was so angry that I wanted to reach across the table and cut out his tongue so he couldn't continue speaking.

Joseph explained that he could not sleep the night before and was wide awake at four o'clock in the morning when the Lord gave him his revelation. Joseph began by stating that I needed to trust God. He explained that God would not have convinced me through a prophet on an airplane about his promise if he didn't expect me to trust him to fulfill that promise. He had provided a promise, and it would take time to fulfill, which required trust, faith, and obedience in the process.

Throughout the Bible, God made many promises to his children, but the fulfillment of his promises was never immediate. God told Eve in the Garden of Eden that he would redeem the world through her lineage;

however, the nation of Israel waited hundreds and thousands of years for the birth of the Messiah. God promised Noah that he would save his family from a flood that didn't end up happening for a century. God promised to lead the Israelites to the Promised Land, but it took forty years of wandering through a desert before they would enter. Even after the Israelites crossed the Jordan, they would have to defeat the current inhabitants of their land before they could settle. God told the Israelites that they would eventually defeat all of the nations who currently occupied the Promised Land, but that it would not all happen at once. In fact, it took years before Israel subdued and defeated the opposition in their land.

In each of these scenarios, God provided a promise and then provided an opportunity for the receiver of that promise to display his or her trust in God's faithfulness. This was never an overnight process. If God promised to deliver Alissa's hand in marriage, he would be faithful based on his flawless track record, but this promise would require a process.

Joseph did his best to illustrate these truths through scripture while we waited to order breakfast. The fact that our God is a God of covenants who hates divorce and loathes broken promises as stated in Malachi 2:16, really tugged on my heartstrings.

God had made a promise to me, but I had also made a covenant before him. I needed to fulfill my covenant before entering into a new one with Alissa. Joseph explained that the Bible states how God desires obedience more than sacrifice (1 Samuel 15:22). This particular situation provided an opportunity to give God both obedience and sacrifice. By sacrificing my relationship for God, I would also walk in obedience by honoring something considered holy and sacred in his sight.

The walls that were currently guarding my heart began to crumble as Joseph explained how God desired to bless his children for their obedience to him. He finished with the assurance that God would be faithful to fulfill his promise, but that I needed to completely consecrate myself in this covenant by cutting off all communication with Alissa.

At the end of our conversation at the Bear Beach Café, I admitted to Joseph that I understood what he was trying to tell me and did feel the Lord's conviction, but that I could not help but hate him for delivering the message. Joseph then admitted that he had been arguing with God all morning about sharing the message that God had delivered to him. He told

God that he had been attacked time and time again for delivering these messages and that his heart could not take it anymore. God comforted Joseph telling him to be faithful and to watch his Spirit work.

I did feel the Spirit work. My heart melted as I listened to the message Joseph delivered, and my feelings of hatred for him were replaced by an overwhelming sense of peace and repentance.

Revisiting Mount Everest

Our car ride from the restaurant to the hotel was nearly silent. Joseph had a satisfied grin on his face as if he could tell that I was sitting there stewing in the Spirit's conviction. Joseph said a few encouraging words about his being proud of me and how God was going to bless my obedience, but I remained silent.

When we got to our room, I felt the need to take a shower. As I stood under the hot hotel water, I prayed aloud to the Lord asking for his comfort and guidance. I told him that I wanted to fulfill this covenant and that I was willing to give up Alissa for him. I begged him to be faithful to me in returning Alissa upon the completion of our commitment, and I felt a sense of peace as I climbed out of the shower.

After drying off and walking into the bedroom, I could see the majesty of the Sierras piercing through our panoramic windows. Coincidentally, this was the same hotel, same floor, and same view we had had exactly a year ago. Although we had first talked about the commitment journey in China and Thailand, it wasn't until our trip to Tahoe last year that I finally went "all in" with the no dating portion.

I don't think it was a coincidence that I found myself recommitting to our covenant once again in the same place that God had initially put the desire in my heart to start this journey. God sparked a fire and later rekindled my desire to focus on him at the same time and place. My journey continued up the mountain, my Mount Everest.

While in the shower I had counted the cost of my decision, as we all must do when deciding to follow Jesus, and I knew that I was in for opposition from Alissa, her family, and my own family as well.

How could I expect them to understand my choice? I was the one in this situation, and it was incredibly difficult for me to understand. However, I needed to walk by faith, not by sight. Faith is hoping in the unseen and trusting that God will fulfill what he has promised. Holding on to Alissa was not an act of faith, because I could see the end result if we continued our relationship during this season. By letting her go, I would have to put my hope and faith in the Lord to bring her back in his perfect timing.

I needed to implement faith like that of Abraham. God promised Abraham a son despite his old age, and he was told he would have more descendants than there were stars in the sky or grains of sand on the seashore. As is stated in Romans 4:3, "Abraham believed God and his faith was credited to him as righteousness." Simple faith was all God required for Abraham to be "credited with righteousness." Thankfully, faith is the same requirement necessary to receive salvation. Works aside, to receive the forgiveness of sin and eternal life in heaven, God simply requires us to place our faith and life in his son Jesus Christ. When we follow in the footsteps of Abraham, "our faith will be credited to us as righteousness."

Communicating My Conviction

Upon returning home from Tahoe, I knew that I had to follow through with the conviction I had been confronted with on the trip. I asked the Lord to give me the words to explain this situation in a way that would make sense to Alissa. I also asked that he would protect her heart from discouragement, depression, and the lies that I knew the devil would be telling her. After much prayer, I composed the following letter:

> Happy New Year, Alissa! I can't tell you how difficult it was watching the "countdown" on my couch at home, with only Steve to share the celebration with. I am so excited for the day when God will allow us to share all of our holidays together. You may be wondering why I am e-mailing you, seeing as we have agreed to only connect once a month.

Well, as you know, I spent the weekend in Tahoe snowboarding with different friends (thank you again for the goggles; they were amazing!), and reflecting upon the past year, when God spoke to me. I didn't expect the conviction that he brought or the timely message he delivered, but I did receive revelation this week.

It was revealed to me in Tahoe that God did not need to send his son Jesus to die for our sins. God has the power to save us on his own, but Jesus was a crucial part of his perfect plan. Like the part that Jesus plays in our salvation, God does not necessarily "need" us to go through this two-year separation period. God has the power to give us the relationship that we both want, right now, but this separation is a crucial part of his perfect plan.

I was extremely convicted upon reflection of the verse that says, "God cannot be mocked." These were powerful words when applying them to the covenant I made with God. I am claiming to be fulfilling my covenant to God by not pursuing a romantic relationship with anyone, yet I find myself head over heels in love with you. Do I regret spending Christmas together? Absolutely not! I loved every minute of our time together, but reflecting back upon the boundaries we established in October, I am only deceiving myself in saying that I am not pursuing you. By no fault of your own (because you have done an amazing job honoring our boundaries) I still find myself madly in love with you. Whether we talk once a month, once a day, or once every six months, it does not change the fact that you have my heart. I love you, Alissa Griehshammer, and I honestly view you as my girlfriend. I told my family that you are my girlfriend, I tell anyone that asks that I'm not single, and if anyone were to see my Facebook, they would also know that we are more than "just friends." This is an undeniable truth that I can no longer overlook.

Pursuing a relationship in itself is not the issue. What is the issue, and what has always been the issue, is the timing. I promised God two years of my wholehearted, undivided attention, and I have yet to offer that.

At the end of this two-year journey God wants the glory for himself to say, "Look what I have done for my children. They were obedient to me, and I remained faithful to them as promised." God wants all the glory in our lives, Alissa. If we continue to talk, even once a month, I cannot wholeheartedly say that I trusted him completely. God would not receive all the glory because of our active efforts to stay in touch. It is so cliché, but we must "let go and let God." As much as I enjoy talking to you, even once a month, it is not something that we can continue doing.

I was forced to reflect upon my motives this weekend. By keeping in contact with you, I was assuring myself by my own efforts that we would one day be together. I need to completely trust God with this and place my hope and faith in him. By doing so, I know that he will deliver the desire of my heart upon completion of this commitment as promised in prophecy. Not only was this promised in prophecy, but was confirmed and reaffirmed many times over the following weeks. "Blessed is she who believes what the Lord has said to her will be accomplished" and "Have faith in the Lord your God and you will be upheld; have faith in his prophets and you will be successful."

Remember those confirmations?

God is and has always been faithful to fulfill his promises. Trust him, Alissa! I apologize for putting you through this once again, but I want God's blessing. I know that by giving him 100 percent now, he will honor that and bless us 1,000 percent in the future (the very near future lol; two years is nothing—I've only been Christian for two years). I want his blessing for our life, our family, our ministry, and our testimony, and I know he will do all of these things if we are obedient.

Another portion of this revelation came through the teaching of the difference between achievement and blessing. Can I achieve a master's degree, become a counselor, and have a relationship with you all at once? Of course I can, but will I be blessed? This weekend God spoke to my heart once again, as he did back in July and also October. He said, "Matt, I love you. I have already told you what will come of your commitment and obedience to me, but you have to let it go now. Do not limit me. My blessing knows no bounds. You think you know what I have planned for you, but you have no idea. Release this desire to me, and I will fulfill it tenfold." The words were deafening.

I love you, Alissa. I love you so much that I'm willing to give you up to the Lord and trust him 100 percent to fulfill what he has promised. I have asked you before, and I will ask you again. Will you trust him with me?

By wholeheartedly trusting in the Lord, this means that we trust God and God alone to bring us back together. This means cutting off all contact as discussed in the past, relinquishing any human effort at salvaging our relationship, and trusting God with it completely. When we are brought back together, I want us both to be able to say, "To God be the glory; thank you, Jesus, for remaining faithful to us. Not to us, but to God be the glory!" This is the desire of my heart, and I hope and pray that you will keep me accountable by honoring this request. Let us fully commit ourselves to God and trust our love story to the author of life!

I am excited for this challenge, Alissa, and I sincerely hope and pray that you will accept it with me. I do understand, however, that this commitment was one that I have made to God on my own. I also understand that I cannot ask you to wait for me, and I will hold nothing against you if you decide otherwise. No matter what happens, I trust that God has a plan to give us a hope and a future. Remember: "Seek first his kingdom and his righteousness and all these things will be given to you as well." What a wonderful God we serve. Call me if you wish; otherwise, I look forward to seeing the fulfillment of God's promises in December 2012!

Your best friend,
MJ

After receiving this e-mail, Alissa asked to speak with me one last time on the phone. As usual, I was nervous, but she was both supportive and encouraging. She reiterated her agreement that she also wanted God's best for our relationship and that she understood that I needed to fulfill my vow.

Although I needed to trust God without worrying about Alissa's response, I was thankful to have a relationship with a God who knows what we need and always provides. God knew that I needed to hear those words, and I was thankful to have received them.

This being our third "final" conversation, we both prepared our hearts to say good-bye. Before hanging up the phone for the final time, I told Alissa that I loved her and she returned the sentiment.

That girl has made my heart pound since the third grade, and this conversation was no exception.

After hanging up the phone I once again sighed with a sense of relief. I had peace knowing that the Lord was in control and that he had a path for each of us to walk, a cave in which to abide and growth for us to experience before we were reunited.

It was an exciting time filled with endless possibilities. What would become of us? How would God use this period of waiting to mold us, shape us, and use us for his purposes?

It was a mystery.

Honestly, I was walking without clear direction, but the comforting part was knowing that God was guiding my steps.

CHAPTER 9

WALK IT OUT

Although I had completely removed myself from Alissa's life, my family and friends did not follow suit. My sister, mother, and a close friend from church all made efforts to continue their relationships with Alissa.

One would think these ties would alleviate the pain of our living apart, but on the contrary, it only made matters worse. I remember one interaction with my sister as a direct attack from Satan himself …

While we were alone in my parents' kitchen, my sister proceeded to tell me how badly my commitment journey was paining Alissa. "You are literally killing her, Matt! What are you doing? If you really loved her, you wouldn't treat her like this."

The barrage continued. "Do you even understand how many guys have been asking her out? If you don't stop this whole commitment journey thing, you are going to lose her."

And it continued some more. "If you called her right now, she would forgive you and take you back. What are you waiting for?"

Looking at my sister in the eyes, I said with my best Jesus impression, "Get behind me, Satan!"

Confused, my sister responded, "What does that even mean? Weird."

Jamie didn't understand, but I knew that the devil was using her to discourage me.

Whatever your commitment, know that resistance will arise and may even come from those who care about you the most.

Heaven or Hell

This may sound random, but follow me for a second …

Would you be okay living in heaven if Jesus wasn't there?

Think about this …

According to the Bible, heaven is a place without evil, death, tears, pain, hunger, or thirst. All animals, including lions and lambs, will get along, and children can play next to cobras without fear. The streets are paved with gold, and there is an unending supply of awesome food. The list goes on and on from there.

Sounds pretty incredible, right?

So let me ask the question again—would you be okay with heaven, as the Bible describes, if Jesus wasn't there?

I was.

Before committing to the two-year journey, I would have been happy to inherit a godless eternity. I mean, the list of heavenly perks is pretty extensive; what's not to love?

However, I've since come to the biblical understanding that God is love. Therefore, choosing a godless and consequently loveless eternity would essentially be hell, right? Who would ever want to visit a place void of love, let alone live there for an eternity?

It wasn't until I was confronted by a trusted friend that my heart started to change. Did I really love God, or did I just like his stuff? In other words, did I truly love Jesus, or did I simply enjoy what he could do for me?

The answer was haunting.

Enjoying a relationship with God and basking in his glory didn't even make my "top ten awesome things about heaven" list. How could I claim that God was my Father, friend, Savior, Lord, and king, and not even want to spend time with him in heaven?

Something was wrong here.

In my mind, I had plenty of things to look forward to in heaven other than God. For me, heaven was a place with unending powdery snowboarding trails, ceaseless stretches of sandy beaches, and the fattiest fried foods that kept me looking like a bodybuilder 24/7. In most of my fantasies about heaven, God was simply an afterthought.

You can imagine the conviction I experienced when reading the psalmist's poem, "Whom have I in Heaven, but you?" (Psalm 73:25). This passage in the Bible was written by someone who truly loved God and understood the purpose of it all.

Our entire life from birth through death and into eternity is all about enjoying a relationship with God. Sin had separated me from that relationship until I placed my faith in Jesus, but now that I was saved, my outlook needed to change. If my goal wasn't to enjoy God, I was missing the mark.

It was then that I realized what Jesus meant in Revelation when he rebuked the church for "losing their first love" (Revelation 2:4). I too had lost my first love.

I was starting to see things a little more clearly. This journey was more than a waiting room. God needed to remove some distractions so he could regain his rightful place in my life. Once God was the center of it all, he knew that I would be able to truly enjoy this life and his gifts.

Taking Alissa from me was an incredible act of love from God. I now understood that if God wasn't number one in my heart, I would place others there and hold that person to standards that only God could meet. Naturally, feelings of disappointment would turn into discouragement, discouragement into despair, and despair into destruction. Anything that takes God's place in our lives will eventually destroy us. As my savior, God was once again protecting me from destroying a gift, a relationship with his daughter, that was meant to be a blessing.

To resolve this heart problem, the Physician (aka God) brought me to Psalm 37:4: "Delight yourself in the Lord and he will give you the desire of your heart." This simple psalm became my prayer for the remainder of the commitment journey.

If you are being honest, where does God rank in your life? Often, even good things like family, friends, jobs, commitments, and education can become "god things" when they take his rightful place in our lives.

Like me, some of you might also need to consider a reprioritization party.

It's All in the Process

Not to compare myself with King David or Jesus (Who does this guy think he is—always comparing himself to people in the Bible?), but I think it's interesting how God often puts his people through a process before fulfilling his promise.

David, Israel's greatest king, was anointed king of Israel while he was still a shepherd boy. He then had to wait until age thirty before he took the throne. In the meantime, David tended his father's flock, fought lions and bears, mastered the harp, and killed the giant Goliath. All of these things prepared David to receive God's promised position.

Before Jesus was even born as a human, he already knew his identity as God, King, Messiah, and Savior. Despite knowing his identity, Jesus accepted God's process and lived as a humble servant and hardworking carpenter for thirty years before performing a single recorded miracle.

In good company, I too received a promise, but first I had to endure a process. Trust me: I would have loved to spend two years playing Call of Duty and going to the gym every day, but my waiting period was never meant to be passive. As is demonstrated in the subsequent sections, God had a process and projects for me to complete in order to prepare me to receive his promise.

Life and Death

One of my pastors, Jentezen Franklin, said, "When something in your life dies, God births something new."

Just weeks after my relationship with Alissa died, I began volunteering with the high school ministry at my church. On any given Sunday, around two hundred students gathered to grow closer to God. These students and the high school volunteers became my family. We met together multiple times during the week, shared meals, went on fun outings, worshipped God, and served our community.

It was incredible to see Jesus's promise fulfilled; he claimed that "if anyone gives up family, property or anything else" for his sake they would be "repaid 100 times in this life and the life to come" (Mark 10:29).

Yes, I lost an incredibly significant relationship for God's sake, but he gave me over two hundred new relationships in return. Jesus is faithful to fulfill his promises!

Looking back, I realize that I met some of my best friends during that season in the high school ministry, and all because of an act of obedience. Had I clenched my fists and held on to Alissa, God could have never blessed me through these other relationships. He wanted to give me an abundance, but I needed to open my hands to him first.

My time serving in the high school ministry was a process that God used to prepare my heart for the fulfillment of his promise. Not only that, but God also had me working full time at a community college, completing a graduate school degree, participating in a Monday night men's group, and meeting with my mentor every Wednesday, Friday, and Saturday—not to mention all the traveling, snowboarding, and Caribbean cruising I did during my mentorship. This was one packed process!

Hearing the Voice of God

Part of my journey was learning how to hear the voice of God.

What does God sound like anyway?

Anytime I share about having a relationship with God, talking to him, and hearing his voice, people are curious to know what the voice of God sounds like.

I've heard people say that God sounds like Jiminy Cricket. Some say God sounds like your conscience, that still small voice in your head. Others have described his voice like thunder, while some have described Aslan the lion or even Morgan Freeman.

Outside of my initial encounter with God in December 2008, my most memorable experience of hearing the voice of God happened at a gym in Castro Valley, California, in 2011.

It was a standard Friday evening. After work, I drove from Oakland to Castro Valley, where I would meet Joseph at his gym.

When I walked through the door, the receptionist, whom I had seen in the gym for years without having ever spoken to her, politely greeted me with a smile and scanned my membership card.

I walked to the elliptical machine and began my workout. As I was gliding in gazelle-like fashion, my mind kept returning to the receptionist. I was not attracted to this girl, I didn't know this girl, I'd never even talked with her, but I couldn't stop thinking about her.

Then, the thoughts turned into words. Although not audible, I could hear the voice of God as clear as crystal. "Matt, I want you to tell the front desk receptionist that God has someone who will love her and serve her, not use and abuse her."

Me: Yeah, I'm not saying that.

God: Matt, go talk to her.

Me: Are you kidding me? You want me to walk up to a complete stranger, a girl I have never said more than a "hi" to before, and tell her that God has a message for her?

God: Yes.

Me: Do you understand how crazy that sounds? I don't even know this girl's name.

I thought that watching TV or listening to my iPod would drown out God's voice, but that failed, so I continued fighting with him until I finished my cardio session. All I could think about was how this scenario might possibly play out.

Would she be by herself? Surely I wouldn't talk to her unless she was alone. What if she freaked out and called her manager, or even worse, the cops! "There is a crazy customer here who is apparently hearing from God and wants to talk to me about the voices in his head; we need an ambulance and a straitjacket *stat*!"

How would I even start that conversation? "Hey, I know we've never talked before, but God just told me something extremely personal about your life, so here it goes …"

I was playing out these scenarios in my mind as I considered the possibility of obeying God.

I have prayed countless times to hear the voice of God, to experience God's presence, to feel his power, to be used by him for his kingdom, and here was my chance.

I got off the elliptical machine and walked toward the weight room. There was a glass window in the weight room that peered into the reception area. As I walked past the window, I noticed that the receptionist was alone. This was the perfect opportunity.

Me: Come on, God. You can't possibly expect me to …

God: Matt, you only have two choices: obedience or sin. "If anyone then, who knows the good they ought to do and doesn't do it, it is sin for them" (James 4:17).

Understanding my lack of options, I walked over to the curl rack for a set of confidence. After a few reps, I racked the weights and headed to the reception counter. I could hear my heart beating in my chest, and I started to get that nervous feeling in my throat like I'm either going to throw up or choke. Without making eye contact I walked past the receptionist and continued on to the water fountain down the hallway.

"You coward. Where is your faith?" I told myself.

After my pit stop at the fountain, I prayed, asking God for confidence and boldness. Then as I walked back toward the receptionist, I stopped at the reception counter.

Me: Hi.

Laura: Hello. Can I help you?

How do you even start this conversation? "Hi, I'm Matt and I have a message for you from God"?

Me: I've been attending this gym for years now and just realized that we have never actually met. I'm Matt.

Laura: Nice to meet you. I'm Laura.

After our introduction, I asked about her job, school, and a couple other random questions to break the ice.

Me: It's nice to finally meet you, Laura.

Laura: Likewise.

Me: Before I take off, I need to tell you something.

Laura: …

(I'm positive Laura thought I was ready to ask her out at this point. Her face looked like she was bracing herself for something really awkward, which was super-distracting because I was about to say something awkward.)

Me: I'm a Christian and often pray while I work out. On the elliptical today I very clearly heard God tell me that he has a message for you.

Laura is now glaring at me with skeptical eyes that clearly said, "You must be joking!"

Laura: …

Me: God has a man for you who will love you and serve you, not use and abuse you.

There was silence.

Then more silence.

Followed by even more silence …

Although Laura didn't say anything, I could tell by the tears in her eyes that these few words were impactful.

There were no phone calls to the police department, screams for help, or any of the imagined responses I had earlier conjured … just tears.

I stood there waiting for Laura to say something.

Laura: (sniffling) How did you know to say that?

Me: Honestly, I don't know. That's what I heard God tell me in the cardio room. I didn't want to tell you, because I thought you would think I was crazy.

Laura then explained that the guy she was currently "dating" had another girlfriend and that he was only using Laura for sex. Meanwhile, he was promising that once he broke up with his current girlfriend, they could be in an exclusive relationship.

Wiping the tears from her eyes, she continued to tell me that she was sick of how every guy she met only wanted to have sex with her, and none of them was willing to commit to her.

I don't know why I was shocked, like God got lucky or something, but nonetheless, I did not expect this encounter to unfold as it did.

I talked to Laura for a little while longer, counseling her and sharing a little about my own testimony before walking away and finishing my workout.

After that encounter at the gym, Laura avoided conversation with me when I would see her at the reception counter. I don't really blame her; she must have felt uncomfortably vulnerable around me, which is totally understandable. However, conversation or not, we both knew that a miracle had occurred that day. God was not dead; he was very much alive, and he was speaking to a woman in the gym much like he did the woman at the well (John 4).

Be careful what you pray for; God listens and he is faithful. Also, I would encourage you to ask God to speak only if you plan on listening. I've already mentioned the story of Jonah, who ran away from God when he called him to preach to the Ninevites. I'm not trying to spend anytime inside of a fish like he did.

Unwelcomed Adventure

What's your favorite Christmas memory?

Before December 2011, I would have probably said the time my neighbor drove eight hours at midnight to cover our front yard with snow from Tahoe. Since it never snows in Pleasanton, you can imagine our surprise when we opened the front door to our first-ever white Christmas.

How about your worst Christmas memory?

Hands down, my worst Christmas memory was when I told my parents that I would be overseas that year for Christmas. I felt horrible dropping this Grinch-sized bomb on my parents, but it was the opportunity of a lifetime.

It all started over Easter …

Joseph and I had flown back to Hawaii for the second time that year.

While driving the dangerously windy Hana Highway, Joseph received a phone call.

It's crazy how one call can change your life. Have you ever received a phone call like that?

After hanging up the phone, Joseph turned to me and asked, "How would you like to spend a month with me in Myanmar?"

Me: A month in Myanmar, huh? For what?

Joseph: Vacation. We can spend a month on the beach—writing, working on homework, visiting my family, and …

There's always a catch.

Joseph then told me about the Hand of Hope seminar, which would train church leaders to provide pastoral counseling to those in their congregation.

Me: Sure, that sounds awesome! When is it?

Joseph: December 15 through January 10.

Me: Whoa, whoa, whoa! Pump the brakes. You want me to miss Christmas and New Year's Eve with my family and friends?

Joseph: It's one year, and this is a once-in-a-lifetime opportunity. When else will you be offered an all-expenses-paid, monthlong vacation to Myanmar while doing the Lord's work? Besides, this is part of the commitment journey., I'm training you to be a counselor, remember?

He had a point.

"Ok, I'm in …"

Agreeing to Myanmar was easy. Telling my parents was an entirely different story. They already shared a disdain for Joseph. They despised how much time we spent together and detested Joseph for taking me away over Easter. However, this was Christmas, the holy grail of family holidays. Surely this would push them over the edge.

As I expected, my parents weren't happy.

If you've ever been told, "I'm not mad, just disappointed," then you know how I was feeling at that moment.

Once again, I was faced with a situation where my commitment journey caused pain and resulted in resistance from those I loved.

Eventually, my parents pushed past their disappointment to give me their blessing, along with new luggage for the trip and a ride to the airport.

A Not So Silent Night

Have you ever questioned whether or not you were dreaming or hallucinating, like, "Is this real life? Is this really happening right now?"

I'm talking about a situation that could be a page out of *Alice in Wonderland* but is actually part of your real-life script.

Welcome to my Christmas Eve in Myanmar …

After dinner with Joseph's family, it was time for church—not just any church, but a Pentecostal church. The last Pentecostal church I had visited was in Oakland with Jenette the prophet. I guess you can say that my expectations were a little high.

For the Christmas Eve service, Joseph's church had invited a pastor from Singapore to speak. This pastor didn't pull any punches. He claimed to have a healing gift from God, and not only that, but he proclaimed that it was God's Christmas gift to the church to have anyone with an illness, injury, or impairment receive healing at tonight's service.

Not to say that I didn't believe in miracles, but this was a lofty claim. I mean, my entire life story is surrounded by miracles, but I had never heard anyone make bold statements like this.

As I sat in the back row skeptically listening to the sermon, the speaker very specifically asked if there was anyone in the room who needed healing from injuries or impairments in their legs. An elderly Asian woman raised her hand and was asked to stand up. She was struggling to stand, so her neighbors assisted her out of her chair. As she stood up, the preacher pointed at the woman and commanded with authority, "In the name of Jesus, be healed!" Immediately this elderly woman collapsed to the ground.

What in Jesus's name had just happened? Was she dead? Had that pastor just killed an old lady in Jesus's name? Was this real life? What was I witnessing?

Thankfully, she wasn't dead. She was, however, still lying on the floor seemingly unconscious, now covered by a blanket.

I didn't know whether to laugh or call the cops. This old lady had just passed out in the middle of a church service, and instead of getting her medical attention they brought her a blankie? Something was definitely wrong with this picture. Old ladies should not be falling over like that!

Without blinking an eye, the pastor then asked if anyone else wanted to experience Jesus's healing power.

Jesus's healing power? That woman had just passed out quicker than a freshman pledge at a frat party. No way was anyone else going to stand up after watching Grannie Smith on the ground over there.

But, to my surprise, people actually began to stand up, and almost like clockwork, people began to collapse.

I had never seen anything like this before.

As people were passing out around me, I could sense that Joseph wanted me to experience the power of God as well.

Naturally, I was hesitant.

I mean, everyone that stood ended up unconscious on the floor. Why would I want that?

Joseph's niece did …

Earlier in my visit to Myanmar, I spent time with Joseph's sister and her husband. They had three kids; however, I rarely ever saw their daughter. Apparently Joseph's niece was sick and did not want to leave her room in fear that she would pass the virus on to their elderly, quite fragile grandmother. Joseph's niece responded in faith for healing from her illness that night. When she walked to the stage, the pastor placed his hands on her face, praying in the name of Jesus.

I kid you not, instead of falling to the floor this young girl began to vomit in front of the whole congregation. Literally, white foam flowed out of her mouth and onto the church floor. Tears began to flow from her eyes as she continued vomiting foam from her mouth. I have seen projectile vomiting before, but nothing like this. She could have started a car wash with all the foam that was flying from her face. What the heck was going on in this place?

When Joseph's niece finally stopped throwing up, she began to praise God in another language. Although I didn't speak Mandarin, Burmese, or Cantonese, I knew this wasn't an Asian language. It sounded so foreign, yet so familiar. Instead of vomit, angelic words now began to flow from her lips. Where these words were coming from I had no idea, but it was beautiful. She was seemingly harmonizing with a choir of angels as she belted these wonderful words of praise to the Lord. I would later learn that like Alissa, Joseph, and many others in this church, Joseph's niece had the gift of tongues.

My attention was then diverted back to the old woman. She was now off the floor and walking around claiming a healing miracle over her injured legs.

God had healed her! And so publicly, right in front of us.

Another guy then climbed onto the stage, grabbed the microphone, and testified that God had also healed him. All around me people were being healed. It was the most amazing, miraculous thing I'd ever seen!

The pastor then offered his final invitation. "If you are in need of God's healing touch tonight, take a step of faith and walk down to the altar."

This was my chance.

After seeing God's healing power in this place, I too wanted to be touched by him. In all honesty, more than anything I was hoping to receive the gift of tongues out of this experience.

I walked down the aisle not knowing what to expect. Now standing at the altar, the pastor came down to place his hands on my head. As he began to pray over me, I started to praise God. "Hallelujahs" and "Praise the Lords," followed by "Holy, holy, holys" came from my mouth as he asked the Spirit of God to fill my mouth with praises.

I recognized my words and began to feel discouraged that I wasn't speaking in tongues yet. Why wasn't it happening?

As the pastor continued to pray, I could sense a loss of feeling in my legs. My entire body then felt frozen, and I could no longer move. At some point in his prayer I fell backward, completely unable to brace my fall, as my arms were cemented at my side. Two people were apparently standing behind me the whole time in case of such an event.

As they placed me on the ground, I could feel an electrical current surging through my body. Although I could hear the conversations around me, I could not respond. My lips couldn't even move. My arms and legs were frozen as well. I just lay there as the peace of God flooded over my body.

Like the old lady, I too was covered with a blanket as I remained on the ground. I'm still not sure what the blanket had to do with anything.

Anyway, after around fifteen minutes I regained mobility and was able to sit up. All I could feel was a peaceful glow. The pastor explained that I had been "slain in the spirit." I didn't know what this meant, but I was confident that I had just experienced the power and presence of God once again.

Confirmation of the Crazy

Before leaving the church I was able to talk with Joseph's niece. I asked her what had happened, and she explained that she felt the Holy Spirit fill her until foam started to pour from her mouth. She reported that once the foam had exited her body, the sickness was gone as well.

Although my eyes had witnessed these miracles, they still seemed crazy in my mind. It just didn't make sense. But, after experiencing what I experienced and witnessing what I witnessed, I didn't need it to make sense. Our God is incomprehensible. What kind of God would he be if we could figure him out? I am thankful that God is more complex than our human understanding. If we could comprehend the complexities or miraculous happenings of God, we would ourselves be considered gods. However, as God states in Isaiah 44:6, "I am the first and I am the last; apart from me there is no God." Again in Isaiah 44:8 God says, "You are my witnesses. Is there any other god beside me? No, there is no other rock; I know not one."

I remember walking away from that church service with a reverent fear of God in my heart. He was so real to me. After the occurrences in this service and my conversion experience in December 2008, I could never deny his power, his presence, or his love. God was real. I witnessed his miracles, felt his peace, and was completely in awe of his existence. It was truly edifying to know without a shadow of a doubt that God existed, and he was present with me and loved me. It's a feeling that words cannot describe.

Lying in bed that night I couldn't help but think about my recent decisions. If I had chosen to disobey God and keep Alissa or had I stayed home for Christmas, this night would have never happened. Before falling asleep I thanked God for giving me the grace to make these difficult decisions during my commitment journey.

The cost of this commitment had been great, but the payoffs were even greater. Speaking of payoffs, it was also in Myanmar where Joseph promised that if I completed the commitment journey he would fly me anywhere in the world to propose to Alissa. Talk about an incentive.

The Bratty Kid at Christmas

Nobody likes a crybaby.

Especially at Christmas.

You've seen this, right? The kid who has all their needs met, but didn't receive the newest gadget or game for Christmas. That kid then cries, complains, and even threatens to call child protective services to report his neglectful parents.

I'm guessing that never happens in Haiti. Just sayin'.

As crazy as this may sound, even after such an incredible experience with the Lord in Myanmar, I wasn't satisfied. I was given many gifts, but one was missing. Like the people in Joseph's church, I too wanted the gift of speaking in tongues.

Without this gift, I began to feel like a second-class Christian. I felt left out, unworthy, loved less than others because God had given them something that he hadn't given me.

I was the bratty kid at Christmas. God had given me so many things, but I wasn't happy, because I didn't get the gift that the other Christian kids had.

Maybe that's why God didn't give me the gift of tongues. Maybe God was trying to gift me with the attitude of gratitude by helping me focus on all he had already given me. Novel concept.

For the next two years I spent much time in prayer, confusion, and conversation with others about the gift of tongues. According to the Bible, this gift encourages, builds, and strengthens the individual in ways that are otherwise impossible to obtain.

I wanted it.

After two years of silence, during the spring of 2013 I was introduced to a preacher from Santa Barbara named Britt Merrick. He was in the middle of a ten-sermon series all about the Holy Spirit when I began to podcast his messages. Specifically, his sermon titled, "Baptism in the Holy Spirit" caught my attention.

During this sermon I immediately connected with Britt because we shared a very similar testimony. I then began to reflect on the story of my life and how it related to Britt's.

I was raised in the church by a God-fearing woman who desperately wanted me to know Jesus. She had me in church every Sunday morning and made sure that I attended as many church events as possible. I eventually accepted Jesus as my Lord and Savior in middle school at a church retreat and was baptized in high school. I continued to struggle with sin, mainly pornography and masturbation, but I also lied to my parents, got drunk and high, and messed around with women.

I may have believed that Jesus was my Savior, but he definitely wasn't the Lord of my life. Jesus was simply a life raft that I used when storms, trials, and tribulations threatened the peace in my life. However, all that changed when Jesus confronted all of my sin and invited me to follow him in 2008.

As you will recall, after feeling the weight and conviction of my sin, I repented asking Jesus to save me, heal me, and forgive me. The moment I did these things I felt the Holy Spirit of God flood over me as if I were drinking him into my body. This "stream of living water" came in the form of a bright green glowing Nalgene bottle of water. Jesus was calling me to drink of him because he is the fountain of life, the source of living water.

The moment that water entered my mouth, I was actively drinking in his Holy Spirit. It was the most incredible, indescribable feeling I had ever had.

At the time I didn't know what I was experiencing. I lacked the theological understanding to label my experience. However, I have since come to understand this as my Holy Spirit baptism. In Luke 3:16, John the Baptist said, "I baptize you with water, but one is coming who will baptize you with the Holy Spirit and fire." Although I didn't have the gift of tongues, I had been baptized in the Holy Spirit and was gifted by God in other ways—healing, for example (i.e., Mitch Hannegan from my college days).

For me, the greatest physical evidence of my encounter with the Holy Spirit was the immediate freedom from my most enslaving sin.

All my adolescent "Christian" life I struggled with masturbation and pornography. Can anyone relate? I would finish the act and immediately feel guilty. I would then beg God to forgive me and make promises never to look at porn or touch myself again. It then happened the next night, and the cycle started all over like a broken record.

There were times when I would abstain for weeks, months, and even years (yes, years), but I always fell right back in. However, after being baptized in the Holy Spirit, I was immediately released from my addiction to porn and other sexual sin. Since my experience with Jesus in 2008, I have yet to look at another piece of porn. Not even once.

Not only that, but after my baptism in the Holy Spirit I had new desires and a new fire to talk to people about Jesus. Before, I had been embarrassed to publicly proclaim my faith, but now I couldn't shut up about him and wanted everyone to be saved.

My purpose in adding this portion of my commitment journey is not to boast, but to encourage you. God is the giver of amazing gifts. His Holy Spirit is one of those gifts. Jesus died to give this gift to you!

After Jesus rose from the dead, he told his followers that he had to return to heaven so he could send the Holy Spirit. As believers, once we put our faith in Jesus, we receive God's Holy Spirit, and when you encounter the Holy Spirit of God, you will never be the same again. It's just not possible. Inviting the Holy Spirit into your heart is essentially like inviting a construction worker into your house who plans to remodel the entire structure beginning with the foundation. Demolition is inevitable.

All of this is to say, if you have received the gift of tongues, that's awesome. Praise God! If you haven't received that gifting but you are producing the fruit of the Spirit—namely, love, joy, peace, patience, kindness, goodness, faithfulness, gentleness, and self-control—even better! (Galatians 5:22–23). Not all of us will receive the same gifts from God, but we can all be encouraged by the promise that if our lives are looking more and more like Jesus's, we are on the right path.

This is a great time to take a moment and evaluate your life. Seriously, stop for a moment and think about this:

If I claim to be a Christian, do I look more like Jesus today than I did five years ago? Five months ago? Five weeks? Five days? Am I growing in the attributes of God, in the fruit of his Spirit? Jesus said, "You will know a tree by the fruit it produces." What type of fruit are our lives producing?

This isn't an exercise to create guilt but one to encourage you forward in your faith. Press on, my friends! God promises that when we draw near to him, he will draw near to us. It is impossible to be close to God and not become more like him (James 4:8).

Air Jordan

I once heard a story about a young boy who encountered the spirit of Michael Jordan. This boy was reportedly playing hoops at the local court when he encountered the spirit of Air Jordan, which this boy claimed changed his life forever. He reported that he now had the same ball handling, shooting, and dunking ability as Michael Jordan himself.

What would you say about this boy if you saw him play and he couldn't even make a free throw? I guess you would call him Shaq ... but seriously. What if this boy claimed to have Jordan's power but couldn't dribble a ball, jump more than three inches off the ground, or make a layup?

That is essentially what we are looking at when we see people who claim to be Christians yet look nothing like Christ.

People want proof. Yes, we are all works in progress, but even construction sites gradually look different.

When I was in high school, I believed in Jesus, but I wasn't following him; consequently, my life looked nothing like his.

I have to stop here for a moment. This thought has often kept me up at night ...

What would have happened to me if I had died before having mushrooms with the Messiah?

Despite my having been raised in the church and baptized in middle school, and even my claiming to have faith in Jesus, on December 19, 2008, God told me I was going to hell if I didn't repent and follow him.

My religion did not save me. Checking ritualistic boxes didn't save me. I was saved only when I personally encountered Jesus, repented of my sins, and received his Holy Spirit—because once that happened, my life started to change. Some things changed faster than others, but my life was drastically transforming.

Where is the proof in your life that Jesus is changing you? If you can't think of anything, you have some business to take care of.

Go ahead. God is listening.

What are you waiting for? This isn't a game! Some of you reading these words right now are on the path to hell.

It doesn't have to end that way. God doesn't want it to end that way. He sent his son to die in your place so that it wouldn't end that way. Jesus loves you!

If you have any doubt, here's a biblical promise for you: "Ask and it will be given to you, seek and you will find, knock and the door will be opened to you" (Matthew 7:7). Jesus promises to pour out his Holy Spirit on anyone who desires to experience true life and transformation.

If you want an encounter with God, stop what you're doing, repent of your sins, receive God's forgiveness, and ask to be filled with the Holy Spirit.

Remember what Jesus's brother James taught us in the first chapter of his book: "When you ask, you must believe in order to receive." Have faith that God can change you, that he will give you his Holy Spirit, and that he will save you. According to Romans 10:13, "All who call upon the name of the Lord will be saved."

It's simple but by no means easy.

CHAPTER 12

HELL ON HALF DOME

Of all the physical feats I've accomplished up to this point in my life, climbing Half Dome in Yosemite was definitely the most difficult. Granted, the first time I climbed to the top I was ten years old; each time after seemed only to get harder and harder.

It must have been temporary amnesia, because after each summit I promised myself never to voluntarily put my body through such grueling pain again. Yet, three times over I have seemingly forgotten my promise along with the soreness and exhaustion that follows.

Is Half Dome really that bad? Yes. Yes, it is. The average hiker takes ten to twelve hours to complete the sixteen-mile round-trip; yes, it's hard!

Funny story: before Alissa and I split, she told me that her family hiked Half Dome every year. All my bragging rights immediately flew out the window. I thought four times was something to write home about, but every year? Wow. I was impressed. That is, until I discovered that she thought "climbing Half Dome" was actually hiking the Mist Trail. Yeah. Only nine miles short, but close. One day she'll finish the second half of that trek and I'll stop telling this joke. Maybe.

What Alissa had yet to discover was that the worst part of the Half Dome hike is when you are nearly at the top. At this point you have already hiked for nearly seven hours in the hot sun. Your journey has taken you up a massive staircase known as the Mist Trail, through endless switchbacks, and up a near-vertical set of granite steps.

You can now see the finish line, but before you cross, you must pull yourself up a vertical slab of granite by the infamous and sometimes slippery steel cables. Serious talk: surviving this last leg of the journey is almost better than the breathtaking views at the top.

The last two months of my commitment journey were no different. It was now October 2012, and my December finish line was in plain view. However, like the Half Dome hike, I had some final fierce obstacles to climb.

Before attempting to reconnect with Alissa on December 1, I wanted to complete my graduate course work. I had only two classes left, but each class was accelerated. This meant that I would be completing two sixteen-week graduate-level courses in just eight short weeks. Against the advice of my academic advisor, I enrolled in both courses.

Then, one week after beginning my final two classes, I received a sixty-day eviction notice from my landlord. We now had until November 30 to vacate the house.

Not only did I have a large academic load due at the end of November, but I also now had to move and clean out my current house.

Cleaning the house doesn't sound like an overly burdensome challenge; however, this was not your average rental. The home I shared with my best friend, Steve, had been occupied by many tenants throughout the last fifteen years. After the tenants moved out, they would leave old furniture, kitchen items, broken appliances, children's toys, art materials, and other items in the garage. Random junk from fifteen years of tenants was strewn about and stored in our backyard, garage, kitchen, and atrium. We were essentially living in a flea market, and according to our landlord, every item on that property was our responsibility.

Our first step was bug bombing the house. I am terrified of spiders and was certain that our garage was a nesting ground for black widows. We bought the bombs, threw them grenade style into the garage, and slammed the door. Steve and I then made our way to the back room to play some Madden Football.

It didn't take long for the toxic gas from the garage to seep its way through the ventilation system and into Steve's bedroom. What we thought was a safe room turned into a toxic box of torture in a matter of minutes. The way I like to tell the story, "We barely escaped with our lives …," but really we were fine.

After the bug bomb it took Steve and me the entire two months to clear the house. This chore took countless trips to the dumps and the Salvation Army, as well as filling our neighbors' trash cans before the garbage trucks arrived.

It was now November 20, ten days before the eviction deadline. I still had nowhere to move and a handful of assignments to finish. Talk about stress.

With this proverbial gun to my head I had no time to think about reconnecting with Alissa. What should have been the most exciting time of my life was overshadowed by worry and fear.

Then finally, with only seven days before homelessness or having to move back into my parents' house, I found a place of my own.

Learning to trust God's timing has been one of the most frustrating and fruitful lessons of this journey. Over the years, I've gained the understanding that God is always on time, but he is rarely early, at least according to our own timeline.

So I now had a place to live, but I had yet to complete my classes, and there was no way I could possibly finish with a move now in the mix.

That same day I checked my e-mail and found a message from my professor. In my three years of grad school I had never seen this message before, but today of all days I received the following: "For only $150 you can purchase a sixty-day extension on your course work. Order now."

Another lifeline. Thank you, Jesus!

So my timeline wasn't God's timeline. Sound familiar?

I wanted to finish my classes before December 1, but God had another plan and provided accordingly.

Why do I even make plans? God already knows how the whole thing plays out anyway.

Preparing to Receive My Promise

Now that I had moved into my new apartment, I could start planning my reunion with Alissa.

Unbeknownst to Joseph, I received Disneyland tickets from my parents for my birthday. The plan was to fly down to Orange County where Alissa lived and surprise her at midnight on December 1. My hope was that we would then spend the early morning talking at a local diner like old times, getting caught up and reacquainted before spending the day at Disneyland celebrating God's faithfulness.

I had made all these plans behind Joseph's back, hoping that he wouldn't find out. In my heart, I didn't trust that he would actually honor the commitment deadline of December 2012 and would instead concoct some crazy reason why I hadn't waited long enough.

My mind was set on December 1, and no one was getting in my way.

Breakfast Blowout

Sure enough, while at a late-night Denny's dinner, Joseph asked me point-blank about the weekend of December 1. To my surprise, Joseph assumed that I would want to spend the first weekend of December with him snowboarding in Utah instead of reuniting with Alissa. He was hoping that we would spend the weekend celebrating the last two years of our commitment journey together.

Are you kidding me? After two years away from Alissa, Joseph now wanted me to blow her off for a vacation? No way!

"Thank you, Joseph—such a generous offer! Unfortunately, I already have plans to visit Alissa that weekend." I then divulged my plan about Disneyland.

Dead silence ensued.

I knew Joseph too well. A familiar fury, comparable to that during our conversation in Tahoe, began to build. I could see it all over his face.

Why was he so mad? I had spent the last three years hanging out with him every weekend. Having completed the commitment journey and now free to pursue the woman of my dreams, he should have been happy for me!

I started to see what I thought were his true colors.

"I'm done!" Joseph yelled in the middle of the diner. "You have learned *nothing* about commitment. These three years have been a complete waste. You have completely wasted my time and yours! You make all these plans without even talking to me about them. Don't you think that

I wanted to be a part of something so important to you? Of course not, because you think only about yourself! Go ahead then, Matt. Do what you want to do. It won't last. You have learned nothing!"

After this verbal assault I was ready to throw my plate of pancakes in Joseph's face. At that moment I would have been perfectly content to walk away and never see him again.

I had completed my commitment journey; there was nothing more for us to discuss. If he couldn't be happy for me and instead wanted to take me away to Utah without allowing me the freedom to reconnect with Alissa, then I was ready to wash my hands of him. My only problem at this point was that my car was parked at his house and he was my ride home.

As his "captive" audience, I listened to Joseph's reasoning.

To my surprise, I slowly began to grasp the concept that he was trying to communicate.

Finish Your Fruit!

Our commitments will all be judged by the fruit they produce, the final product of our efforts. No one cares how much time, effort, blood, and sweat you poured into the beginning of your marriage, career, fitness goal, or hobby; if the fruit of that tree is rotten, no one will eat it. So finish well.

The most important day of your marriage isn't the first, but the last. How did you finish?

It truly won't matter how beautiful or expensive your wedding was if the marriage ends in divorce.

If you have ever seen the TV show *The Biggest Loser*, you know exactly what I'm talking about. How often are we moved by the sad story and inspired by the progress only to be disappointed when all the pounds are regained after the cameras have stopped recording?

How about the high school student with promising grades and a bright future? That same student gets caught up in the party scene at school, loses the scholarship, and ends up dropping out of college to move back home. We've all seen it.

Thankfully, if you're not dead, God's not done and will give you a second, third, tenth, and millionth chance to finish well. People would much rather hear the story of redemption than one of destruction.

The fruit of our lives will speak louder than our words or intentions. Anyone can make a commitment, but only kept commitments are commemorated and celebrated.

I couldn't give up now. I had come too far. If celebrating our completed commitment would preserve my relationship with Joseph and allow me to finish strong, it would be worth the sacrifice of waiting a few more days to reconnect with Alissa. I can only imagine the regret I would feel after spending two years of my life committed to something, only to walk away with it in shambles.

After I reconciled with Joseph, we headed to Utah for the weekend.

New Wine into Old Wineskins

Although the snow in Utah during the first weekend of December left much to be desired, our dinner at the Ruth Chris Steakhouse did not. To celebrate the completion of our two-year total commitment journey, Joseph treated me to one of the best meals of my life. To top things off, Joseph wanted to discuss my plans with Alissa.

For the first time in the three years, Joseph actually wanted to talk about my relationship in a positive way. Strangely enough, he even had a smile on his face. Joseph then proceeded to tell me how proud he was of me for finishing the journey and how excited he was for my time with Alissa. Joseph then asked how I intended to contact her.

I told him all about my "white knight" approach. How I had planned to surprise Alissa in Orange County, on her doorstep at midnight. I thought that after two years I would just show up unannounced with flowers in hand, ready to ride into the sunset with the girl of my dreams.

Of all the possible responses, Joseph confronted my plans calling them both prideful and presumptuous. He then proceeded to quote Jesus by accusing me of "pouring new wine into old wineskins" (Matthew 9:17).

What did that even mean?

I'd heard the saying before, but I never understood its meaning and definitely not in this context. Thankfully, Joseph explained.

The definition of insanity is doing the same thing over and over again expecting a different result. Joseph pointed out that in my past, I used romance to secure relationships. This approach, however, failed time and time again because all of these relationships were built on a flimsy foundation. Romance alone cannot sustain a lasting relationship.

Although I had learned a lot in the last two years, I was still preparing to use the same approach with Alissa that I had used countless times in the past. I wanted a lasting relationship on a firm foundation, but I was building with sand, not solid rock.

Joseph explained that emotions are fickle and fading, but true friendship endures the test of time. If I wanted a lasting relationship with Alissa, I needed a new approach. I needed to build a friendship—slowly and steadily, over time. Not diving in too quickly. Not allowing my emotions to take center stage.

Joseph also pointed out another flaw in my plans for reuniting with Alissa. "How long can you keep the fire burning at that temperature? Your plan is to woo her with this Prince Charming, white knight, Disneyland fairy-tale approach. This will undoubtedly create a high emotional climate. Both of your emotions will inevitably skyrocket. How long can you maintain those emotions?

"If you make things too hot too quickly, your emotions and inevitably your relationship will eventually cool off. Your approach is provoking the law of gravity. Remember, Matt: what comes up must come down.

"Sustainability is key.

"A foundation of friendship will provide the sustainable climate in which to maintain your relationship."

Joseph also reminded me that we had been apart for two years. Not that I needed a reminder; I thought about that every day. "The height at which you intend to bring your emotions by means of this fairy-tale encounter will also deceive you by clouding your judgment."

Joseph continued, "The beginning stage where friendship is built can become clouded by your emotions, which will also prevent objectivity. You want to see and assess Alissa without emotionally installed blinders. People change over time, and two years is a long time. This is your chance to assess Alissa and count the cost of continuing this relationship. Once you commit to her, there is no going back. Take your time by building a friendship. Rushing into a relationship will not allow you to accurately observe this woman whom you are considering as a life partner. Your marital vow will supersede any dissatisfaction you may have with her character. Take time to study her, understand her, and learn as much about her as you possibly can to ensure that you have all the information necessary to make a wise decision. You have only one shot at this."

Without a firm foundation of friendship—Joseph was right—we would have nothing to fall back on. I couldn't possibly sustain a lifelong relationship built solely on romance and emotion.

Starting to see his point, I swallowed my pride and told him that I'd pray about it. My mind was already made up, but I had to at least maintain the appearance of having control over the situation. As much as I wanted a fairy-tale beginning, I'd much rather have the fairy-tale ending.

A Most Frightening Phone Call

Sitting on the edge of my bed, I bowed my head to pray. "Lord, thank you. These past two years have been hard as heck, but you have been faithful to walk me through the fire. I can't believe the day is finally here. My moment has arrived. I am finally free to contact your daughter. I honestly have no idea what I'm going to say. Holy Spirit, please give me the words, bless me with peace, and help our conversation flow. God, work a miracle here. I trust that you will fulfill your promise, Lord. Thank you for being so faithful. I love you."

Pacing around my room, I thought of what I might say.

Nothing satisfactory came to my mind.

It felt as though the words were frozen in my brain, as if my mental word processor was paralyzed.

After five minutes, I realized that pacing wasn't helping.

I just needed to dive in; there was no wading here. This was an all-or-nothing endeavor.

Dialing her number, I realized that my heart was ready to burst through my chest. Alissa would probably hear my heartbeat through the phone if she picked up.

Two rings passed, and I panicked. Hanging up the phone, I tried catching my breath. *Are you really hyperventilating right now? Come on, Matt, you've been waiting for this moment for two years.*

I hadn't been this nervous in my entire life.

Now standing in my prayer closet, I grasped the reality that I would never be 100 percent ready. Dialing her number again, I held my breath.

Each ring lasted an eternity. What if she didn't pick up? Should I leave a voice mail? A voice mail after two years?

Sure enough, on the last ring, Alissa picked up.

"Leave a message!"

Voice mail!

I didn't leave a voice mail.

After five minutes, I received a text message from Alissa. She was at a Christmas party for work and would be leaving soon. She asked me to call back a half hour later.

I waited the half hour and called again. No answer.

Really? Almost immediately, I received another text message from Alissa. She was still at the party and had to help clean up.

Not at all what I was expecting.

Thankfully, God had taught me enough about waiting during the last two years; what was another hour?

When Alissa finally returned my call, the nerves were gone. God once again had used the waiting period to prepare me. From our first hello to the final good-night, our conversation flowed flawlessly.

Alissa and I then slowly reestablished rapport from December 4 until Christmas Eve over the phone. Alissa wouldn't be home from Southern California again until Christmas, and I was encouraged to wait until her homecoming for our first face-to-face encounter.

To my surprise, Alissa was fiery on the phone. She was seemingly ready to jump right into the relationship that had been on hold for the last two years. I, however, was trying my best to keep a slow and steady pace. Alissa quickly caught on to this and pushed the issue. "So what is this? Do you want to be with me or not? Why are you holding back? You're either in this or you're not. Don't waste my time."

I have to give the girl credit—she doesn't play games. It was comforting to know from the start that Alissa wanted a relationship. I mean, she had waited two years, but hearts change. I hadn't known what to expect.

Surreality

Alissa's homecoming over Christmas sealed the deal.

Our first date since 2010.

I nearly had a heart attack pulling up to her house.

Two years.

Two years and I was finally here.

Now that I had developed my relationship with God and committed to making him the Lord of my life, I was now free to pursue the woman of my dreams.

When Alissa opened the front door, I felt the light of heaven shining on my face.

My angel without wings.

Alissa approached me and threw her arms around my neck.

I could have died at that moment and been perfectly satisfied.

It was like no time had even passed.

We spent the next two weeks celebrating together and with our families, as well as processing the past and trying to figure out our future.

Then, on New Year's Day, 2013, I finally asked Alissa to be my girlfriend.

Our celebration continued through the weekend as Alissa and I prepared for the journey ahead.

One thing we knew for sure—this was not the finish line but simply the starting gate.

Although we were now walking together, we were walking right up the base of another mountain.

Our climb up the mountain of commitment together could finally begin ...

101 Questions

For many, long distance can be the death of a dating relationship. Thankfully, we didn't really mind. In fact, talking on the phone long distance was a significant improvement from our previous season of complete silence. I would argue that our season of long-distance dating may have been one of God's greatest blessings to us.

Not only did long-distance dating keep us pure and prevent us from physically touching each other, it also forced us to develop our communication skills. The option of sitting around idly for hours watching movies together was off the table. Instead we spent hours each day getting to know each other, asking difficult questions, and discussing marriage books that we decided to read together.

Before contacting Alissa in December, I purchased a book called, *101 Questions to Ask before Getting Engaged.* Almost nightly, we opened this book to discuss a question. There were some hard-hitters, mind you. Everything from "What's your biggest regret" to "Divulge the entirety of your medical history."

The topic for tonight's discussion was "What loss have you yet to mourn?"

Ladies first!

Alissa's answer was quick. She felt that she had successfully dealt with all the losses in her life, including the relatively recent death of her grandfather.

I, on the other hand, had some skeletons in my closet that surprised even me when they came crawling out. While processing this question with Alissa, I discovered that I had yet to forgive Joseph or grieve the last two years of my commitment journey.

Out of all the positive things that came from our relationship, why did I need to forgive Joseph?

The commitment journey with Joseph was the best thing that could have happened for my faith, family, relationship with Alissa, career, and development as a man.

Honestly, before this journey I was a mess. I suffered from people pleasing, addiction, a noncommittal spirit, selfishness, immaturity, and a lot of other things. I'm not saying that this journey had made me a perfect person, but I was definitely a long way from where I started.

There were so many good things that came from this journey, but I still held some ugly emotions and thoughts about Joseph and the journey, which I now faced with Alissa on the phone.

What atrocities had this man committed against me that warranted forgiveness?

The two-year commitment journey, though beneficial, was the most painful experience of my life. There were times when I loved the journey and other times when I absolutely hated Joseph, hated the journey, and would have rather eaten a bullet than finish the two years.

There were times when I did not trust Joseph, times when I thought I was being lied to, manipulated, and strung along by false hope. There were many times when I wanted to quit and actually cried out to God with tears streaming down my face for him to take me away from this situation. I begged God to remove Joseph from my life; I begged God to provide the peace I needed to leave the commitment journey. There were even times when I literally wanted to die.

I hated the awkwardness I experienced with my parents. My relationship with Joseph was a serious source of pain for them, especially my dad, who felt that he was being replaced by Joseph as my father figure, which couldn't have been further from the truth.

In fact, it was Joseph who encouraged me to forgive my dad for his affair and spend time working to reconcile our relationship.

I hated having to defend my relationship with Joseph to others, which admittedly looked extremely strange from the outside.

I also hated wearing a commitment ring. I hated having to explain why I was wearing a ring on my wedding ring finger when I wasn't married. The explanation of "I'm learning to commit so I can one day commit in marriage" made sense, but it resulted in some of the most uncomfortable conversations.

The girls at church literally nicknamed me, "The Betrothed One."

Worst of all, I hated feeling like I was hurting Alissa. There were even times when I actually knew she was in pain but couldn't contact her.

I remember receiving notice one summer during our two years of separation that Alissa had been in a high-speed car accident on the freeway, resulting in her hospitalization. I so badly wanted to call and comfort her, but I was instead convicted by my commitment to remain silent and trust that God would take care of her.

I needed to mourn the loss of my Friday nights and the relationships that were strained because of them. My relationship with my best friend, Steve, was extremely strained during this time. I also missed out on a lot of opportunities to develop other relationships besides the one with my mentor.

I had never grieved those losses, but I have since learned that commitments carry inevitable losses. You cannot retain your current lifestyle and complete your commitment journey. Commitment means change.

Processing all of these things gave me closure and a proper perspective on the situation.

I did decide to forgive Joseph.

In fact, I am downright thankful for him. Besides Jesus, Joseph was the greatest influence in my life that brought me closer to God. Without our journey together, only God knows where I would be, but I guarantee it wouldn't be with Alissa, working my current job, being free from debt, or being reconciled to my family.

The benefits far outweighed the cost. In the end, I am eternally grateful for Joseph and the commitment journey.

CHAPTER 13

MY THAI VALENTINE

My first trip to visit Alissa in Southern California after our reunion occurred over Valentine's Day weekend. After I arrived in Orange County on Saturday morning, Alissa and I spent most of our day talking poolside at her friend Kathy's house where I would stay for the weekend. It was a beautiful February day, warm enough to sit in the sun but cool enough to stay out of the pool.

While we were lounging on Kathy's comfortable patio furniture, Alissa asked if I wanted something to drink.

Her trip took longer than usual, so I capitalized on the opportunity and made dinner reservations for our Valentine's Day celebration. I wanted Alissa to have a new experience and quickly remembered that she had never tried Thai food before. This idea worked out well, since I had a gift pack for Alissa that included a Thai elephant souvenir I had bought for her two years ago while traveling in Thailand.

After I locked in our reservations at Silk Thai, Alissa came back outside with our beverages and we continued soaking up the sun and enjoying the cool coastal breeze.

Alissa eventually announced that she had a surprise for me.

Interestingly enough, Alissa surprised me with a professional Thai massage as my Valentine's Day gift. We both received hour-long Thai massages before our Thai dinner. Only God could have planned such a beautifully themed event.

Changes

The next day began as planned. I woke up to my devotional time with God as I prepared for another day with the girl of my dreams. We had plans to attend church, grab lunch, and possibly visit the beach.

Before Alissa arrived for breakfast, my devotional encouraged me to view unexpected changes as divine interruptions. It also said to trust that God will use unforeseen circumstances to grow, stretch, and bless those willing to submit to his plans. I thought that was a strange message considering that Alissa and I had plans for the day that would glorify him. I mean, we were planning on attending church together; why would God be preparing me to change that?

Sure enough, I received a text from Alissa that morning informing me that her stomach was really upset and that she didn't feel well enough to do much more than lounge around the house all day.

Thinking that I knew what God had in store, I began to excitedly anticipate a lazy day with my girl. The possibilities were looking pretty choice: Maybe some cuddling on the couch, movie watching, ice cream, and possibly even a nap? This was about to be an awesome day.

Alissa eventually arrived, and we began to make breakfast together. While waiting for her coffee, Alissa received a phone call.

It was her sister, Janae.

Crying could be heard from the other end of the phone as Janae informed Alissa that their grandmother had just died. Devastated, Alissa ended the phone call.

Immediately afterward, we started the six-hour drive back home to Pleasanton to be with her family.

I often underestimate God. My assumptions about his plans are rarely correct. Just when I think I've figured him out he throws me a curveball.

Even in these sad circumstances, I was looking forward to our road trip together. I enjoyed spending quality time talking with Alissa, and this six-hour drive would provide plenty of that.

We covered almost every topic imaginable—her grandmother; our hopes, fears, failures, past relationships, wounds, and scars; Jesus; our faith walk; our testimonies; and many others. Things were going really well. It was a smooth ride with fun conversation.

Then, somewhere along Interstate-5, Alissa mentioned a letter I had sent her nine months prior. She asked me if I felt comfortable discussing the contents of the letter, which completely caught me off guard. Granted, I had known this conversation would come up eventually, but I wasn't prepared to discuss it at this moment. I needed a little time to gather my thoughts. I desperately needed the Holy Spirit to give me the right words to explain the letter. I needed God's peace to fill my heart before diving into this difficult topic.

The Thorn in My Flesh

It was in December 2010 that I made a life-altering discovery while in the shower. Shocked, confused, and scared, I made an appointment to see my doctor.

A brief examination confirmed my greatest fear.

Alissa needed to know.

Unfortunately, at this point in our relationship we were only connecting on the phone once a month, and the next time I was scheduled to speak with Alissa was on Christmas.

There was no way that I was going to ruin her Christmas with this news. If ever there was a bad time, Christmas was it.

I reasoned that there was no rush to tell Alissa about my diagnosis during our holiday together. The news would have to wait until our monthly conversation in January.

The conversation never came.

On January 4, 2011, Alissa and I broke up so that I could complete my two-year commitment journey.

The decision not to tell Alissa ate away at me for sixteen months. I hated myself for not telling her about my diagnosis. The guilt was too much to bear.

There was no way that I could allow Alissa to spend another eight months waiting for me without hearing the news.

She deserved to know.

She had a decision to make.

I remember the night like it was yesterday. In my prayer closet on knees and elbows I cried out to the Lord for help. "I can't take this anymore, Lord! I can't do this; I need you, Jesus! Please, Father, I need your wisdom. What should I do? Should I tell her now or wait until December? What is the right thing to do?"

What happened next is an anomaly.

I don't want to mislead anyone into thinking that I'm some super-spiritual dude who hears the voice of God on a regular basis, but in my prayer closet, Jesus spoke to me clearer than ever before.

"Who am I?" God said.

"What?" I responded.

Usually when I pray, I'm not expecting to hear an immediate response, but the Lord repeated, "Who am I, Matt?"

I thought about this for a moment until his words filled my mind.

"I am the truth."

Silent pause ...

He continued, "I am the truth, and the truth will set you free" (John 8:32).

It made perfect sense. Alissa needed to know the truth. Then and only then would I experience freedom.

There have only been a handful of times in my life that I have heard God speak so clearly.

"Thank you, Lord!" I exploded.

Praises and thanksgiving filled my closet as his words continued to fill my mind. "I am the truth, and the truth will set you free."

As I began to contemplate the ramifications of this concept, God's promise from the airplane prophecy resurfaced. God had prepared me for this exact moment when he sent a prophet to me on an airplane who provided a promise from God about my relationship with Alissa. Then it hit me. God is responsible for the outcome; I am responsible for obedience. It was my responsibility to be truthful; it was God's responsibility to fulfill his promise.

God had known that I would be in this situation. He had known exactly what I needed and provided it well in advance. If I was going to have a testimony, I would have to endure a test. This was certainly a test.

It was time to tell Alissa the truth and trust God with the outcome. By my telling Alissa about my diagnosis, the future of our relationship would be completely in God's hands.

I confidently climbed out of my prayer closet to tackle the task of writing Alissa the most painful letter I had ever composed.

After a few weeks, many drafts, and continual prayer, I was ready to send the letter:

Alissa,

Please forgive me for prematurely breaking our silence; however, there is an urgent matter that must be addressed. Since the December of 2010 I have been suffering in silence regarding the discovery of a certain "thorn in my flesh." Initially I was encouraged to conceal this information, as the potentiality existed that my immune system would eventually heal itself. However, I can no longer keep quiet in good conscience. I have been battling through this decision for months and have finally found peace regarding the appropriate course of action.

Before I begin, I ask that you would please keep this confidential, as my family does not know about my current health condition. While weighing the options of this decision, I was forced to ask the clichéd yet convicting question, "What would Jesus do?" In my prayer closet this evening amidst my many anxieties, I was reminded of our Savior's identity. Jesus is the truth, and the truth will set us both free. I have been in bondage to this truth for the past sixteen months, and I can no longer remain silent.

Last December, as previously stated, I literally discovered a thorn in my flesh—something that I must deal with for the rest of my life. I discovered this thorn right before the Christmas that we spent together. Upon hearing this news my heart shattered; I was honestly terrified and completely confused, not knowing what to do with this information. The shock was paralyzing, and I chose to suppress the reality instead of gathering the courage and strength to reveal this news to you. Although this does not excuse my delayed disclosure, I sincerely apologize.

I was officially diagnosed with the human papillomavirus on December 15, 2010. During my freshmen year of college I recall seeing a small bump that eventually disappeared. I did not have any further signs or symptoms for four years until another small bump revealed itself in early December 2010. I went to the doctor, and he confirmed that I had HPV. It doesn't hurt, and I barely notice it, but it's there and it's contagious. There is no cure for the human papillomavirus, although as previously stated the potentiality exists for my immune system to defeat this virus. However, there is also a chance that this virus will remain with me for the rest of my life. Despite the fact that there is a vaccine available (Gardasil) to prevent someone from contracting this virus, I cannot ask you to walk this journey with me. I can only provide you with the information necessary for you to make an informed decision.

You need to think very seriously about your future, Alissa. This is your life and your health. The reason I am telling you now is to protect your heart and mind as you process through this information and the decision at hand. I did not want the emotionality of our reunion in December and the excitement of the Christmas season or family pressure to cloud your judgment. I ask that you will pray about this and seriously count the cost of your decision. Please, do not worry about me; whatever choice you make, I will understand. Through this journey, God has helped me to discover the peace that surpasses all understanding; in other words, "it is well with my soul."

This is my fault, Alissa, a consequence of my past sin, and I cannot ask you to endure this with me. I would never forgive myself for making you feel obligated or trapping you into a relationship with me, which is why I could not wait until December to inform you about this. My hope is that telling you now will provide enough time for you to process this decision thoroughly. I will happily support any decision you make, whether you decide to walk away or join me in this journey.

My covenant ends in December; however, there is obviously no time restraint to your decision-making process. Please take as much time as needed to pray, fast, consult with your doctor, and research this virus before making a decision. All that I ask is that you would eventually inform me of your decision so that I can either move forward with you or move on without you. If you make a decision before December, feel free to e-mail me, but understand that I must complete this covenant before engaging in further conversation. However, if your decision happens after December, I will gladly speak with you then.

As I previously stated, your continuance in this journey is your choice alone, and I will wholeheartedly support your decision. You deserve the best, Alissa. Please never settle for anything less than God's best. No matter what happens, I will always be your brother in Christ Jesus and will continue to rejoice in the promise that one day God will make all things new and we will celebrate this together in our heavenly bodies! Praise Jesus!

Eternally,
Your brother in Christ,
MJ

Before the diagnosis, I was certain that Alissa would wait for me to finish my commitment journey. After my initial visit to the doctor, I wasn't so sure. Could God really work a miracle in my body to heal me or in Alissa's heart to accept me as I am?

I didn't know.

What I did know was this: the *Planet Earth* scene from 2008 with the underwater crabs finally made sense. This was not a warning, but a prophecy. God was trying to prepare my heart when he showed me those crabs. It was then revealed to me that repentance doesn't always cancel our consequences. Our sins will always be forgiven by God, but they often result in natural repercussions.

Even after this revelation there were times when I was mad at God about my diagnosis—not because it affected me but because it would affect her.

I understood the law of the harvest, "You reap what you sow." I had this coming. I wasn't mad at God for the emotional and psychological pain I was experiencing. I was mad at God for allowing his daughter to experience this potential pain on my behalf.

Alissa didn't deserve this.

She was saving herself for marriage. She was keeping herself pure.

Why would God want his daughter to end up with someone in my condition?

It wasn't fair.

She didn't sow this, I did.

I quickly learned that our sin doesn't affect just us; it harms those that we love as well. Ask any child of divorced parents, and they will tell you.

I mailed the letter in the beginning of May after a family trip to Costa Rica. I'm not exactly sure what I expected in return, but I didn't expect this ...

A Toilsome Trimester

The month of May passed without any confirmation that Alissa had either received or read my letter.

Surely she would respond in June.

I heard nothing.

There was no way that it would take two months to respond. July would be the month that I heard back from Alissa.

Not a word.

I really thought that I would have heard something by July. Even bad news would have been better than no news. The silence was deafening. I started to believe that she had no intention of responding to my letter at all.

Then, on August 5, 2012, I received an e-mail from Alissa titled, "I hope you get this."

Matthew,

Thank you for your letter. I'm sure it wasn't easy to reveal this sensitive information to me. I want you to know that I've taken the last few months to seek wise counsel and the Lord's wisdom about how to move forward. There's so much on my heart that I want to share with you, but have been convicted to the truth that now is not the appropriate time to do so. As your sister in the Lord, I am honored that you trusted me with such information and am glad that I can be praying about this specifically. However, as a woman who continues to have strong feelings for you and a desire to be in your life as more than a friend, I have to be honest in saying that I wish you had told me either when you were first diagnosed or that you would have waited until we potentially ventured into a dating relationship again. Reason being, because those would be the only times that I would have any sort of right to know this kind of personal information about you. But unfortunately, right now, I don't have that right.

This is the whole reason why we went our separate ways. The covenant you made to the Lord disabled you from having the right to know anything about me and my life, or my right to know anything about you and yours. The news of your condition isn't and won't be the only serious issue that we'd have to face as a couple. Lord knows I have my own burdens from the past to share at some point with the man I'm committed to. I really do hope you have found relief in telling me, but I also can't help but feel frustrated with your choice in timing and the manner in which you relayed this weighty information. Put yourself in my shoes. Would you have really wanted me to tell you something so serious as this through an e-mail and at a time when you couldn't call me with any questions that may have arisen?

Please hear me when I say that I understand why you thought waiting to tell me until December wouldn't have been fair or right, that you wanted to give me time to process and pray before then. I believe you made that decision because you thought it was the best thing for both of us, that your motives were of pure and good nature. I don't for a second doubt the sincerity behind your words or the implications behind the letter. Again, I just don't agree with the timing. I've tried my best to respect the promise you made to the Lord by not reaching out to you, even when things came up that I thought you should know about. In those times, God always reminded me that he knew all that was going to happen to us during this season, yet he still called us to obey. So what I'm trying to say is as much as I would love to sit down with you and talk about the contents of your letter, I won't be comfortable doing so unless it's in the context of a dating relationship.

I hope you understand what I'm trying to say in all of this. I'm honestly sorry if it at all feels cold. It's taken me days to formulate any words to describe the many thoughts running through my mind, and yet still be sensitive and respectful to where you're coming from and what you've been going through. I continue to care for you deeply, Matthew. And I only hope for God's will and power and best to reign in your life, with or without me.

Praying for you always,
Alissa

These were the last words I would receive from her until December.

During our first few phone calls in December, Alissa eluded to the letters, but the conversation never fully materialized. For me, it felt like a ticking time bomb. When would she want to talk about the letter? Surely she had an opinion.

Day after day passed, but the conversation never occurred.

It wasn't until the six-hour road trip from Costa Mesa to Pleasanton that we broached the topic.

I told her everything from the beginning. The moment I began to speak I realized that God was answering my prayer. My anxiety was gone, the fear was gone, and my worries were gone. I was able to speak confidently and clearly everything I had hoped to say. As promised, the Lord once again gave me the peace that surpasses all understanding. He protected my heart and my speech during our conversation and prepared Alissa's heart for this conversation, which was something that I had been praying about for the last two years.

When I was done speaking, I waited in silence for Alissa to respond.

Her brief milliseconds of silence felt like an eternity.

Before responding, Alissa took a deep breath.

Preparing for the worst, I gripped the wheel with white knuckles.

An Unexpected Response

Are you kidding me? I thought to myself as I listened to her reply.

"Never once did I ever consider leaving you, Matthew … If anything, it made me love you more."

I'm dreaming. This has to be a dream.

I told a virgin that I have a sexually transmitted disease, and it made her love me more?

Ashton Kutcher was nowhere to be found.

I wasn't being Punk'd.

This was the tangible grace of God unfolding before my eyes. Unmerited, undeserved favor.

This should have been a deal breaker.

It would have been a deal breaker had God not been graciously preparing Alissa's heart for this conversation.

The only thing I can say is grace. God's grace. Alissa saved her virginity for marriage while I carelessly cast mine away in high school with consequences.

Trust me—I'm right there with you; this doesn't seem fair.

How can someone with such a horrific past claim that his sins are gone, that his past has been erased and is no longer relevant? How can someone get away from his past sins scot-free? Where is the justice in that?

It doesn't really seem fair that people can walk free with no penalty, but our God isn't fair.

If God were fair, we would all die in our sins because "the penalty for sin is death" (Romans 6:23) and "all have sinned and have fallen short of the glory of God" (Romans 3:23).

If God were fair, we would all be dead and suffering in hell.

Life is not fair because God is not fair, but God is just.

He does not pardon sin either.

As a just judge, God cannot excuse sin or turn a blind eye as though it never happened.

Sin must be punished, atoned for.

There is a bill to be paid, and our sin is costly.

There are no freebies with God.

In God's economy, all debts must be paid in full.

Why am I confident that my sexual sins from the past were paid for? Jesus nailed them to the cross. He nailed them to the cross with the rest of my sins and the sins of the entire world.

My sins were washed clean in an ocean of God's grace. "It is by grace you have been saved through faith, and this is not of yourself, it is the gift of God, not by works so that no one can boast" (Ephesians 2:8–9).

Maybe that's why I had yet to mourn that loss, because Jesus had already redeemed it. In his eyes I was a virgin.

How crazy is that?

I guess *crazy* is the wrong word; it's more scandalous really.

I mean, my past is littered with broken hearts, broken promises, lies, abuse, addiction, impurity, and a whole laundry list of sin, but God no longer sees my sin. He sees the righteousness of his son Jesus in me.

As my propitiation, Jesus substituted himself for me in the judgment seat. My sin accrued the death penalty, but Jesus stood in the gallows in my place; Jesus took the cross for my sins.

It should have been me under the wrath of God.

It should have been I who was fiercely flogged, I who was stripped naked and shamefully exposed to the watching world.

It should have been I who was mercilessly beaten until my face no longer resembled the likeness of man.

I should have been the one who was cursed at, spat upon, and ridiculed.

It should have been my beard that was ripped off my face, my crown of thorns piercing my scalp until the blood seeped in my eyes.

I should have been scourged by a whip that was embedded with glass, bones, and other shrapnel.

My skin should have been torn from its flesh by the cat o' nine tails that would often break and dislodge the ribs of those afflicted by this torture device.

I should have carried my own cross up the mountain of the skull. It should have been my blood that covered the city streets as I fell in the dirt.

That one-hundred-pound crucifix should have fallen on my back as I lay on the ground.

It should have been my hands and feet that were pierced by the railroad-spike-sized nails.

It should have been my body that hung from the cross.

I should have struggled for each and every breath as my lungs were constantly threatened by suffocation and asphyxiation.

It should have been my lips that drank the bitter gall fed to me by my persecutors.

It should have been my heart sack that was punctured by that Roman spear so that blood and water flowed from my side.

It should have been me, but it was Jesus.

Scandalous.

Absolutely scandalous.

The fact that a perfectly innocent man, a man who walked the earth for thirty-three years without ever breaking any law or thinking any negative, hurtful, lustful, or untruthful thoughts, would willingly take my place to cancel my sin debt.

How scandalous it was for Jesus Christ, in all of his purity, righteousness, holiness, and perfection to trade places with a dirty, guilty, condemned sinner.

For him to look at me and say, "I find no fault in you; enter my holy kingdom," is a scandal.

How can this be?

How can a just God allow a sinner such as myself to be considered pure, clean, perfect, and without spot or blemish?

Nothing but the blood of Jesus can explain such a scandal.

The price for my sin was death, and it was paid in full.

Jesus sat under the fierce, relentless wrath of his Father so that I wouldn't have to. He did that for me, and you, and the entire world. "For God so loved the world, that he gave his one and only son, that whoever believes in him shall not perish, but have eternal life" (John 3:16).

This God man, Jesus, was the payment for the sins of the world to those who believe.

God's wrath was satisfied by Jesus's death on the cross.

The bill for our sins was completely paid in full. Jesus died to foot the bill.

Jesus's blood wiped out all outstanding charges on his Father's ledger.

God's budget was perfectly balanced, his checkbook reconciled.

The payment was received, and the Father was pleased.

I love the second half of Romans 6:23, "The penalty for sin is death, *but*, the gift of God is eternal life in Christ Jesus."

Even Sir Mix-a-Lot would say that is a big "but."

Our works have earned us death, but God's work gifts us with life.

Praise God that the verse doesn't read, "The penalty for sin is death, and if you do enough good works, pray long enough, attend church enough, give enough money, punish yourself enough, feel guilty for long enough, *then* you will receive eternal life."

Religion 101 says, "Work hard and God will pay you the wages that you earned from all your religious efforts," but on the cross, Jesus said, "It is finished!"

In other words, Jesus said, "I'm tired of religion. I've done everything that needs to be done. Take this gift; it's free, doesn't cost you a thing, but it cost me everything; you are welcome."

In the words of my favorite Elvina Hall hymn, "Jesus paid it all, all to him I owe. Sin had left a crimson stain, He washed it white as snow."

This is our God.

He has done it all for us.

All we have to do is say thank you.

How do we say thank you?

With our lives.

We follow the way that Jesus lived, we abide by the rules he lovingly established, and we love God and love others.

It's really that simple.

We don't do anything to get into heaven; we do everything he wants us to because we are already going to heaven.

We say thank you to Jesus with our lives.

Icing on the Cake

As if I didn't already have enough reasons to thank God, he surprised me again. After I sent my letter to Alissa in May 2012, a man named K. P. Yohannan visited my church in Livermore.

At the end of his presentation about his nonprofit organization Gospel for Asia, which provides food, shelter, education, and the gospel to orphans in India, he invited anyone needing a healing miracle to receive prayer. I walked up to the stage, and K. P. and my pastor Steve prayed over me. Since that time I have yet to experience another HPV outbreak. No more doctor visits, no painful surgeries, nothing. God answered our prayers, and I've been healed ever since.

God's grace is incredible. It was by his grace that he healed me. Even if God hadn't healed me, his grace would have sustained me through the suffering.

God is so good, full of grace and mercy. We deserve death because of our sins, but God gives grace, free and amazing grace, to those who love him. Hallelujah!

Praise God if he heals you, and praise God if he doesn't. His grace is sufficient for all, no matter the circumstance.

Mystery Vacation

In January, after our commitment ended, Joseph mentioned that he wanted to take me and Alissa on a trip to celebrate our journey, and knowing how much I loved and treasured Thailand, Joseph offered to take us there. My obedience during the commitment journey was already turning out as a blessing for me and Alissa.

One thing I came to discover about Joseph was that he was a man of action. When he said that something was going to happen, he followed through without any reminders. However, it was now April, and three months had gone by without Joseph making any reservations for our trip.

Back in February, Joseph had told me that he was preparing for retirement. When I think of retirement, my mind goes to summers on the sand and winters on the slopes … but not Joseph. He was preparing to transition into another employment position. I guess after working for thirty-plus years the guy didn't know what else to do with himself. This large life transition could have explained Joseph's delay in planning our summer vacation.

In early May I asked Joseph if he still planned on taking the trip to Thailand. Alissa needed to request time off from work, so I needed to know. He told me to trust God and practice patience.

Really? Trust and patience; that's all you have for me?

Midway through May, Joseph was offered a job across the continent. That same week Joseph called me to his home to talk. He had a mischievous look on his face. I knew something was up. He asked me to sit down as he began to address the July Thai trip. He said that he needed more time to situate himself now that he would be moving across the continent, and he would have to postpone the Thailand trip.

He then said, "You know, I've been thinking a lot about this trip. I've spent a lot of time seeking God through prayer and examining the significance of this trip. I think we can do better."

"Better? What do you mean by better?" I asked.

"Well, there isn't a whole lot of meaning in the July trip. We can do better," Joseph said plainly.

I was honestly lost trying to figure out what all this "better" talk was about.

Joseph continued, "We'll still go on a trip in July—trust me about that—but let's wait on Thailand until November."

Seeing my confused and disappointed face, Joseph again repeated, "We can go on another trip for the Fourth of July holiday, but in November we will fly Alissa to Thailand, where you can propose to her. That way there will be more meaning to the trip."

Propose to her? I couldn't believe what I was hearing! Throughout our entire commitment journey I had yet to hear Joseph support my desire to marry Alissa, and now here he was planning my proposal. I was blown away. I'd never actually believed that he wanted me to get married despite all the talk about "preparing me for the next commitment."

Wow. A Thai proposal! That would be amazing! We'd started our commitment journey in Thailand; it was only fitting that I start my new commitment journey with Alissa in Thailand as well.

The following Friday, Joseph and I went to the gym as usual and had Panda Express before going to see a movie. In line at the Panda Express, Joseph and I discussed our Fourth of July plans. Although I didn't yet know where we were going, I told Alissa to ask for the week of the Fourth off for a mystery vacation.

Joseph asked if I would want to take Alissa to Canada for the Fourth of July. I'd always wanted to visit Canada, and I was sure that Alissa would love the beautiful snowcapped mountains, glacier-filled water, hiking, biking, fresh fish eating, and bear sighting. It sounded like the perfect vacation.

As we were discussing the options of the trip, it dawned on me that I could turn this awesome trip into the adventure of a lifetime. Previously in the day, Joseph had me research how to ship his Jaguar to Canada, and it hit me. Alissa and I could drive his car to Canada for the most epic road trip of all time.

Joseph was surprised that I offered to provide him with personal car-delivery service and agreed to let me drive. I then spent the night researching how long it would take, where I would stop, how much it would cost, etc.

I was excited about my cross-country adventure with Alissa. We loved long drives together. I mean, in reality, our only experience was driving from her home in Costa Mesa back up to Northern California, but still, it was a memorable and enjoyable six hours in the car together. This of course paled in comparison to the fifty-six-hour drive to Canada, but we could totally do it.

Full of excitement, I texted Alissa:

Me: (April 26, 2013) Are you ready to have the adventure of a lifetime?

Liss: As long as it's with you

Insert "Awwws" here. Yeah, she's cute.

Me: Our July trip just got so much more exciting …

Liss: Is it a bad time to mention that if this is a vacation with Joseph, that I'm not sure I'd be down for that just yet?

Me: lol you need to learn to trust me.

Yes, I actually said "lol."

And then my heart completely deflated.

Here I am, excited about this amazing adventure, and Alissa tells me that she doesn't want to go if Joseph is going.

Panic ensues.

I just told Alissa to trust me, yet I was still planning a vacation that went against her one and only qualifier for our trip. She was never going to trust me again. I couldn't do this to her. Not only that, what the heck was I going to tell Joseph? "Sorry, Joseph, Alissa doesn't want to go on a vacation with you"?

I found myself in quite the conundrum on Friday night. This was definitely the proverbial rock-and-a-hard-place situation.

"Lord, deliver me from this," I prayed in desperation as I thought about the implications of Alissa's last text. This was going to create havoc in my relationships with both Joseph and Alissa. It was a lose-lose situation.

Joseph and I headed to the movie after our Panda Express conversation. Neither Joseph nor Alissa had any idea about the turmoil I was experiencing. I felt alone. Continuing to cry out to God in prayer, I asked for a ladder to lift me out of this pit. How could I make it out of there without hurting anyone's feelings or betraying anyone's trust? *Lord, only you can make this happen; please work a miracle.*

I have no idea what movie we watched that night. All I could think about was texting Alissa to trust me and how she would never trust me again if I brought her to Canada. On the flip side, I couldn't stop thinking about the arguments I would have with Joseph about Alissa not wanting to spend time with him. Two people I cared about would both be hurt by this situation. Jesus, help me!

I went to bed with terrible anxiety and worry on my mind. Before lying down to sleep I once again lifted up my concerns to the Lord and asked for his mercy and grace. Thankfully, he gave me peace and the ability to fall asleep.

The next morning Joseph and I had breakfast at his house and talked about the cross-country car conversation. Joseph said, "I'm not sure how good I feel about you and Alissa driving all that way by yourselves with no accountability. If anything happens to you guys—whether you get hurt, in an accident, or mess up sexually—I won't be able to forgive myself." I tried my best to convince him that he had nothing to worry about, and he quickly dropped the conversation.

Later in the morning when I was doing some chores around the house, Joseph asked a question that I will never forget. "If you and Alissa don't want to go to Canada for the Fourth of July, is there anywhere else that you would like to go?"

Seriously? Like, you're actually asking me this question right now? I couldn't believe my ears. Just like that, God provided my ladder. "Well, my aunt and uncle invited me to visit them at their beach house in Florida for the Fourth, but I didn't want to say anything because we already had Canada plans."

"Is that what you want to do?" Joseph asked. "It's honestly fine with me if you don't come to Canada; I just want you guys to have a good time without all the stress of having to drive up there."

"Well, if you don't mind … yeah, that would be really fun to visit my family in Florida."

"Done. Call the airline now, and I'll book your tickets."

My prayers were answered. There was no prompting or prying, uncomfortable conversation, or confrontation. Jesus just answered my prayer perfectly.

Traveling Blind

My favorite part of our trip to Florida was the mystery of it all. At the very beginning of our relationship, Alissa told me that it was impossible to surprise her. Accepting her challenge I made it my mission to constantly find ways to surprise Alissa.

She literally had no idea where we were going when we boarded our plane from San Francisco to Houston. It wasn't until two o'clock in the morning at the Houston terminal when Alissa discovered that we were headed to her mother's hometown in Pensacola, Florida. Alissa was ecstatic.

Actually, she had motion sickness.

No, seriously.

I'd never heard anyone throw up so loudly in my life. I was probably thirty yards from the women's bathroom, and I could still hear the echoes ring through the terminal.

Déjà Vu II

As I began my morning Bible study in my uncle's beautiful beachfront condo, it hit me that today was the Fourth of July. Not only that, but I was in Florida with the girl of my dreams, on a beach, with family that I loved and plans to watch fireworks.

The scene looked all too familiar.

Just three years ago, Alissa and I spent our last Fourth of July together on a beach with family and fireworks. Only last time it was our last time together before having to break up. This time was different. This time was miraculous. After our spending two years apart, God redeemed our

Fourth of July and allowed us to experience the blessing of our obedience and commitment. It was incredible to see God bring everything full circle and make it even more beautiful than before.

The Cocoon and the Christ

Of all the diseases in the world, the "itis" is by far my favorite. Most often experienced in the southern parts of America, the itis can be identified as a comatose state of food euphoria. Common side effects of the itis are laziness, lethargy, stomach pain, cramping, bloating, long naps, and snoring.

Lying on my uncle's couch after our breakfast at Waffle House, Alabama BBQ for lunch, and alligator-on-a-stick with a giant turkey leg and a Sonics milkshake for dinner/dessert, the itis was in full effect. As I lay there in my comatose state, I thought about my favorite children's book by Eric Carle, *The Very Hungry Caterpillar.*

Page after page we follow the very hungry caterpillar on a journey through all the food he consumed in ever-increasing quantities until, like me, he ended up in a food-induced coma. Although my coma occurred on a couch and his in a cocoon, our stories are quite similar.

The very hungry caterpillar had to allow his old life of crawling on the ground to die before he was transformed into a beautiful butterfly. What went into the cocoon was introduced to a transformational process that required a unique waiting period.

Also like the cocoon, Jesus had to enter a cave for three days before experiencing his transformation. The great king of heaven had to die to his kingly nature to become a servant on earth who was then murdered on a cross and buried in a cave. Three days later Jesus was resurrected to new life. Like the caterpillar, Jesus was clothed in a resurrected body, more glorious than before.

Both Jesus and the caterpillar rose from their cocoons with new abilities. The caterpillar received wings, while Jesus received a glorified body that reigned victorious over death, ushering in new life to all who are willing to undergo the same transformation. Jesus makes new life available to all who are willing to die to their old self, receive the Holy Spirit, and allow God to make them new creations in Christ.

Consistent with all of these examples, Alissa and I had our own cocoon/ cave to enter. Only by allowing our original relationship to die, could God transform and resurrect a more beautiful, impactful, meaningful, and God-glorifying relationship. This trip to Florida was no different. Our Fourth of July 2010 had to die so that our resurrected Fourth of July in 2013 could speak to us about God's faithfulness, redemption, and transformational power.

CLIMBING YOUR OWN MOUNT EVEREST

Mountaintop Experience

Throughout the Bible, mountains were places where people went to meet with God. It was on mountains where people felt "close" to God. His presence was often manifested on mountains. From Abraham to Jesus, many of the most notable Bible characters experienced God on a mountain.

Moses first met God on Mount Horeb through the famous burning bush. Moses then spent forty days and forty nights with God on Mount Sinai before receiving the Ten Commandments.

Abraham encountered God on Mount Moriah, where he was commanded to offer his son Isaac as a sacrifice. Thankfully, God stopped Abraham before he killed his son and provided a ram for slaughter instead. This of course foreshadowed the sacrificial death of God's son, which would happen on that same mountain.

Mountains are significant when it comes to connecting with God.

Jesus knew this and was found many times throughout his ministry connecting with God and teaching others while on mountains.

Before selecting his twelve disciples, Jesus spent an entire evening on a mountain praying to God the Father. Jesus was transfigured before Peter, James, and John on Mount Tabor. One of Jesus's most famous teachings was even titled the Sermon on the Mount. It was on the Mount of Olives where Jesus cried out to his Father about his impending crucifixion, which occurred the following morning on Abraham and Isaac's Mount Moriah.

Following the pattern of the Bible, if you want to experience God, climb a mountain. Whether you literally go climb Mount Everest in Nepal or choose to pursue that Everest-sized, God-given dream in your heart, God will meet you on the mountain. Some of you have known about your mountain for years, while others are only now thinking that God has more in store for your lives, but the truth remains the same—each of us has a mountain to climb.

So, What is Your Mountain?

What is God asking you to do in order to fulfill his purpose for your life?

We each have a journey to walk, a mountain to climb, but as with any worthwhile endeavor, your "Mount Everest" begins with a commitment. You may be reading this as a high school student looking to pursue a college degree, a single individual interested in marriage, someone desiring to enter full-time ministry in the church or mission field, an entrepreneur desiring to begin a business, a couple looking to start a family, or someone seeking general purpose and direction in life. Some reading this book may want to commit to overcome an addiction, heal a broken relationship, or find answers to life's toughest questions about God, to discover his purpose for your life, but in any case, your journey begins with a commitment. "Commit thy way unto the Lord, trust also in him, and he shall bring it to pass" (Psalm 37:5, KJV).

To begin a commitment journey, you must be willing to consecrate yourself. In other words, you must dedicate yourself to this special purpose. Consecration requires that you count the cost of your commitment with the following questions:

Are you willing to sacrifice your time, money, and energy to completely pour yourself into this journey? Will you invest yourself knowing that temptation, trials, pain, exhaustion, and failure will come? Are you prepared for persecution, setbacks, and uncertainty? Are you prepared to fall down, scrape your knee, sweat, bleed, and cry? Are you ready to throw away your map, GPS, and compass to be completely reliant on

God's presence, direction, provision, comfort, wisdom, companionship, and purpose?

Even if you cannot answer yes to all of these questions, but you are willing to take an initial step of faith and ask God for help, then you are ready to begin your journey. God compares us to clay for a reason; if we will submit our lives into his hands, he will mold us into the vessel that he will use for his glory. He truly does all the hard work.

Lose Some Weight

That's right, lose some weight! The lighter you are, the easier your climb will be, so shed some pounds.

Start with your backpack.

Whether you are climbing a mountain or walking through the supermarket, everyone carries a backpack.

The backpack I'm talking about is the place where we hold our burdens, commitments, relationships, worries, cares, and dreams. We carry these things around on our backs wherever we go. For some, our backpacks are light, while others are forced to move at snaillike speeds as a result of all the excess baggage we are carrying.

Carrying a backpack is a necessity when climbing your Mount Everest. All of your supplies for success are carried in your backpack. Sometimes, however, we manage to place unnecessary items in our backpack that only weigh us down and make our journey more difficult.

To finish your commitment journey, you must empty your backpack of all unnecessary weight. All items in your backpack must serve a purpose. You don't have the strength to carry all the luxury items at your disposal. Consolidate and cast away anything that may hinder you from completing your commitment. Hebrews 12:1 says it this way: "Let us throw off everything that hinders and the sin that so easily entangles. And let us run with perseverance the race marked out for us ".

Before starting my Mount Everest I was a people-pleasing, appeasing addict. I could never say no to anything. It didn't matter how busy my schedule became, there was always room for another coffee date, lunch meeting, Bible study, or church event. Were these things bad? No.

However, I couldn't focus on God's call for my life, because I kept saying yes to other things.

While we were journeying together, Joseph continually reminded me to "clear my backpack." There was way too much unnecessary weight holding me back from running my race well.

On your Mount Everest climb, this process is just as crucial. Learning to say yes to the best and no to the rest will give you an advantage and eagle-eyed focus.

What's in your backpack? Take an inventory. Can you carry all of that across the finish line?

Whatever your commitment, there are some things that simply cannot stay in your backpack. Evaluate what is manageable and necessary to carry while climbing your personal Mount Everest. I promise you, there is freedom in this exercise.

When we understand our purpose, we are free to say no to the many things that compete with our commitments.

Let me warn you now—people will not take kindly to your newfound use of the word *no*. However, if God has called you to complete a task or commitment, "no" may be your greatest defensive and offensive tool for obedience. Let people criticize. You won't be answering to them in heaven. Our obedience to God is the only thing that counts in the end.

Peeping Tom

In any commitment, there will be unending opportunities and reasons to back out. One of the greatest reasons for quitting your commitment is that the grass looks greener elsewhere. You will inevitably see people prospering without the process you are experiencing. In other words, some people's paths will simply appear easier than yours.

Throughout my journey, I watched the majority of my peers enjoying freedom on Friday nights, engaging in romantic relationships, and seeming to experience immediate blessings that were supposedly on back-order for me. In other words, I spent a significant amount of time peering over the fence admiring my neighbor's lawn and wishing that we could trade places.

The grass is always greener on the other side.

I often told myself that life would be better outside and away from my commitment journey. I could have my weekends back, stop wearing the commitment ring, start dating Alissa again, and have true freedom. Life would be so much simpler on the other side of the fence; I didn't need this commitment journey.

I was believing the "garden snake lie."

In the Garden of Eden, Satan (in the form of a snake) made Adam and Eve focus on the one thing that God banned, while forgetting all the ways that they were blessed. They had a perfect relationship with God, great sex in their marriage, unlimited food, and stable employment. However, Satan focused their eyes on the lie that the grass would be greener if they were their own gods. They didn't need someone telling them what to do; they could decide for themselves with one bite of fruit. Adam and Eve fell for the snake's lies and ate, only to discover that the grass was not as green as they had hoped.

Mr. Green Thumb

It has been said that "the grass is greener on the other side only because it was planted over a leaky septic tank."

I personally believe the author of that saying attended college with me at Sonoma State, where the air was constantly filled with the "Sonoma aroma." By Sonoma aroma, I of course mean "cow poopourri." I'm serious—the entire countryside smelled like a bakery of fresh cow pies. It was absolutely disgusting. Yet, year after year, the wineries of Sonoma County covered their soil in cow manure.

Most would agree this career would qualify as a contender on Mike Rowe's *Dirty Jobs*. However disgusting, the farmers didn't mind the smell so much, because that manure made them some serious money. In fact, the grapes that grow from that fertilizer are known worldwide. Sonoma wines are tasted and tested across the globe with accolades and awards spanning across the equator.

Like the saying about the septic tank, fertilizer is required to make green grass and fruitful ground.

People often covet green grass, but they forget about the process and ingredients that were required to get that grass green.

This is true in any commitment. We look at the success of a company, the letters after someone's name, and the physical fruit of a fit body, and we admire their grass. It's okay to admire and appreciate the hard work of others, but a comparison trap waits for us if we linger around the fence line for too long.

When we allow dissatisfaction over the dung in our lives and the admiration of others' green grass to turn into bitterness, resentment, or jealousy, we have fallen into the comparison trap.

Instead of complaining about the manure in our lives and focusing on the green grass that our neighbors have, let's take that manure and make it into something beautiful, useful, fruitful, and successful. Remember: when waste comes our way, God is giving us the resources necessary to grow a garden.

Now, we can't just take fertilizer, spread it around our backyards, and expect flowers to miraculously spring up overnight. Manure must be mixed into the existing soil with some elbow grease and effort. It's not easy to fertilize a garden. We often end up dirty, sweaty, tired, and sometimes bloody, but this is the work required to grow a garden. We need to work with the waste that has been given to us. Wasting what others view as garbage is to waste a growth opportunity.

No matter what the commitment, fertilizer will follow.

Fertilizer could be failure, disappointment, loss, marital discord, arguments, distrust, unfaithfulness, hurt, betrayal, injury, low test scores, illness, or any other negative experience. Either we can accept these circumstances as waste, or we can work with the situation, work through the circumstances, and offer our garbage up to the great gardener to make something beautiful out of a smelly, inconvenient pile of manure.

Your growth and overall success depend on what you make of that manure. If the stuff just sits around, it will start to stink, attract flies, and become a health hazard to you and those around you. However, if you take the fertilizer, work through it, and see it as a blessing instead of a curse, you will eventually see the fruits of your labor.

Ask any successful businessman, professional athlete, famous artist, doctoral student, or happily married couple, and you will hear countless stories of failure, disappointment, missed shots, and fights that ended up propelling them deeper into their commitment, eventually resulting in success. Failure is not an enemy of the successful. Failure merely provides more fertilizer to enrich your garden.

If I wanted to have a successful marriage, thriving ministry, and fulfilling career while overcoming my noncommittal spirit, I had to give all my fertilizer to the great gardener. Only God could take the opposition, family division, awkward conversations, and unfulfilled longings and turn them into something beautiful, powerful, fruitful, and glorifying to God, the great gardener.

Preventative Measures

As we've already covered, our commitments will be tested by temptations. Other opportunities will arise, the grass will look greener elsewhere, and we may even become bored during a season of commitment keeping. Besides using guardrails, how can we stay committed to God's calling on our lives?

Pack the power of the predecision!

In 2007, the New England Patriots' head coach Bill Belichick was allegedly caught videotaping his opponents' play calling signs. The Patriots were given an unfair advantage by knowing the plays that their opponents were planning to use. Although this constitutes cheating in the National Football League, predeciding how you will respond to your enemy's obvious attacks is an ingenious strategy to utilize during your commitment journey.

When God places a calling on your life, the enemy will do everything in his power to prevent the fulfillment of that purpose. He will attack your health, finances, relationships, purity, security, and anything else in order to distract you from completing your call of duty. Knowing how the enemy plans to attack gives you a defensive guide to predecide how to respond when the obvious attacks arise.

I remember one instance during my commitment journey when a woman from my past contacted me via text message. She very blatantly offered me an illicit sexual opportunity. This woman assured me that no one would find out and that there was nothing wrong with two friends engaging in mutually beneficial activities. She then followed her messages with provocative pictures and sexual innuendos.

Her tactics were textbook. The predecision to keep myself pure for my future wife propelled me to flee from this sexually enticing invitation. I understood what was at risk and anticipated the encounter.

The choice was clear: I could enjoy the momentary pleasure and become enslaved to sin, guilt, and shame or flee from her devilish advances and conquer the snake who was trying to sabotage my salvation. I chose not to enslave myself by holding fast to the truth of scripture—"Resist the devil and he will flee from you" (James 4:7).

I know that my enemy understands my struggle with lust, so I set up boundaries in advance around areas where I am weakest.

To conquer temptation in your commitment journey, tap into the power of the predecision. Know how to respond before a response is required.

While in a committed relationship, how will you respond to the friend request of an old flame? How about the flirtatious coworker or the attractive girl/guy in the gym giving you attention? Predecide now.

If you're committed to saving money, getting out of debt, or preparing for retirement, what will you do when the opportunity arises to break your budget? Predecide about your expenditures.

What about when those late-night TV commercials come on, or the sensual ads on social media that tempt you to surf into deadly waters? You don't have to drown; predecide now!

Before arriving at the Christmas party, predecide how you will respond to the temptations of abandoning your diet or caving in to your chocolate cravings. Eat a meal before you go; make sure you're full of good things so the temptation won't touch you.

Like Bill Belichik, know your enemy's playbook. Create strong defensive and offensive weapons to overcome your opponent before the opening kickoff.

Storms

Storms can destroy homes, sideline your beach vacation, and devastate an entire country. Storms can also water thirsty crops, provide the snow necessary to bless your ski vacation, and shape mountains into masterpieces.

Jesus promised that storms are coming. He said, "In this life, you will have trouble." In other words, grab your raincoat and umbrella because it's about to get wet!

Instead of our dreading the storms of life, God wants us all to learn that we can embrace them.

Why?

Because storms shape mountains.

When people look at Mount Everest, they marvel at its majesty. Being in the presence of something so large and fierce strikes a sense of fear and reverence into the hearts of people. Many forget that it took years of violent storms, turbulent winds, and the collision of relentless forces to form the character of that mountain. Every ridge, cliff, peak, and indent of the mountain is a scar from the storm.

To this day, glaciers, rivers, landslides, earthquakes, and snow are shaping mountains around the world. From the Himalayas to the Sierra Nevadas, not a single mountain was created without a series of storms to carve out its character. It is the process of storms occurring over a long period of time that makes people marvel at a mountain's beauty today. Why would a storm be any different in our marriages, dreams, jobs, and educational pursuits?

Without the storm, we would not have a mountain to marvel at. It is our resilience through the storm that tells our testimony.

In order to endure the storm, we must first develop the perspective of purpose. This is the vantage point that God has a plan and purpose for every storm in life. The perspective of purpose helps us understand that God can use anything for our good and his glory if we hold fast to his promises.

The Bible literally contains thousands of God's promises.

Regarding the perspective of purpose, Romans 8:28 says, "In all things God works for the good of those who love him, who have been called according to his purpose." This is a promise that God can use anything, literally "all things" that happen to us, for our good because he can bring good out of any and every bad situation or circumstance.

This does not mean that God brought the cancer to your body, affair to your marriage, lawsuit to your company, broken leg, failed exam, or financial downturn, but God does promise that he can use the bad situation and circumstances for our good.

This promise reminds me of a bad-tasting medicine or painful surgical procedure. It might leave a bad taste in our mouth, inflict temporary pain or discomfort, or even leave a scar, but it is ultimately used to heal us, help us, and benefit our lives.

I tread lightly, however, when bringing up such a sensitive topic.

There are some things in life for which we may never have the answers. I honestly don't understand what good came out of the Holocaust, genocide in Darfur, or other mass killings that have occurred throughout history. I don't understand why millions of people starve to death or die of curable diseases. I do, however, believe that if Christians were actually obedient to God's commands and were to steward their resources well and tithe on the money God gave them, things like world hunger would be nonexistent. But why God doesn't choose to intervene and stop millions from starving and dying on a daily basis, I just don't know.

Without answers to these daunting questions, I have to hold fast to God's promise in Romans 8:28, along with the understanding in Isaiah 55:9, that "God's ways are higher than our ways and his thoughts are higher than our thoughts." If our finite minds could understand the mind of an infinite God, we would transcend the limitations that make us human. We may never know, on this side of eternity, why some of the tragedies we experienced had to happen. I believe with all faith that one day God will give us either understanding, or such a grandiose heavenly inheritance that we will be too enamored with God's glory to care.

The Volcano Climber

While looking back on my mother's life, I could not understand why God would allow her to experience the suffering that she endured for our family. My mom endured an affair, emotional neglect during her first years of marriage, and my dad's substance abuse problem, which destroyed his career and almost swallowed the lives of both children.

I remember walking past my mom's bedroom after my dad announced that he was leaving our family. She was lying in bed sobbing with her Bible tightly clenched in her hands as though she were holding on to God for dear life (which she was). It's heart-wrenching to remember my mom's pain during that time. Not only did her husband walk away, but I was verbally abusive toward my mom, blaming her for my dad leaving. These are terrible memories for all of us.

Even so, I don't believe my mom asks why it had to happen.

Why am I so confident?

Since then, Jesus has completely changed and restored our whole family. He forgave and saved both me and my dad and resurrected her dead marriage after a seven-year separation; her relationship with my sister is better than ever, and our family is now unified like never before.

Did she walk through fire and experience the crucible of family pain? Yes.

Were her hopes and dreams fulfilled by God's miraculous power and faithfulness? Absolutely.

Through that season of suffering, my mom witnessed miracle after miracle, answered prayer after answered prayer. Even in seasons of silence, God was drawing her closer to him than ever before. She was hearing his voice, feeling his comforting hand upon her, and being strengthened with God's power to endure. My mom has never been closer to God than when she walked through that fire with him. Does my mom wish God's will could have been easier or taken a different form? Probably, but so did Jesus in the garden of Gethsemane before his crucifixion—"Father, if you are willing, please take this cup of suffering away from me. Yet I want your will to be done, not mine" (Luke 22:42).

Nonetheless, my mom had a Mount Everest to climb, and she endured the storm. She was committed to her husband and committed to our family no matter how much pain her commitment caused her. Her marriage is one at which people now marvel. The relationship she has with her children is coveted, as is our family's enjoyment of one another.

What they don't know is that our family is a product of a perfect storm. The scars are a testament of God's glory.

I actually believe that if you asked my mom how she felt about that season of storms, she would tell you that every tear, every sleepless night, and every agonizing moment of despair was worth it. In fact, my mom would tell you that she would gladly endure the same pain again if it meant saving her family. My mom reminds me of Jesus in that way—"who for the joy set before him endured the cross" (Hebrews 12:2). Gain at the cost of pain.

You want a strong marriage? Relational pain. You want a better body? Physical pain. You want that baby? Birth pain. Remember your coach from high school or college? "No pain, no gain."

Nothing worth having comes without a cost. Your commitment will cost you something. The storms in life that come to test your commitment will hurt, but hold on; there is purpose in the pain.

The Original Promise Keeper

Holding on to God's promises through the perspective of purpose is the key to overcoming the storm.

The foundation of our faith is Jesus and his promises. No matter the storm, no matter the circumstances, no matter the score, our Father in heaven is faithful, and he alone has the final word.

Biblically speaking, Jesus promised his disciples three times that he would be handed over to the leaders of religious law to be arrested, beaten, and crucified. He also told them not to worry, because on the third day he would rise from the dead. Jesus promised that he would be victorious over the grave. Jesus promised that death couldn't hold him down. Jesus gave his disciples a promise so they wouldn't lose hope when the rest of the world was left with confusion, disappointment, and disillusionment. When the world looked upon Jesus's body torn open on the cross, they mourned the loss of their hope. They were hoping that Jesus was in fact the Messiah, the savior of the world, but when they saw him dead, their hope died too.

Jesus knew this would happen. This was his plan all along, and in an effort to spare his disciples from despair, he gave them his promise to rise again.

If Jesus's disciples held on to the perspective of purpose, if they remembered his promises during their darkest day, they could have remained hopeful and victorious over their circumstances. The disappointment of Jesus's death would not have defeated them. They could have carried their heads high in confidence, even when the waves of doubt were pounding against their doors. I'm sure people were asking the disciples, "If God is such a good and loving God, why would he let this happen?"

Have you heard that one before?

When approached with this age-old question, the disciples could have responded with the perspective of purpose anchored in God's promise. "This isn't the end of the story. Just hold fast to hope for a few more days, and you will see. Jesus is coming back!"

People will think you are bat dung deranged for holding on to God's promises during your darkest hour.

"Come again? He's what? Coming back from the dead?"

Zombie Jesus always raises an eyebrow.

I can hear the haters now:

"Your marriage is dead, that goal is gone, the dream is done. Wake up! Can't you see, your hope has been crucified; there is no cure for this cancer. Move on."

I remember the voices of friends and family telling me, "If you let Alissa go, she's gone. You have seen her, right? She's gorgeous. Guys want her. You let that bird fly away, and she is never coming back. Two years? Are you insane? No one is waiting two years for you, Matt. Don't be stupid."

This was my Mount Everest. I had a calling on my life, and I had to climb if I wanted to have a lasting relationship with God. As I've stated time and again, we all have a mountain to climb in this life. I had mine, my mom had hers, Jesus had his, and you have yours.

Victory

For those who hold fast to God's promises there is victory. This faith, our hope is an anchor for our soul that assures us of victory. When you have a promise from God, you can confidently claim the victory even when the win is nowhere in sight.

Let me say that again—when God calls you to accomplish a task on his behalf, you have already won.

Game over.

Done.

Why?

Because God does not lose.

He is the victorious one.

It is in God's very nature to be victorious. Winning is in the fabric of his being.

God's purpose will always prevail.

You cannot look at the promise in Romans 8:28 without noticing the second portion of this scripture. "In all things God works for the good of those who love him, who have been called according to his purpose."

If you have been called according to his purpose, you cannot lose. *God's will always wins.*

I wish this had been my perspective as I climbed my Mount Everest. It's easy looking back. Hindsight is always 20/20, but this thought is a total game changer. If God is calling you to climb a mountain, whatever it may be, he will get you to the top. He never said it would be easy. In fact, Jesus promised that it wouldn't be. Jesus promised storms. That's why the perspective of purpose and the vision of victory are so important. *Don't miss this.* When you understand that you have already won the victory and every setback and storm along the way is simply preparing you for victory, you become unstoppable.

This is what we call faith … "being sure of what we hope for and certain of what we do not see" (Hebrews 11:1). By faith, we claim the victory over any obstacle standing in the way of our success. By faith, we embrace the storm, trusting that our character is being formed so that we can handle the victory when it comes.

If only Hollywood could grasp this idea. How many times have we seen childhood stars receive the success they have always dreamed of only to have the entire world watch that success destroy them? God loves us and does not want this for our lives. He is preparing us for the victory so we can actually handle and enjoy it when victory comes.

Looking back on my commitment journey, Alissa and I praise God that he didn't give us the victory in our timing. We are both confident that had God given us the relationship we wanted in 2010, it would have self-destructed. Neither of us was ready. He had to bring us through the fire, through the storm to prepare, equip, build, and chip away at our character until we trusted him fully with every part of our lives and were prepared to handle the victory he had in store for us.

In Christ, you can behold the perspective of purpose. Embrace the storm.

In Christ, you already have the victory. Keep climbing.

In Christ we have the confidence that "In all things God works for the good of those who love him, who have been called according to his purpose" (Romans 8:28). Let faith be the anchor for your soul as the storms in life test your ship. God may seem like he's sleeping on the boat, but remember that he has the power to calm the storm, and he will do so in his timing. You will never drown when Jesus is the captain of your ship. Keep sailing.

Thanking God for the Storm

With the perspective of purpose and vision of victory in place, we can now thank God and praise him during the storm. Understanding that God is actually blessing us with trials gives us a completely new way to view our worries. They are simply opportunities for God to show up, increase our faith, build our character, and prepare us to handle more responsibility and blessings. I'm sure people will accuse me of preaching a prosperity gospel at this point, but on the contrary, only in Western culture do we see the word *blessing* from a purely monetary perspective. It is a blessing to be close to God, to experience him, to know him, to really know that he is present. Storms provide that opportunity, so praise God for them!

Your blessing may be the loss of a relationship.

Mine was.

Although I didn't realize it at the time, I was so blessed by God when he took Alissa from my life. In the beginning of our relationship, I told her that I had made a commitment to God not to date anyone, yet there I was, dating her! How could Alissa ever marry me and believe my "oath" before God to love her and her alone, forever and ever, when I had already broken an oath to God in order to date her?

God taking Alissa away afforded me the ability to become a man of quality character, a man of my word, a man who can keep his commitments even when it hurts. God was building me into a man that Alissa could trust, but for that to happen, I was blessed with a tremendous hurt. The loss of Alissa cut my heart deeply. It was one of the most painful losses I have ever experienced, but it was a blessing.

Another blessing was the agonizing trial and test of my purity with Alissa. When God brought us back together, the sexual tension was always high. We wanted each other. Badly. After two years of waiting, through fourteen months of long distance, and seeing each other only once a month, the sexual tension was tight. Keeping my hands off Alissa was probably the greatest test of our faithfulness to God and one another. This test, as painful and frustrating as it was, strengthened our testimony and trust of one another. The test of not touching Alissa sexually before our wedding night showed her that I was a man of self-control. If I could keep my hands off her, she could trust that I would be able to keep my hands off other women as well.

This test was costly and painful, but it was a blessing that strengthened our character.

CHAPTER 15

LET'S REVIEW

Throughout our journey together, we have covered counting the cost of our commitments, completing the tasks God gives us, building a strong foundation, and the inevitable storms that will test all of the above. This final portion is, in my opinion, the most important element of the entire book.

Lemonade

Home run records have been set, bike racing championships have been won, and other mountainous commitments have been fulfilled by men and women who sacrificed everything, including their convictions and character, to achieve their goal.

In the end, when the truth of their wrongdoing was unveiled to the world, what was their gain? Instead of enjoying the fruit of their labor, they were confronted with consequences. Some were forced to give up their gold medals, others had to remove their names from the record books, and some were even convicted of criminal charges.

These examples are the rare cases, of course, but they beg the question: was it worth it? Was the juice worth the squeeze?

In one of Jesus's most pointed and impactful sermons, he asked the same question. "What good will it be for a man if he gains the whole world, yet forfeits his soul?" (Matthew 16:26). In other words, what do you really gain if you have accomplished all your goals and accumulated all of your treasures and trophies, but have given up what is most important in the process?

Did you know that it's possible to do something "good" for God in a way that displeases him and hurts others? In the book of 1 Samuel, chapter 13, the first king of Israel, King Saul, learned this lesson the hard way. He wanted God's blessing and provision during a battle against the Philistines, so he sacrificed a burned offering to the Lord.

This sounds spiritual and good, but Saul sinned greatly against God by offering this sacrifice. According to God's law, only a priest could sacrifice such an offering, and Saul was not a priest. Saul wanted to achieve success by circumventing God's established order. Unfortunately for Saul, this action resulted in the loss of his kingship. Not everything we sacrifice is good, even in the name of God.

Let's bring this home practically: Is this educational endeavor, career aspiration, hobby, or fitness goal worth sacrificing your family for? If you fulfilled your commitment to build a Fortune 500 company but have a bankrupt heart, did you really gain anything in the end? If you lost all that weight, earned your doctorate degree, fulfilled that lifelong dream, but neglected your wife and kids, was it worth the damage done to your loved ones?

Remember: attempting to honor God in a dishonorable way can have dire consequences.

Character Counts

Along with counting the cost of our actions, we should consistently evaluate our character. It may be beneficial to ask yourself and others, "Am I sacrificing my character to keep this commitment?"

Is this commitment making me a better person, parent, partner, spouse, sibling, or son? What am I becoming? Have I lost myself along the way? Is the juice still worth the squeeze?

It's easy to lose ourselves in the process of keeping our commitments. But stay focused on your goal, and remember that your character counts. If your climb isn't building your character, consider cutting your losses before you truly lose yourself.

Remember: "What does it benefit a man to gain the whole world and lose his soul?" (Matthew 16:26).

In Case You Didn't Know ...

Ultimately, my hope is that everyone reading this book will understand that a loving God exists. He created everything, and he wants to save you from the sinful state that has separated you from his presence. God has provided a way to be reconciled to him through the sacrifice of his only son Jesus, and he wants to adopt you into his family to love you forever. Honestly speaking, if you haven't already figured it out by now, surprise! There's my "hidden" agenda.

Secondly, an adventure is waiting for you beyond your wildest dreams. A commitment journey the size of Mount Everest is beckoning, calling you to climb. However, one greater than Gandalf the Grey is knocking at your door this time. Jesus is calling you to something far more adventurous than any *Lord of the Rings* fantasy. This is a journey that will last an eternity.

Jesus is offering a journey that has already been paid in full, but it will cost everything you have. Jesus, your tour guide, is waiting with his map, compass, provisions, and protection. Everything you need for this journey can be found in Jesus, and all he is looking for is a willing heart that will follow him. Jesus wants you to trust that he will lead you through this life, up mountains, down into valleys, through the darkness, through fires and trials into his glorious, eternal light and heavenly home. Your personal Mount Everest with Jesus is calling. Are you ready to start climbing?

Write Your Own Ending

We are all living out our life's story. What do you want yours to say?

I'll tell you how I don't want my story to read: "Matt had a dream, started to follow it, but was quickly distracted by things that didn't matter. He then settled for a life of complacency and mediocrity, and he never accessed the faith that he so unconvincingly proclaimed. Matt lived his life in fear of others' opinions and chose to seek after others' approval instead of God's glory. In the end, Matt wasted the precious opportunities that

God presented on a golden platter and spent his final years reflecting on a life full of regret."

A. No one wants to read that story.
B. I would rather die today, right now, than leave that kind of legacy.

Someone said, "The greatest failure in life is to succeed in things that don't matter." Congratulations, you watched every episode of *The Bachelor* and *American Idol*, you read the entire *Harry Potter* series, and you had the best kill-to-death ratio on Call of Duty. Congratulations, social media star, you had the most likes on Instagram, most followers on Twitter, and most friends on Facebook. Congrats for pinning the most "repinned" item on Pinterest. Congrats on going viral with your YouTube video. Congrats on collecting the most stuff and having the biggest house and fastest car. You have succeeded in nothing of importance.

Jesus said that whatever we build our lives on will be tested by fire, and only that which remains will matter. If you are building with perishable materials, your life will burn. We have been given ninety years to live, give or take a couple decades. Jesus's brother James said, "What is your life? You are a mist that appears for a little while and then vanishes" (James 4:14). In light of eternity, our life vanishes like smoke, in the blink of an eye—the snap of our fingers and it's gone. What will you do with your time?

Make a commitment to leave a legacy. Do something that matters. Make your mark. Don't settle for easy success. If your goal didn't require God, it wasn't big enough. If your goal wasn't large enough to require the help of the Almighty Creator, it wasn't worth it.

If your goal didn't cost you blood, sweat, tears, or sleep, it wasn't worth the investment. If your goal didn't bring glory to God, if it was self-serving, it will burn. Build with fireproof materials. Build with love, sacrificial service, peacemaking, justice-seeking, hunger-ending, thirst-quenching, slave-freeing, orphan-adopting, prisoner-visiting, others-centered living. Build with kind and encouraging words, generosity, and caring acts toward undeserving people; clothe the naked, feed the hungry, shelter the homeless, teach the illiterate, and volunteer your time. Instead of working on your golf game, perfect your ability to love your wife and kids. Seek the good of others; build relationships. Help those who cannot help themselves. Plant trees for the next generation so that they can enjoy their fruit.

Don't be deceived; busyness does not equate to productivity. Invest your time, talents, and treasures in people. Help others by doing good for them and loving them the way that God loves us.

No one wants to settle for mediocrity, and none of us has to. We can write our own ending by God's grace. He gives us the free will to choose how this whole thing plays out. When you die, desire to attend your own funeral. Write your own eulogy. Start today.

So How Does This Thing End Anyway?

If you can remember, while in Myanmar for Christmas I received a promise from Joseph. He vowed to take me anywhere in the world to propose to the girl of my dreams. I'm guessing that it's not a surprise that I selected Thailand.

As usual, our plans are rarely God's plans.

A week after we had purchased our hotel and airfare, Alissa's sister announced that she was pregnant. And wouldn't you know it, she was due during our vacation to Thailand, so I canceled our trip.

Determined to propose in Thailand, I booked another trip over the Thanksgiving holiday. In all the planning excitement, I failed to ask Alissa if she would be okay with traveling over Thanksgiving. She wasn't and explained the importance of being with her family during the holiday season. I then promised, Lord willing, to never make her miss a family holiday and consequently canceled our trip, again.

I started to think that God was closing the door on the Thai proposal. My suspicions were seemingly confirmed when my parents suggested that I propose to Alissa on our family vacation in Belize.

It wasn't Thailand, but Belize would have been just as tropical, beautiful, romantic, and memorable, so I accepted their offer.

Joseph eventually caught wind of my new plan and asked, "Where is the meaning in your proposal? Anyone can propose on a cruise ship. That's been done before. There is no significance in Belize. Without the commitment journey, there would be no proposal. Why can't you just trust God to finish what he started in Thailand?"

He was right. This thing started in Thailand and would end in Thailand.

Now committed to the Thailand trip, I booked our third and final reservations for February, the week of Valentine's Day.

Third time's a charm ... Alissa and I set off for our Thai adventure on Sunday, February 9, 2014.

During our time in Thailand we explored the jungle on ATVs, cruised the coastline on scooters, ate a ton of delicious Thai food, took advantage of the ten-dollar hour-long massages, enjoyed the beautiful beaches, and I even got a tattoo. Sound familiar?

Redemption.

Again, God brought everything full circle.

What had once died was resurrected into something even more beautiful than before. I had always longed to bring Alissa to Thailand, and now here we were. Alissa and I were now experiencing the fruit of my commitment journey and her support through that journey firsthand.

On Wednesday, February 12, I told Alissa that I needed to drop Joseph off at a local school to conduct some business. Little did she know I was actually planting Joseph at the proposal scene to take pictures of the event.

Joseph and I rode our rental scooter fifteen minutes through familiar villages and back country roads before reaching the national park. After parking the bike, we set out on a thirty-minute hike toward the waterfall where I planned to propose. This was the same place that Joseph and I had visited twice before during our commitment journey. Not only that, but I had tattooed a picture of this waterfall on my ankle to signify the commencement of the commitment journey.

When we finally reached the top, I found the perfect place for Joseph to hide. Before I left to pick up Alissa, Joseph and I prayed. This was a popular tourist destination, so we asked that God would bless us with privacy for the proposal.

After praying, I ran back down the hill, jumped on the scooter, and drove back to the hotel, where Alissa was waiting.

When I finally reached Alissa's hotel room door, I was soaked with sweat and covered in dirt. Alissa asked why I was such a mess. Of course

I lied. Alissa heard a story about the long dusty roads and hot sun required to access Joseph's job site.

After I quickly cleaned up, we set off for our morning hike. To capture our adventure, Alissa wore a Go-Pro camera on her new chest harness. She recorded our scooter ride through the backcountry villages and through the jungle as we ascended toward the waterfall. When we finally reached the base of the waterfall, I discovered that Alissa and I were not alone as I had hoped. Instead, two Japanese girls were standing in the exact spot where I had planned to propose.

Frustrated, I froze, staring at the waterfall and thinking fast about an alternative location. I then noticed that the two girls were taking photos of one another with the waterfall in the background. Realizing the opportunity, I quickly asked the girls if I could take their photo, hoping that they would return the favor.

While Alissa was photographing the girls, I grabbed the ring out of my backpack. With my free hand, I flipped my iPhone camera to video mode hoping to catch the moment. The two girls, who were now holding my video camera, did not understand my intentions, but when I dropped down on one knee in front of the waterfall, they knew exactly what they were witnessing.

From a third-grade classroom to a two-year waiting period, followed by fourteen months of long-distance dating, I was now on bended knee in Thailand asking for Alissa's hand in marriage.

She said yes, we kissed, and the girls caught the whole thing on camera. As it turned out, the Japanese girls were a godsend, because Joseph was nowhere to be found until post-proposal. He apparently couldn't get a good shot of the action, but God foresaw this and gifted us with these two pseudo-videographers instead. Why do I ever worry? God always has my back!

If that wasn't enough, just moments after our celebration ended, hordes of tourists began to scramble up the rocks toward us as we made our way back down the mountain. It was perfect timing for a perfect proposal, and God provided everything.

That night, Alissa and I celebrated our engagement with a candlelit dinner on the beach followed by a Thai sky lantern ceremony. Nicholas Sparks couldn't have created a better ending.

After arriving home, we then began our six-month engagement journey toward the altar, where we finally tied the knot on Saturday, August 23, 2014.

God fulfilled his promise.

What was prophesied on an airplane in October 2010 was fulfilled nearly four years later. Not only that, but shortly after the honeymoon, I was hired as a counselor. I had finally made it to the top of my Mount Everest. One commitment was completed while another one had just begun.

God is faithful. He fulfills his promises. You can trust him with your life. I learned this during my commitment journey.

Trust Jesus with your life. Allow him to guide you through a life of commitment keeping.

My journey isn't over, and neither is yours. I have many more mountains to climb, and so do you.

If you're not dead, God's not done.

Climb on, my friends …

Famous Last Words …

If I could walk away with one lesson from this entire journey, it would be that commitment is a choice.

From the time of Adam in the garden until today, we are continually blessed with the free will to choose. No matter what your commitment journey, you have a choice. No one will force you to stay; you must choose to remain.

Commitment is a freewill offering. Whether it's God's free gift of salvation, your marriage, or that Everest-sized dream, commitment is a choice. Every day provides a new opportunity to stay committed or walk away.

For those who continuously choose to remain committed, God will bless you with success and fulfillment. But in the end, the choice is always yours.

What will you choose?

BIBLIOGRAPHY

Life Application Study Bible, New International Version, 1673. Grand Rapids, Michigan: Zondervan, 1984.

Shipman, B. *WWJD Today? Daily Time with Jesus: A Devotional.* Nashville, Tennessee: Broadman & Holman, 1998.

ABOUT THE AUTHOR

Matthew Jones currently works as an international student specialist and academic counselor at a community college in Oakland, California. Matthew holds a master's degree in clinical psychology, volunteers with the high school students at his church, and spends his free time with his beautiful wife. Matthew enjoys hiking, camping, collecting tattoos from other countries, and playing competitive activities with his wife, such as softball, poker, and chess. Matthew and his wife live in Pleasanton, California, where they hope to one day adopt children from around the world.